Corps Camping

RV Camping at Corps of Engineers Public Recreation Areas

Published by:

Roundabout Publications
PO Box 19235
Lenexa, KS 66285

800-455-2207

www.TravelBooksUSA.com

Published by Roundabout Publications, PO Box 19235, Lenexa, KS 66285 / 800-455-2207

Library of Congress Control Number: 2009935550

ISBN-10: 1-885464-31-2
ISBN-13: 978-1-885464-31-6

Contents

Introduction

"This land is your land. This land is my land...
This land was made for you and me."
—Woody Guthrie

Camping on public lands is a long-standing American tradition. Huge portions of public lands, managed by a variety of government agencies, are available to the general public for recreational use. These are located on federal, state and county properties. The many camping choices nationwide – from primitive to semi-primitive camping areas to developed campgrounds – are too numerous to list in a single volume.

The U.S. Army Corps of Engineers provides over 30 percent of the recreational opportunities on federal lands. This book is designed to guide you to more than 600 Corps-managed campgrounds around the country.

How This Guide Is Organized

This book lists U.S. Army Corps of Engineers projects alphabetically by state – Alabama through Wisconsin. Included are only those projects and locations that have campgrounds with developed sites that are suitable for RVs. Walk-in or boat-in primitive camping areas that are not vehicle accessible are not included...this book is geared primarily to RVers.

Each Corps of Engineers project area typically covers thousands of land and water acres and, in many cases, projects cross over state lines. Project listings may appear in both state sections or will be cross-referenced. The Corps of Engineers itself is not organized by state, but rather geographically into eight regions of the U.S., with a number of districts in each region. Consequently, most states have more than one Corps district managing projects within the state. All district offices are listed in Appendix E; managing districts are listed with each project.

Project Listing

Each project's section begins with the name, address, phone number and managing district, followed by a general description of the size and/or scope of the project. Directions are provided to the project office and visitor center, if applicable. Visitors will find it helpful to stop at the office or visitor center before going on to the campground in order to obtain maps, fishing reports and information about locations of boat ramps, marinas, fishing piers, swimming beaches and other recreational facilities at the project. At some projects, check-in and collection of camping fees (for non-reservable camping) is done at the project office, while others may handle this process at the campground.

The *Activities* chart summarizes the major recreational opportunities at each project, but it is not all-inclusive. Types of recreation offered in and around Corps lakes are many and tend to vary from project to project, depending on locale, equipment, facilities and local needs.

Also included in the text before campground listings will be general information about points of interest in the area and other unique features of the project.

Campground Listings

Campgrounds at the project are listed in alphabetical order. Each listing includes the following features where available:

1) Season: The campground's season of operation.
2) Total number and types of sites: Types of sites include primitive, basic, and developed. Primitive sites are usually for tent camping only. Basic sites provide a pad (gravel or paved) but no hookups. Developed sites include a pad, picnic table, lantern post, and usually electric and/or water hookups.
3) Pull thrus: Where available.
4) Hookups: Includes electric, water, and/or sewer.
5) Non-reservable: Where applicable, this indicates that some or

all sites at the campground are available on a first-come, first-serve basis and cannot be reserved through recreation.gov. Note that many campgrounds have non-reservable sites available off-season. Call the project office for information about availability of non-reservables.

6) *Daily Fee*: Range of daily fee(s) for an individual, single RV-occupancy site. If using a Senior Pass or Access Pass, the amount listed will be reduced by 50%. Fees are as of 2008.

7) *Basic Amenities*: drinking water, dump station, restrooms, showers, laundry – listed where available. Other amenities and features may also be noted here.

8) *RV length limit*: Rare. Most Corps of Engineers campgrounds can accommodate big rigs, although at some locations the number of big rig sites is limited. Call early for reservations and request one of the longer sites.

9) *Directions*: Directions from a nearby town; generally the directions supplied by recreation.gov.

10) *Phone*: Direct line to the campground where available, or the direct line to the project office.

11) *Address*: Physical or street address of campground (where available).

Camping Reservations

You can check availability and make reservations online anytime at www.recreation.gov.

-or-

Call toll free 1-877-444-6777 to check availability and to make reservations over the phone: Mar 31 to Oct 31, 10am to midnight EST and Nov 1 to Feb 28, 10am to 10pm EST.

Detailed information about camping reservations can be found in Appendix B.

Alabama

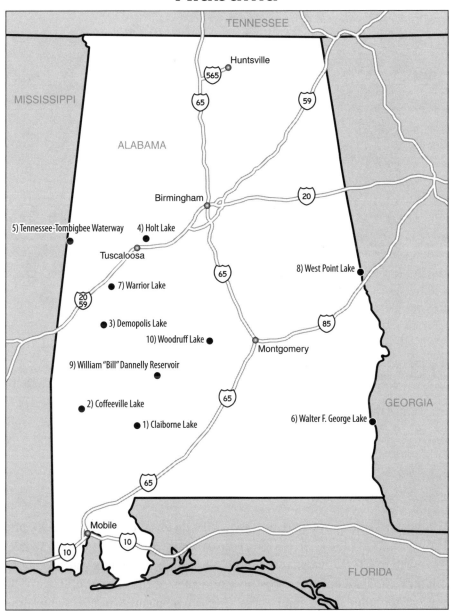

1) Claiborne Lake
2) Coffeeville Lake
3) Demopolis Lake
4) Holt Lake
5) Tennessee-Tombigbee Waterway

6) Walter F. George Lake
7) Warrior Lake
8) West Point Lake
9) William "Bill" Dannelly Reservoir
10) Woodruff Lake

Map #	Auto Touring	Biking	Boating	Climbing	Cultural/Historic Sites	Camping	Educational Programs	Fishing	Groceries/Supplies	Hiking	Horseback Riding	Hunting	Lodging	Off Highway Vehicles	Visitor Center	Page #
1		♦	♦			♦			♦	♦		♦				8
2			♦			♦			♦			♦				9
3		♦	♦			♦			♦	♦		♦			♦	9
4	♦	♦	♦			♦	♦		♦	♦		♦				10
5	♦	♦	♦			♦	♦	♦	♦	♦		♦			♦	11
6	♦		♦			♦	♦		♦	♦		♦	♦		♦	12
7			♦			♦	♦		♦	♦		♦				13
8			♦			♦		♦	♦	♦		♦			♦	14
9		♦	♦			♦	♦		♦	♦		♦			♦	15
10		♦	♦			♦			♦	♦		♦			♦	16

1) CLAIBORNE LAKE

U.S. Army Corps of Engineers
1226 Powerhouse Road
Camden, AL 36726
Phone: 334-682-4244
District: Mobile

Claiborne Lake is located north of Mobile in southwestern Alabama. From junction US-43 & US-84 in Grove Hill, go east on US-84 to SR-41, north to CR-17, west to the dam. Nestled in the state's southwest hill country, the lake encompasses over 60 miles of the Alabama River. The project includes 2,743 land acres, 5,850 water acres and 204 shoreline miles. Much of the lake's surrounding park land is being allowed to revert to its natural state, providing habitation for abundant wildlife. Claiborne is noted for being the most pristine of the Alabama River lakes. It has great appeal to sportsmen, bird-watchers and naturalists.

Isaac Creek campground has a playground, boat ramp, fishing pier, fish cleaning station and a convenience store nearby.

Isaac Creek: All year, 60 sites with electric (50amp) and water hookups, $16–$18, dump, restrooms, showers, laundry. From Monroeville, Alabama, travel 8 miles north on SR-41 to CR-17 west and follow signs. 251-282-4254, (5030 Lock and Dam Rd, Unit 4, Franklin, AL 36444).

2) COFFEEVILLE LAKE

U.S. Army Corps of Engineers
384 Resource Mgmt Drive
Demopolis, AL 36732
Phone: 334-289-3540
District: Mobile

Coffeeville Lake is located 60 miles south of Demopolis on US-84. It is the third largest lake in the Black Warrior-Tombigbee chain of lakes in western Alabama. It has a surface area of 8,800 acres and a length of 97 miles. The 4,000-acre Choctaw National Wildlife Refuge at Coffeeville Lake is managed by the U.S. Fish & Wildlife Service primarily for migratory waterfowl.

The Corps operates a modern campground at the lake where boating, fishing and picnicking are the major activities. Campground gates close at 10pm. Off road vehicles are prohibited. The campground has a boat ramp and playground.

Service Park: All year, 32 sites with electric & water hookups, some pull thrus, $16–$18, dump, restrooms, showers, laundry. From Coffeeville, Alabama, 4 miles west on US-84 to the campground. 251-754-9338, (451 Service Park Rd, Silas, AL 36919).

3) DEMOPOLIS LAKE

U.S. Army Corps of Engineers
384 Resource Mgmt Drive
Demopolis, AL 36732

Phone: 334-289-3540
District: Mobile

Demopolis is the largest of the Black Warrior-Tombigbee chain of six lakes. Located at the confluence of the two rivers, Demopolis Lake covers 10,000 acres and extends 48 miles upriver on the Black Warrior and 53 miles up the Tombigbee. The lake is situated 50 miles south of Tuscaloosa. From the town of Demopolis, take US-80 west for 2 miles to Lock & Dam Road to the Black Warrior & Tombigbee Resource Center where maps and directions to various lake areas are available.

Fishing is the most popular activity on the lake. Whether by boat or along the banks, anglers will find bass, crappie, bream and catfish. Corps-managed campgrounds at Demopolis include Forkland and Foscue where boat ramps and courtesy docks are available. Off road vehicles are prohibited. Campground gates close at 10pm. A highlight of the year at Demopolis Lake is the week-long "Christmas On The River" celebration featuring a night time parade on the river viewed by huge crowds from the white bluff above the Tombigbee River.

Forkland: All year, 42 sites with electric & water hookups, $18, dump, restrooms, showers, laundry. From Demopolis, go 9 miles north on US-43, follow signs, turn left on the county road (unpaved) for one mile. 334-289-5530, (1365 Forkland Park Rd, Forkland, AL 36740).

Foscue Creek: All year, 49 full hookup sites, 5 sites with electric & water hookups, (50amp throughout), $18–$20, dump, restrooms, showers, laundry. From Demopolis, go west for 3 miles on US-80; turn right, follow signs. 334-289-5535, (Lock Dam Rd, Demopolis AL 36732).

4) HOLT LAKE

U.S. Army Corps of Engineers
Box 295
Peterson, AL 35478
Phone: 205-553-9373
District: Mobile

Holt Lake is 6 miles northeast of Tuscaloosa and just northwest of the town of Peterson. From Tuscaloosa, go 10 miles east on AL-216 to the Resource Office. The lake is a narrow, winding body of water that stretches for 18 miles and encompasses 3,200 surface acres. It is part of the Black Warrior-Tombigbee chain of lakes.

Two Corps-managed campgrounds, Burchfield Branch and Deerlick Creek have fishing piers and boat ramps. Water skiing is a popular activity. Burchfield and Deerlick have swimming beaches; Deerlick also has hiking and bicycle trails. Off road vehicles are prohibited. Two privately managed marinas are located at Holt Lake. Restaurants and sightseeing can be found in nearby Tuscaloosa.

Burchfield Branch: All year, 36 sites with electric (50amp) and water hookups, $18, dump, restrooms, showers, laundry. From Tuscaloosa take I-59 exit 86 to CR-59 toward Brookwood. Right at the traffic light in Brookwood to Hwy-216, then left (NE) on to CR-59. Left at the stop sign on to Lock 17 Road. Turn left at Lock 17 Grocery and follow Lock 17 Road (approximately 23 miles from Brookwood). 205-497-9828 or 205-553-9373, (15036 Bankhead Rd, Adger, AL 35006).

Deerlick Creek: Mar-Nov, 40 sites with electric & water hookups, some pull thrus, 6 basic sites, $10–$18, dump, restrooms, showers, laundry. From I-59 exit 73, take Hwy-82 (McFarland Blvd.) west for 4.2 miles then right on CR-30 (Rice Mine Road) for 3.4 miles. Right at the stop sign to CR-42 (Lake Nicol Road) for 3.4 miles to CR-89 (Deerlick Road) Right for 3.2 miles. 205-759-1591, (12421 Deerlick Rd, Tuscaloosa, AL 35406).

5) TENNESSEE–TOMBIGBEE WATERWAY

Tom Bevill Visitor Center
1382 Lock & Dam Road
Pickensville, AL 35447
Phone: 205-373-8705
District: Mobile

The 234-mile long Tenn-Tom Waterway stretches through western Mississippi and, for a short distance, into Alabama. The 1820-1850 era antebellum-style Bevill Center welcomes visitors to the Alabama portion of the waterway. From Tuscaloosa, go west on US-82 for 18 miles, turn left (southwest) on SR-86 for 24.4 miles, then left on SR-14 for .4 mile, then right on Lock & Dam Road. The U.S. Snagboat Montgomery (National Historical Landmark) is located at the Center.

Two Tenn-Tom recreation areas with RV camping are in Alabama (near the MS state line.) Pickensville Campground at Aliceville Lake is just north of the Visitor Center and Cochrane Campground at Gainesville Lake is about 15 miles to the south. Public boat ramps, swimming, playgrounds, multi-use courts and fish cleaning stations are available. Campground gates are open 6am-10pm.

Cochrane: All year, 60 sites with electric and water hookups, some sites have sewer, some pull thrus, drinking water, $16–$20, dump, restrooms, showers, laundry. Plenty of shade. From Pickensville, south on SR-14 to the town of Aliceville, then SR-17 south for 10 miles. Approximately 2 miles from the Huyck Bridge, turn right at the sign for Cochrane area and travel about 2 miles, entrance on left. 205-373-8806, (707 Tenntom Park Rd, Aliceville, AL 35442).

Pickensville: All year, 176 sites with electric (some 50amp) and water hookups, 29 sewer hookups, drinking water, $16–$20, dump, restrooms, showers, laundry. From Tuscaloosa, take US-82 west to SR-86, turn left, travel west on SR-86 west to Pickensville. The entrance road to the campground is 2.5 miles from the yellow caution light. 205-373-6328, (61 Camping Rd, Carrollton, AL 35447).

6) WALTER F. GEORGE LAKE

U.S. Army Corps of Engineers
427 Eufala Road
Ft. Gaines, GA 39851
Phone: 229-768-2516
District: Mobile

W.F. George Lake, sometimes referred to as Lake Eufala, extends 85 miles along the Chatahoochee River and borders Alabama and Georgia. From Fort Gaines, GA, take Hwy-39 north for 2 miles; the W.F. George Resource Building is on the left. With 640 miles of shoreline the lake has plenty of room for water-related activities. The project consists of 34,853 land acres and 45,181 water acres.

The quiet campgrounds are ideal for enjoying the natural beauty of the lake and the Chatahoochee River. Campground gates are open 7am-10pm. All camping areas have boat ramps, fishing piers and playgrounds. Swimming is available at Hardridge and White Oak Creek. Lakepoint State Park, 7 miles north of Eufala, has camping, cabin rentals and restaurants. Gracious antebellum mansions are located in nearby historic towns, including Eufala.

Note: Campgrounds at W.F. George Lake will be upgraded during the 2010 season. The work will be done one campground at a time. Please call ahead to verify availability at the facility of your choice.

Hardridge Creek: Mar-Nov, 57 sites with electric & water hookups, 20 sites with full hookups, some pull thrus, $20–$22, dump, restrooms, showers, laundry. From Eufala, US-431 south, then east on SR-95, then left on CR-97, follow signs. 334-585-5945, (592 U.S. Government Rd, Abbeville, AL 36310).

Bluff Creek: Mar-Dec, 88 sites with electric and water hookups, $20, dump, restrooms, showers, laundry. From Eufala, north on US-431, then right on SR-165 for 18 miles, follow signs. 334-855-2746, (144 Bluff Creek Rd, Pittsview, AL 36871).

White Oak Creek: All year, 130 sites with electric & water hookups, $20, dump, restrooms, showers, laundry, fish cleaning station. From Eufala, US-431 south, then east on SR-95 for 2 miles, follow signs. 334-687-3101, (395 Hwy 95, Eufala, AL 36027).

7) WARRIOR LAKE

U.S. Army Corps of Engineers
384 Resource Mgmt Drive
Demopolis, AL 36732
Phone: 334-289-3540
District: Mobile

Located on the Black Warrior River, just outside of Eutaw, Warrior Lake is 36 miles south of Tuscaloosa, AL. Activities include river fishing, swimming, hiking trails (difficult) and wildlife viewing.

Mound State Monument is located on the lake at mile 303.4. Forty

Indian temple mounds rise from a bluff overlooking the Black Warrior. The area is maintained by the State of Alabama and features a village site, burial grounds and museum.

The Corps-managed campground, Jennings Ferry, is also known as Roebuck Landing. Boat ramps and fish cleaning station are available. Gates open at 6am and close at 10pm.

Jennings Ferry: All year, 54 sites with electric (50 amp) hookups, some pull thrus, $18, water, dump, showers, laundry. From I-29/59 take exit 40 (Eutaw/Aliceville, Hwy-14) toward Eutaw. Follow Hwy-14 for about 9 miles. 205-372-1217, (1001 Jennings Ferry Rd, Akron, AL 35441).

8) WEST POINT LAKE

U.S. Army Corps of Engineers
500 Resource Management Dr.
West Point, GA 31833
Phone: 706–645–2937
District: Mobile

West Point Lake straddles the AL/GA border, just north of I-85. From Alabama, take I-85 north to Georgia exit 2 to US-29 north. The Visitor Center is on the left. Information and maps are available. The project includes 32,282 land acres, 25,864 water acres and 539 shoreline miles. Surrounded by deep forests and rolling hills, West Point Lake extends along the Chattahoochee River. A wildlife management area of 10,000 acres is located at the upper end of the lake, providing a habitat for many kinds of game and non-game wildlife.

Fishing is the most popular activity at the lake. A dozen creeks and more than 40 square miles of lake provide plenty of good fishing spots. The lake abounds with bass, catfish, crappie and bream. Bank fishing is excellent at most locations. Personal watercraft and water safety courses are offered from February to September in the Visitor Center.

Note: Three other West Point Lake campgrounds are listed in the Georgia section of this guide.

Amity: Mar-Sep, 93 sites with electric & water hookups, 3 tent only sites, $16–$22, drinking water, dump, restrooms, showers, laundry, boat ramp, basketball, tennis courts, playground, hiking trails. Campground gates are open 7am-10pm. From Lanett, Alabama, go 7 miles north on CR-212, follow signs. 334-499-2404, (1001 Country Road 393, Lanett, AL 36863).

9) WILLIAM "BILL" DANNELLY RESERVOIR

Millers Ferry Resource Office
1226 Powerhouse Road
Camden, AL 36726
Phone: 334-682-4244
District: Mobile

From I-65 exit 128, take SR-10 west for 40 miles to Camden, then Hwy-28 west 9 miles to the dam. Maps and directions to various camping and recreational areas are available at the Resource Office. Bisecting Alabama's Black Prairie Belt, the William "Bill" Dannelly Reservoir includes 105 miles of the Alabama River, a reservoir of 27 square miles and a shoreline of more than 500 miles.

Three Corps-managed campgrounds have boat ramps and courtesy docks. A swimming beach is at Millers Ferry and multi-purpose courts are at Six Mile Creek. Camping is also available at Roland Cooper State Park. Numerous fishing tournaments are held during the year. Annual festivals and Civil War enactments are also held in the area.

Chilatchee Creek: All year, 53 sites with electric & water hookups, 6 basic, drinking water, $16–$18, dump, restrooms, showers, laundry. From Alberta (west of the reservoir) CR-29 southeast for 11 miles. Turn left on Chilatchee Creek Road for 2 miles. 334-573-2562, (2267 Chilatchee Creek Rd, Alberta, AL 36720).

Millers Ferry: All year, 60 sites with electric and water hookups, 9 basic, one pull thru, drinking water, $16–$18, dump, restrooms, showers, laundry, swimming. From Camden (south of the reservoir) 12 miles northwest on SR-28. Turn right before the Lee Long Bridge, follow signs. 334-682-4191, (111 East Bank Park, Camden, AL 36726).

Six Mile Creek: All year, 31 sites with electric & water hookups (most waterfront), $16–$18, dump, restrooms, showers, laundry. From Selma (north of the reservoir) follow Hwy-41 south for 9 miles and turn right on CR-139, follow signs. 334-875-6228, (6485 County Rd 77, Selma, AL 36701).

10) WOODRUFF LAKE

U.S. Army Corps of Engineers
8493 U.S. Hwy-80 West
Hayneville, AL 36040
Phone: 334-872-9554
District: Mobile

Woodruff Lake is just 30 miles west of Montgomery; the Project Office is located along US-80. The project includes 21,814 land acres, 12,300 water acres and 372 shoreline miles.

There are two campgrounds managed by the Corps of Engineers, Prairie Creek and Gunter Hill, where campers can enjoy playgrounds, basketball, biking and hiking. In addition, swimming, canoeing and water skiing are available at Prairie Creek. Boat ramps are at both campgrounds. Excellent fishing at both campgrounds and Gunter Hill has good bow hunting opportunities for whitetail deer. Prairie Creek is on the banks of the Alabama River beneath moss-draped oaks, while Gunter Hill offers a peaceful setting of trees on the backwaters of the river.

Gunter Hill: All year, 65 sites with electric (50 amp) & water hookups, some non-reservable sites available, $18, dump, restrooms, showers, laundry. Overlooking the backwaters of the Alabama River. From I-65 exit 167, go 9 miles west on SR–80, then 4 miles north on CR-7, follow signs. 334-269-1053, (561 Booth Rd, Montgomery, AL 36108).

Prairie Creek: All year, 62 sites with electric (50 amp) & water hookups, some non-reservable sites available, 7 tent only sites, drinking water, $16–$18, dump, restrooms, showers, laundry. 48 sites are waterfront. From Montgomery, west on US-80 for 25 miles, then 5 miles north on CR-23, and 3 miles west on CR-40, follow signs. From Selma follow US-80 east for 25 miles then left on CR-23, follow signs. 334-418-4919, (582 Prairie Creek Rd, Lowndesboro, AL 36752).

Arkansas

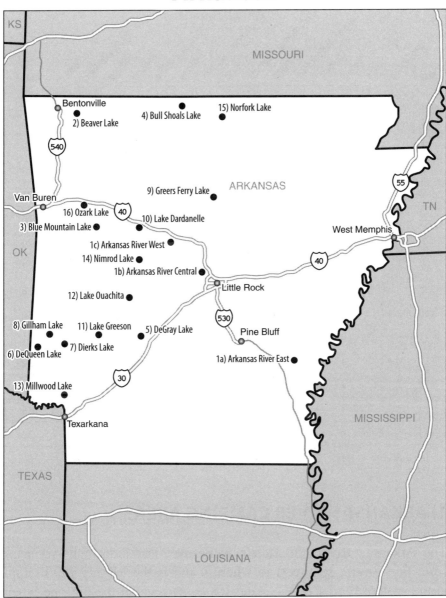

1) Arkansas River	5) DeGray Lake	12) Lake Ouachita
a) East	6) DeQueen Lake	13) Millwood Lake
b) Central	7) Dierks Lake	14) Nimrod Lake
c) West	8) Gillham Lake	15) Norfork Lake
2) Beaver Lake	9) Greers Ferry Lake	16) Ozark Lake
3) Blue Mountain Lake	10) Lake Dardanelle	
4) Bull Shoals Lake	11) Lake Greeson	

Map #	Auto Touring	Biking	Boating	Climbing	Cultural/Historic Sites	Camping	Educational Programs	Fishing	Groceries/Supplies	Hiking	Horseback Riding	Hunting	Lodging	Off Highway Vehicles	Visitor Center	Page #
1	♦		♦			♦		♦		♦						18
2	♦		♦	♦	♦	♦		♦	♦	♦		♦			♦	20
3			♦			♦		♦		♦		♦		♦		22
4			♦			♦		♦		♦		♦				23
5	♦		♦		♦	♦		♦		♦	♦	♦	♦		♦	24
6	♦		♦			♦		♦	♦	♦		♦				26
7	♦		♦		♦	♦		♦	♦	♦		♦				26
8			♦			♦		♦	♦	♦		♦				27
9			♦			♦		♦	♦	♦		♦			♦	28
10	♦	♦	♦	♦		♦		♦	♦	♦		♦	♦		♦	30
11		♦	♦		♦	♦		♦	♦	♦		♦				31
12	♦		♦		♦	♦		♦	♦	♦	♦	♦	♦			32
13			♦			♦		♦		♦	♦	♦				34
14			♦		♦	♦		♦	♦	♦		♦				35
15			♦			♦		♦	♦	♦		♦			♦	36
16			♦			♦		♦		♦		♦				38

1) ARKANSAS RIVER CAMPING AREAS

The Arkansas River, the state's namesake, flows through Arkansas from Fort Smith, southeast to where it meets the Mighty Mississippi at the eastern border of the state. It's easy to catch the big one when fishing in Arkansas. The entire stretch of the Arkansas River is popular among anglers seeking largemouth bass. Camping areas along the river are listed below, east to west: five campgrounds are between the MS/AR line and Pine Bluff, three are near Little Rock and three are west of Little Rock (accessible from I-40.) All have boat ramps. River campgrounds are within the Corps Little Rock District. Project Offices for river campgrounds include: Pine Bluff Project Office at 870-534-0451, Toad Suck Ferry Resource Office at 501-329-2986 and Greers Ferry Office at 501-362-2416.

1a) East (AR/MS state line to Pine Bluff)

Merrisach Lake: All year, 59 sites with electric & water hookups and 6 basic, $11–$19, drinking water, dump, restrooms, showers, interpretive trail, playground. From DeWitt, Arkansas, south on US-165 for 8.1 miles, then east on SR-44 for 5.3 miles to Tichnor Blacktop Road, 8.2 miles south to Merrisach Lane, follow signs. Near the Wilbur D. Mills Lock. 870-548-2712, (PFO 35 Wild Goose Ln, Tichnor, AR 72166).

Notrebes Bend Park: Mar-Oct, 34 sites with electric (50amp) and water hookups, $19, dump, restrooms, showers, laundry, sightseeing. On the river. From DeWitt, Arkansas, south on US-165 for 8.1 miles, then east on SR-44 for 5.3 miles to Tichnor Blacktop Road, 8.4 miles to W.D. Mills Road, 7 miles to the campground on the east side of the dam. 870-548-2291.

Pendleton Bend: All year, 31 sites with electric (some 50amp) & water hookups, $16–$19, dump, restrooms, showers, playground. From Dumas, Arkansas, US-165 north 9 miles, then SR-212 east for 2 miles, follow signs. 870-534-0451.

Wilbur D. Mills: Mar-Oct, 21 sites with electric & water hookups, $16, dump, restrooms, showers, pretty scenery. Follow directions to Pendeleton (above) drive through & continue 2 miles to W.D. Mills. 870-534-0451.

Rising Star: Mar-Oct, 20 sites with electric (50amp) and water hookups, $19, dump, restrooms, showers, playground, wildlife viewing. From Pine Bluff, US-65 southeast for 7.8 miles to Linwood, then north 3.5 miles on Blankenship Road. (Located 12 miles from Pine Bluff, home of the Arkansas Railroad Museum.) 870-534-0451.

1b) Central (near Little Rock)

Maumelle: All year, 129 sites with electric (50amp) and water hookups, some pull thrus, $20–$24, dump, restrooms, showers, playground, hiking. From I-430 exit 9, northwest 4 miles on SR-10, then 4 miles north on Pinnacle Valley Road, follow signs. 501-868-9477, (9009 Pinnacle, Little Rock, AR 72223).

Tar Camp: All year, 58 sites (38 with electric (some 50amp) & water hookups), $19, drinking water, dump, restrooms, showers, playground, nature trails. From I-530 exit 20, to Redfield, Arkansas, junction US-65/SR-46, east to SR-46 to SR-365, north 1 block, then 4 miles east to campground, follow signs. (On the river at Pool 5 Lock & Dam.) 501-397-5101, (4600 River Rd, Redfield, AR 72132).

Willow Beach: All year, 21 sites with electric (50amp) and water hookups, $19, dump, restrooms, showers, playground, ball field. From I-440 exit 7, east on US-165 for 2.5 miles, then south for 3 miles on Colonel Maynard Road, then west 1 mile on Blue Heron, follow signs. 501-961-1332, (11690 Willow Beach Park Dr, Scott, AR 72142).

1c) West (along I-40)

Cherokee: Mar-Oct, 33 sites with electric (some 50amp) & water hookups, non-reservable, $12-$16, dump, restrooms, showers, boat ramp, playground, ball field, shady sites. From I-40 exit 108, Hwy-9 south to Hwy-64 to Morrilton, then .7 mile south on Cherokee Street, then .8 mile south on Quincy, follow signs. (At Lock & Dam #9.)

Sequoya: All year, 14 sites with electric & water hookups, non-reservable, $18, dump, restrooms, showers, playground. From I-40 exit 108, south on Hwy-9, cross river, then 1.6 miles southwest on River View Road. On the south side of the river across from Cherokee.

Toad Suck Ferry: All year, 48 sites with electric & water hookups, $18-$20, dump, restrooms, showers, playground. From I-40 exit 129, go 7 miles west on SR-60, follow signs. 501-759-2005, (3298 State Hwy 60 West, Conway, AR 72032).

2) BEAVER LAKE

U.S. Army Corps of Engineers
2260 North 2nd Street
Rogers, AR 72756
Phone: 479-636-1210
District: Little Rock

Nestled in the Ozark Mountains of northwest Arkansas, birthplace of the White River, the project covers 28,000 acres and has 487 miles of natural shoreline. From I-540, take the US-62/SR-102 exit east to the Project Office where you can obtain maps and information on the recreational opportunities available, special events, craft fairs and fishing tournaments.

There are 11 Corps-managed camping areas, as well as Beaver State Park and several private campgrounds around the large lake. River rafting trips are available at Dam Site River Park. Caves, museums and historic sites are nearby.

Dam Site Lake Park: Apr-Oct, 48 sites with electric (50amp) hookups, some pull-thrus, non-reservable, $16-$17, drinking water, dump, restrooms, showers. From Eureka Springs, 9 miles west on US-62, then 3 miles south on SR-187, follow signs. 479-253-5828.

Dam Site River Park: Apr-Oct, 59 sites with electric (some 50amp) hookups, $18-$20, drinking water, dump, restrooms, showers. From Eureka Springs, 9 miles west on US-62, then 2.5 miles south on Hwy-187. 479-253-9865.

Hickory Creek: Apr-Oct, 61 sites with electric (50amp) hookups, $19, drinking water, dump, restrooms, showers, swimming. From I-540 exit at Hwy-264 for 4.5 miles, then right on Cow Face Road, left on Hickory Creek Road. **Note:** Do NOT exit from I-540 on Wagon Wheel Road as there is an almost impossible turn to Hwy-71B. 479-750-2943, (12618 Hickory Creek Rd, Lowell, AR 72745).

Horseshoe Bend: Apr-Oct, 63 sites with electric hookups and 3 tent sites in the East loop; 125 sites with electric (some 50amp) hookups in the West loop, some pull thrus, $14-$16, drinking water, dump, courtesy dock, nature trail. From Rogers, take the New Hope Road/Hwy-94 East exit, then east for about 2 miles, continue across 71B/8th Street on New Hope Road/Hwy-94 east for 4 miles. Turn left on Hwy-94 at junction of Hwy-94 spur & Hwy-94 east. Road dead ends at the park. 479-925-2561, (16165 E Hwy 94, Rogers, AR 72758).

Indian Creek: May-Sep, 33 sites with electric hookups, non-reservable, $16, drinking water, dump, restrooms, showers. From Garfield, 3 miles east on Hwy-62, then right on Indian Creek Road (CR-89) for 4 miles south. 479-656-3145.

Lost Bridge North: Apr-Sep, 42 sites with electric hookups, $18, drinking water, dump, restrooms, showers. From Rogers, Hwy-62 east for 13 miles to Garfield. Right on Hwy-127 for 6 miles, turn on 127 spur, then left on Marina Road. 479-359-3312, (Marina Rd, Garfield AR 72732).

Lost Bridge South: May-Sep, 36 sites with electric (some 50amp) hookups, $19–$20, drinking water, dump, restrooms, showers, public marina, swimming beach. From Garfield, Arkansas, turn off Hwy-62 and take Hwy-127 for 6 miles, follow signs. 479-359-3755, (12001 Buckhorn Circle, Garfield, AR 72732).

Prairie Creek: Apr-Oct, 112 sites with electric (some 50amp) hookups, $18–$25, drinking water, dump, restrooms, showers, laundry, marina, interpretive trail, swimming. Some seasonal sites. From Rogers, turn east at the intersection of 2nd and Locust. Travel east on Hwy-12 for 4 miles, then left on North Park Road. 479-925-3957, (9300 North Park Rd, Rogers, AR 72756).

Rocky Branch: Apr-Oct, 44 sites with electric hookups (some 50amp), non-reservable, $18, drinking water, dump, restrooms, showers, laundry. From Rogers, take SR-12 east 11 miles to SR-303 for 4.5 miles, turn left, follow signs. (15 minutes from Rogers.) 479-925-2526.

Starkey: May-Sep, 23 sites with electric hookups, non-reservable, $16, drinking water, dump, restrooms, showers, marina. From Eureka Springs, 2.5 miles on Hwy-62, then left on Hwy-187 for 4.2 miles. Turn right on Carroll County Road 2176 (Mudel Road) for 4.3 miles. 479-253-5866.

War Eagle: May-Sep, 26 sites with electric hookups, non-reservable, $16, drinking water, dump, restrooms, showers. Campsites are not adjacent to the water. From Springdale, Arkansas, go 14 miles east on Hwy-412, left on Knob Hill Loop (CR-389), then take Washington CR-95 for 2.1 miles, entrance on left. 479-750-4722.

3) BLUE MOUNTAIN LAKE

U.S. Army Corps of Engineers
Route 1 Box 173AA
Waveland, AR 72842
Phone: 479-947-2372
District: Little Rock

Blue Mountain Lake is 50 miles southeast of Fort Smith in west-central Arkansas. Located between two national forests, the area boasts of much natural beauty. From I-540 exit 12, take US-71 south to SR-10 west to Booneville; continue for 17 miles to Waveland, then south on CR-309. The Blue Mountain project contains 14,119 land acres, 2,910 water acres and 50 shoreline miles.

Catch-of-the-day for anglers can be bass, crappie, bream or catfish. The two modern campgrounds have boat ramps and fish cleaning stations. Waveland Park campground has a shady, cypress tree-lined swimming area.

Outlet Area: Mar-Oct, 41 sites with electric & water hookups, $12-$14, dump, restrooms, showers, playground, overlook area – beautiful scenery. From Booneville,

Arkansas, take SR-10 for 7 miles east to Waveland, then south on Hwy-309 for 1 mile, then west on Waveland Park Road, 1 mile to Blue Mountain Dam, follow signs. 479-947-2101.

Waveland Park: Mar-Oct, 51 sites with electric & water, $12–$14, dump, restrooms, showers, playground. From Booneville, Arkansas, go 17 miles east on SR-10, then south on Hwy-309 for 1 mile, then west on Waveland Park Road for 1 mile to Blue Mountain Dam, follow signs. 479-947-2102.

4) BULL SHOALS LAKE

U.S. Army Corps of Engineers
324 West 7th Street
Mountain Home, AR 72653
Phone: 870-425-2700
District: Little Rock

Bull Shoals Lake is located 135 miles north of Little Rock in north-central Arkansas. Take US-65 north to junction US-62, then 50 miles east to Flippin and 4 miles north to the lake. Maps and information can be obtained at the Project Office. Bull Shoals has 62,326 land acres, 45,440 water acres and 740 shoreline miles. Its extensive area straddles the states of Arkansas and Missouri. In the beautiful Ozark Mountains, the lake is known for its exceptional water quality and outstanding fisheries. Bull Shoals has hundreds of miles of lake arms and coves, perfect for boating, water sports, swimming and fishing. In autumn, foliage in the area is known as the Flaming Fall Revue.

Of the 11 Corps-managed campgrounds, 7 are in Arkansas and 4 in Missouri. They are included in their respective state sections. Most campgrounds at Bull Shoals have playgrounds, boat launches and public marinas. ORVs/ATVs are prohibited. Hiking trails can be found in the Lakeview Campground. The marinas have rental boats, supplies and guides for hire.

Buck Creek: Apr-Sep, 39 sites with electric hookups, $12–$16, drinking water, dump, restrooms, showers. From Mountain Home, AR, take SR-5 north for 24.4 miles, then west on US-160 for 21 miles, then south on SR-U for 5 miles to US-125 for 5.7 miles to Buck Creek Park access road. Follow signs. 417-785-4313.

Dam Site Park: May-Sep, 35 sites with electric hookups, $13–$16, drinking water, dump, restrooms, showers, laundry, golf course nearby, a town is within walking distance. From Bull Shoals, southeast on SR-178 for 1 mile. 870-445-7166.

Highway 125: Apr-Oct, 39 sites with electric hookups, $16–$17, drinking water, dump, restrooms, showers, swimming, marina, From Yellvill, Arkansas, take SR-14 for 14 miles northwest, then north on SR-125 for 13 miles, follow signs. 870-436-5711.

Lakeview: All year, 88 sites with electric (some 50amp) hookups, $13–$17, drinking water, dump, restrooms, showers, laundry, swimming, marina. 1.5-mile nature trail. From Mountain Home, Arkansas, SR-5 north for 6 miles to Midway, then west on SR-178 for 7 miles; north on Boat Dock Road, follow signs. 870-431-8116.

Lead Hill: Apr-Oct, 75 sites with electric hookups, $13–$16, drinking water, dump, restrooms, showers, swimming area, marina. From Lead Hill, Arkansas, go 4 miles north on SR-7, follow signs. 870-422-7555.

Oakland/Ozark Isle Park: Apr-Oct, 46 sites with electric hookups, 37 basic sites, $9–$17, drinking water, dump, restrooms, showers, laundry, swimming area, marina. From Mountain Home, 14 miles north on SR-5, then 10 miles west on SR-202, follow signs. 870-431-5744.

Tucker Hollow: Apr-Oct, 32 sites with electric hookups, $9–$16, drinking water, dump, restrooms, showers, swimming, playground, marina, 35-foot RV length limit. From Lead Hill, Arkansas, 7 miles northwest on SR-14, then north on SR-281 for 3 miles. 870-436-5622.

5) DEGRAY LAKE

U.S. Army Corps of Engineers
729 Channel Road
Arkadelphia, AR 71923
Phone: 870-246-5501
District: Vicksburg

DeGray Lake is 8 miles west of Arkadelphia and 67 miles southwest of Little Rock. From I-30, exit 78, take SR-7 north for 2 miles to the Visitor Center. With 13,800 water areas and 207 miles of shoreline, DeGray is a popular fishing destination. The lake is stocked with a variety of game fish and is a world-class striped bass fishery. Other popular activities at the lake include swimming, scuba diving and boating. On the Caddo River, the lake is noted for its geological formations.

Corps-managed campgrounds have boat ramps, playgrounds, swimming and other amenities. The nearby DeGray Lake State Park also has camping and varied amenities including a swimming pool, tennis, 18-hole golf course, equestrian trail, marina, restaurant and lodge.

Alpine Ridge: All year, 49 sites with electric hookups, drinking water, $10–$16, dump, restrooms, showers, playground, swimming. From I-30, exit 73, take SR-8 west for 19 miles to Alpine, then right onto Fendley Road for 8.5 miles. 870-246-5501.

Arlie Moore: All year, 87 sites with electric hookups, $10–$16, drinking water, dump, restrooms, showers, playground, swimming, nature trail, amphitheater. From I-30 exit 78, SR-7 north for 9 miles, then left on Arlie Moore Road, 2 miles. Located about midway of the lake. 870-246-5501.

Caddo Drive: Mar-Oct, 72 sites with electric hookups, $10, drinking water, dump, restrooms, showers, laundry, playground, swimming beach, boat launch. From I-30 exit 78, SR-7 north for 6 miles, then left on to Edgewood Road, 3 miles. 870-246-5501.

Edgewood: All year, 49 sites with electric hookups, $10–$16, drinking water, dump, restrooms, showers, laundry, playground, swimming. Closest to the state park and about 25 miles from Hot Springs National Park. From I-30 exit 78, SR-7 for 6 miles, then left on Edgewood Road, then 2 miles to campground. 870-246-5501.

Iron Mountain: All year, 69 sites with electric hookups, $10–$16, drinking water, dump, restrooms, showers, playground. Closest camping to I-30. From I-30, exit 78, take SR-7 north 2.5 miles, then left on Skyline Drive for 2.5 miles across the lake, then right on Iron Mountain Road. 870-246-5501.

Shouse Ford: All year, 100 sites with electric hookups, $10–$16, drinking water, dump, restrooms, showers, swimming. From I-30 exit 78, SR-7 north to Bismarck, then left on SR-84 for 9 miles west to Point Cedar. Turn left on Shouse Ford Road, 4 miles. 870-246-5501.

6) DEQUEEN LAKE

U.S. Army Corps of Engineers
706 DeQueen Lake Road
DeQueen, AR 71832
Phone: 870-584-4161
District: Little Rock

DeQueen Lake is located just 8 miles east of the OK/AR border. From the town of DeQueen, take US-71 north for 8 miles, then one-half mile west to the lake. The project has 7,112 land acres, 1,680 water acres and 32 shoreline miles. Sportsmen enjoy outstanding fishing and hunting opportunities at the project.

Three Corps-managed campgrounds all have boat ramps and fish cleaning stations. Convenience stores for food, bait and tackle are located at Oak Grove and Pine Ridge.

Bellah Mine: All year, 20 sites with electric & water hookups, $13–$15, dump, restrooms, showers, canoeing. From DeQueen, go 7 miles north on US-71 to Bellah Mine Road, then west for 5 miles. 870-386-7511.

Oak Grove: All year, 36 sites with electric & water hookups, $13–$15, dump, restrooms, showers, amphitheater, swimming. From DeQueen, go 3 miles north on US-71, then 5.5 miles west on DeQueen Lake Road, then .3 mile north, follow signs. 870-642-6111.

Pine Ridge: All year, 55 sites (17 with electric & water hookups), $13–$15, dump, restrooms, showers. From DeQueen, go 3 miles north on US-71, then 5.5 miles west on DeQueen Lake Road, then 1.5 miles west on Country Road, follow signs. 870-642-6111.

7) DIERKS LAKE

U.S. Army Corps of Engineers
952 Lake Road - P.O. Box 8
Dierks, AR 71833
Phone: 870-286-2346
District: Little Rock

The 1,360-acre lake is 72 miles southwest of Hot Springs, north of Texarkana, east of DeQueen and 5 miles northwest of Dierks in southwest Arkansas. From Texarkana, travel 46 miles north on US-71, then 11 miles east on US-70. The project includes 4,139 land acres, 1,360 water acres and 33 shoreline miles.

Three campgrounds are suitable for RV camping and have beautiful swimming beaches. The lake is known for bass and crappie fishing. Interesting places for day trips in the area are Hot Springs National Park and the Diamond Mine at Murfreesboro. Shopping and sightseeing are available in the area.

Blue Ridge: All year, 17 sites with electric hookups, 5 basic sites, non-reservable, $9–$13, drinking water, dump, restrooms, showers, swimming. From Dierks, travel 3 miles east on US-70, then 4 miles north on SR-278, then 2.6 miles west on county road, follow signs. 870-286-3214.

Horseshoe Bend: All year, 11 sites, with electric & water hookups, $10, non-reservable, dump, restrooms, showers, swimming, playground, wooded area. From Dierks, follow US-70 west for 3 miles to the paved access road.

Jefferson Ridge: Mar-Oct, 85 sites with electric & water hookups, $14–$16, dump, restrooms, showers. Numerous waterfront sites, bank fishing access. From Dierks travel 5 miles west on US-70, then 5 miles north on Green Chapel Road, follow signs. 870-286-3214.

8) GILLHAM LAKE

U.S. Army Corps of Engineers
706 DeQueen Lake Road
DeQueen, AR 71832
Phone: 870-584-4161
District: Little Rock

Gillham Lake is located six miles northeast of Gillham, Arkansas, and 15 miles north of DeQueen. From DeQueen go 15 miles north on US-71, then 5 miles east to the lake, which is located near the Oklahoma state line. The Gilliam project has 7,216 land acres, 1,370 water acres and 37 shoreline miles.

There are two RV camping areas at the project: Big Coon is on the lake and Cossatot Reefs is on the river, a wild and scenic stream that attracts adventurous recreationists. Amenities at both camping areas include: amphitheater, playground, boat launch and fish cleaning station. The two-mile Coon Creek Walking Trail wends through the rolling hills next to the lake.

Big Coon Creek: All year, 31 sites with electric & water hookups, $13–$15, dump, restrooms, showers, swimming. From Gillham, travel 6 miles northeast via county roads, follow signs. 870-385-7126.

Cossatot Reefs: All year, 26 sites with electric & water hookups, $13–$15, dump, restrooms, showers, swimming, canoeing, nature trails. From Gillham, go six miles northeast via county road, close to the dam, follow signs. 870-386-7261.

9) GREERS FERRY LAKE

U.S. Army Corps of Engineers
P.O. Box 1088
700 Heber Springs Rd. No.
Heber Springs, AR 72543
Phone: 501-362-2416
District: Little Rock

Greers Ferry Lake is 65 miles north of Little Rock, just three miles northeast of Heber Springs. From Little Rock, go 15 miles north on US-67/167, then 50 miles north on SR-5. The dam stands at the foot of Round Mountain in the Ozark Mountains. The Garner Visitor Center is on Hwy-25/5 just west of the dam and features an information desk, exhibit area and auditorium where visitors can view an audio-visual presentation. Call the Visitor Center at 501-362-9067 for hours and days of operation.

Eleven Corps-managed areas are available for RV camping. Boat ramps are located at all camping areas and some have marinas that provide rental services, food and supplies. The Josh Park Memorial Trail, a multi-purpose trail for jogging and biking, is near the Dam Site Campground.

The Mountain Island National Nature Trail (moderately difficult) is located at the Sugar Loaf campground.

Choctaw: Apr-Nov, 91 sites with electric (some 50amp) & water, 55 basic sites, $14–$19, drinking water, dump, restrooms, showers, swimming. From Clinton, AR, take US-65 south 5 miles to AR-330, then 3.5 miles east, follow signs. 501-745-8320 (3850 Highway 330 E., Clinton, AR 72031.)

Cove Creek: Apr-Oct, 31 sites with electric hookups, 34 basic sites, non-reservable, $14–$19, drinking water, dump, restrooms, showers, swimming. From Heber Springs, Arkansas, go 6.3 miles southwest on SR-25, then 3 miles northeast on SR-16, then 1.25 miles northeast on access road, follow signs. 501-362-2416. (734 Cove Creek Rd, Quitman, AR 72131.)

Dam Site: Apr-Oct, 148 sites with electric (some 50amp), 104 basic sites, some pull thrus, $14–$20, drinking water, dump, restrooms, showers, swimming. Beautiful scenery. From Heber Springs go 3 miles north on SR-25B, follow signs. 501-362-2416. (315 Heber Springs Rd N, Heber Springs, AR 72543.)

Devils Fork: Apr-Nov, 55 sites with electric (some 50amp) hookups, $17–$19, drinking water, dump, restrooms, showers, swimming. From Greers Ferry, Arkansas, go north on SR-16 for .25 miles, follow signs. 501-825-8618. (73 Devils Fork Rd, Greers Ferry, AR 72067.)

Heber Springs: Apr-Oct, 106 sites with electric, 36 basic sites, $14–$19, drinking water, dump, restrooms, showers, swimming, convenience store. From Heber Springs, go 2 miles west on SR-110, then .5 miles north on paved access road, follow signs. 501-250-0485. (89 Park Rd, Heber Springs, AR 72543.)

Hill Creek: Apr-Sep, 25 sites with electric hookups, $14–$17, drinking water, dump, restrooms, showers, swimming. From Drasco, Arkansas, take SR-92 west for 12 miles, then SR-225 northwest for 3 miles. Then south 2 miles on paved access road, follow signs. 870-948-2419. (474 Hill Creek Rd, Edgemont, AR 72044.)

John F. Kennedy: All year, 61 sites with electric hookups and 13 sites with electric & water, $17–$20, drinking water, dump, restrooms, showers, good wildlife viewing. Located below the dam on Little Red River trout stream. From Heber Springs, go north on SR-25 for 4 miles, cross dam, turn right at second road, follow signs. 501-250-0481. (375 Hatchery Rd, Heber Springs, AR 72543.)

Narrows: Apr-Oct, 60 sites with electric hookups, $14–$19, drinking water, dump, restrooms, showers. From Greers Ferry take SR-16 southwest for 2.5 miles, follow signs. 501-825-7602. (7699 Edgemont Rd, Greers Ferry, AR 72067.)

Old Highway 25: Apr-Oct, 89 sites with electric, 36 basic sites, $12–$17, drinking water, dump, restrooms, showers, swimming. From Heber Springs, go 6.25 miles north on SR-25, then west on SR-258 for 3 miles, follow signs. 501-250-0483. (1500 Old Highway 25 (AR), Tumbling Shoals, AR 72581.)

Shiloh: Apr-Nov, 60 sites with electric, 56 basic sites, $14–$19, drinking water, dump, restrooms, showers, swimming. From Greers Ferry, go 3.5 miles southeast on SR-110, follow signs. 501-825-8619. (1350 Shiloh Rd, Greers Ferry, AR 72067.)

Sugar Loaf: Apr-Nov, 56 sites with electric, 39 basic sites, $14–$19, drinking water, dump, restrooms, showers, swimming. Sugar Loaf is 12 miles northeast of Bee Branch on SR-92, then 1.5 miles west on SR-337. 501-654-2267. (1389 Resort Rd, Higden, AR 72067.)

10) LAKE DARDANELLE

U.S. Army Corps of Engineers
1598 Lock & Dam Road
Russellville, AR 72802
Phone: 479-968-5008
District: Little Rock

Lake Dardanelle offers 34,300 acres of boating and fishing waters rimmed by 315 shoreline miles featuring choice picnic and camping areas. From I-40 exit 81, go south on Hwy-7 for 5 miles to Lock and Dam Rd (Hwy-7 spur), then 3 miles west on the spur to the Project Office and Visitor Center.

The lake is in the Arkansas River Valley, a favorite wintering area for the American bald eagle. From late fall through early spring, eagle are often seen perched in large trees and on snags along the river as they hunt for their favorite prey – fish. There is excellent fishing and abundant wildlife viewing year-round. Bream, crappie and largemouth bass are stocked in the lake providing excellent sport fishing. Boat ramps are located throughout and there is a marina at Spadra. A mountain biking trail is at Old Post Campground and Bridge Rock Nature Trail is at Shoal Bay. Varied activities are available at Corps-managed campgrounds. Dardanelle and Russellville State Parks are also at the lake.

Old Post Road: All year, 40 sites with electric & water hookups, prime sites are along the riverbank, $18, dump, restrooms, showers, tennis/basketball courts, softball/soccer/football fields. Located in Russellville, from SR-7 go 1 mile on Lock & Dam Road, follow signs. 479-968-7962, (1063 Lock and Dam Rd, Russellville, AR 72802).

Piney Bay: Mar-Oct, 67 sites with electric hookups, $16–$18, drinking water, dump, restrooms, showers, amphitheater, swimming. From London, Arkansas, go west on US-64 for 3 miles, then north for 3.5 miles on SR-359, follow signs. 479-885-3029, (189 Private Rd 2720, London, AR 72847).

River View: Mar-Oct, 8 sites with electric & water hookups and 10 basic sites, non-reservable, $11, no dump at this location but campers may use the dump across the river at Old Post Road. From Russellville, south on SR-7 across the outlet. Located west of SR-7 in Dardanelle on 2nd St, immediately below the dam. 479-968-5008.

Shoal Bay: All year, 82 sites with electric hookups, $16–$18, drinking water, dump, restrooms, showers, swimming beach, amphitheater. From New Blaine, Arkansas, take SR-197 north for 2 miles, follow signs. 479-938-7335, (Shoal Bay Rd, New Blaine, AR 72859).

Spadra: All year, 23 sites with electric & water hookups, 5 tent sites, non-reservable, $13–$15, drinking water, dump, restrooms, showers, marina with restaurant. Caution, campground is in a high cliff area. From junction US-64 in Clarksville, go 2 miles south through Jamestown on SR-103. 479-754-6438.

Sweeden Island: Mar-Oct, 22 sites with electric hookups and 6 basic sites, non-reservable, $10–$16, dump, restrooms, showers. At Lock & Dam #9, on the bluffs overlooking the Arkansas River, good fishing and waterfowl viewing. From Atkins, Arkansas, take SR-105 southwest for 15 miles through Wilson. 479-641-7500.

11) LAKE GREESON / NARROWS DAM

U.S. Army Corps of Engineers
145 Dynamite Hill Road
Murfreesboro, AR 71958
Phone: 870-285-2151
District: Vicksburg

Lake Greeson on the Little Missouri River is located 69 miles northeast of Texarkana and 6 miles north of Murfreesboro. The project encompasses 8,799 land acres, 7,260 water acres and 134 shoreline miles. From I-30 exit 46, go north on SR-19 for 30 miles to Murfreesboro, then 6 miles north on SR-27.

A nature trail allows visitors to reach the site of a cinnabar mine. A 31 mile long motor bike trail and the Chimney Rock geological formation are located at Lake Greeson. The lake is a wintering site for American bald eagles.

Cowhide Cove: May-Sep, 48 sites electric hookups, $10–$16, drinking water, dump, restrooms, showers, playground. From Murfreesboro, take SR-27 north for 9 miles to Cowhide Access Road, west to the campground. 870-285-2151 (239 Cowhide Cove Rd, Murfreesboro, AR 71958.)

Dam Area: Mar-Oct, 24 sites (18 with electric hookups), $10–$18, drinking water, dump, restrooms, showers, marina, swimming. From Murfreesboro, go north on SR-19 for 6 miles to the dam area. 870-285-2151 (145 Dynamite Hill Rd, Murfreesboro, AR 71958.)

Kirby Landing: May-Sep, 87 sites with electric hookups, $13–$16, some pull thrus, drinking water, dump, restrooms, showers, playground. From Murfreesboro, take SR-27 north for 15 miles, then west on US-70 for 3 miles to Kirby Landing access road, then south to the campground. 870-285-2151 (224 Kirby Landing Rd, Kirby, AR 71950.)

Parker Creek: Mar-Oct, 49 sites with electric hookups, $13–$16, drinking water, dump, restrooms, showers, playground. From Murfreesboro, go north on SR-19 for 6 miles to Narrows Dam, cross the Little Missouri River and continue for 3 miles to the campground. 870-285-2151 (129 Parker Creek Rd, Murfreesboro, AR 71958.)

Self Creek: Mar-Oct, 76 sites (41 with electric hookups), $13–$15, drinking water, dump, restrooms, showers, playground, marina, swimming. From Murfreesboro, take SR-27 north for 15 miles, to Kirby, then west on US-70 for 6 miles to the campground. 870-285-2151 (4206 Highway 70 West, Daisy, AR 71950.)

12) LAKE OUACHITA

Lake Ouachita Field Office
1201 Blakely Dam Road
Royal, AR 71968
Phone: 501-767-2101
District: Vicksburg

Lake Ouachita, the largest man-made lake in the state, is located 67 miles southwest of Little Rock. From Hot Springs, go 13 miles west on US-270, then north on SR-277. The lake's crystal-clear waters make it a popular site for scuba diving. The project includes 66,324 total acres of land and water. There are 975 miles of shoreline, ideal for fishing and water sports…and 20,000 acres of public land are open for hunting in season. World class striper fishing is a popular activity.

Corps-managed RV camping areas are all on the south side of the lake, north of US-270 between Hot Springs and Mount Ida. Campgrounds have boat ramps and fish cleaning stations. Off road vehicles are prohibited. There is a boating trail for viewing geological formations on the shoreline. Other activities nearby include horseback riding, sightseeing, miniature golf and numerous local shops and restaurants. Lake Ouachita State Park has a modern campground. Several marinas at the lake offer boat rentals and other services and supplies.

Brady Mountain: May-Sep, 57 sites with electric (some 50amp), 17 tent sites, $12–$16, drinking water, dump, restrooms, showers, swimming, playground, hiking trail, equestrian trails, amphitheater. From Hot Springs, 13 miles west on US-270, then 6.1 miles north on Brady Mountain Road. 501-760-1146, (132 Brady Mountain Overlook, Royal, AR 71968).

Crystal Springs: May-Sep, 52 sites with electric & water hookups, 32 basic sites, $10–$18, drinking water, dump, restrooms, showers, swimming, playground. From Hot Springs, 16.8 miles west on US-270, then 1.5 miles north on Crystal Springs Road. 501-767-2108.

Denby Point: May-Sep, 59 sites with electric (some 50amp), 8 basic sites, $14–$16, drinking water, dump, restrooms, showers, amphitheater, swimming, interpretive trail, fish cleaning station. From Mount Ida, 9.5 miles east on US-270, then .3 mile north on Denby Road. 501-767-2108.

Joplin: May-Sep, 62 sites with electric hookups, 2 basic sites, $10–$16, drinking water, dump, restrooms, showers, swimming, horse trails nearby. From Hot Springs, approximately 24 miles west on US-270, then north on Mountain Harbor Road. 501-767-2108.

Little Fir: All year, 29 sites with electric, non-reservable, $10–$12, drinking water, dump, restrooms, no showers. From junction SR-27, through Rubie, 3 miles east on SR-188, then 2.2 miles north. Follow signs. 501-767-2108.

Tompkins Bend: May-Sep, 15 sites with electric (some 50amp) & water hookups and 58 sites with electric only, 14 tent sites, $10–$18, drinking water, dump, restrooms, showers. From Mount Ida, 10.7 miles east on US-270, then 2.1 miles north on Tompkins Bend Road. 501-767-2108.

13) MILLWOOD LAKE

U.S. Army Corps of Engineers
1528 Highway 32 East
Ashdown, AR 71822
Phone: 870-898-3343
District: Little Rock

Millwood is located in the southwest corner of Arkansas on the Little River. The project includes 112,147 land acres, 29,500 water acres and 87 shoreline miles. From Texarkana, travel 16 miles north on US-59/71 to Ashdown, then 9 miles east on SR-32.

Millwood Lake provides some of the best fishing in the country, and birders come to Millwood to view the more than 309 bird species that appear throughout the year. RV camping is found at Corp-managed areas and at Millwood State Park.

Beards Bluff: All year, 25 sites with electric & water hookups, 3 full hookup sites, $10–$15, non-reservable, dump, restrooms, showers. From Saratoga, Arkansas, take SR-32 for 3 miles south, follow signs. 870-388-9556.

Beards Lake: All year, 5 sites with electric & water hookups, non-reservable, $9–$13, dump, restrooms, showers, swimming. From Saratoga, Arkansas, take SR-32 for 4 miles south, below dam. 870-388-9556.

Cottonshed: All year, 46 shoreline sites with electric & water hookups, 3 tent sites, non-reservable, $13–$15, dump, restrooms, showers, laundry, hiking. From Mineral Springs travel 7 miles south on SR-355, follow signs. 870-898-3343.

Paraloma Landing: All year, 34 sites with electric & water hookups, some pull thrus, non-reservable, $8–$11, dump, restrooms, showers, fish cleaning station. Located on SR-234, 1.5 miles south of Paraloma. 870-898-3343.

Saratoga Landing: All year, 17 sites, no hookups, non-reservable, $5, restrooms.

From Saratoga go 1 mile south on SR-32, then .4 mile west on access road. 870-898-3343.

14) NIMROD LAKE

U.S. Army Corps of Engineers
3 Highway 7 South
Plainview, AR 72857
Phone: 479-272-4324
District: Little Rock

Nimrod Lake is located in the west-central part of the state. From Hot Springs, travel 40 miles north on SR-7, a National Scenic Byway. The project consists of 21,640 land acres, 3,550 water acres and 77 shoreline miles.

Nimrod is the oldest Corps lake in the state and has been popular for fishing and hunting since it was completed in 1942. Anglers will find crappie, largemouth bass, bream, catfish and white bass tugging on their hooks. Supplies are available at local stores and bait shops along the lake.

Five parks nestled along the north side of the lake provide modern camping facilities and an opportunity to relax amid the groves of tall, sweet-scented pines. Entrances to the parks are from SR-60 on the east and north sides of the lake. Three campgrounds are directly on the lake: Quarry Cove, County Line and Carter Cove. Sunlight Bay is on Wilson Slough, located just off the Fourche La Fave River upstream of the lake. River Road Campground is just downstream of the Nimrod Dam. Boat ramps, fish cleaning stations and playgrounds are conveniently located at the campgrounds. Swimming is available at Carter Cove and County Line areas. Nearby places of interest include Petit Jean State Park, Mount Nebo State Park and Hot Springs National Park.

Carter Cove: Mar-Oct, 34 sites with electric (some 50amp) & water hookups, $14-$16, dump, restrooms, showers, playground, swimming. From Plainview, east 3 miles on SR-60 to access road, then 1 mile, follow signs. 479-272-4983.

County Line: Mar-Oct, 20 sites with electric (some 50amp) & water hookups, $14-$16, dump, restrooms, showers, playground, swimming. From Plainview, east 6 miles on SR-60 to access road, follow signs. 479-272-4945.

Quarry Cove: Mar-Oct, 31 sites with electric (some 50amp) & water hookups, $14-$16, dump, restrooms, showers, amphitheater, playground, swimming. From Ola, go 9 miles south on SR-7, then west on SR-60 for .5 mile to the access road. 479-272-4233.

River Road: All year, 15 sites with electric (some 50amp) & water hookups, 6 electric-only sites, $13-$16, drinking water, dump, restrooms, showers, playground, interpretive trail. From Ola, south on SR-7 for 9 miles to the access road. 479-272-4835.

Sunlight Bay: All year, 28 sites with electric & water hookups, $14-$16, dump, restrooms, showers, playground. From Plainview, go west on SR-28 for .25 mile to access road, then 2 miles south. 479-272-4324.

15) NORFORK LAKE

U.S. Army Corps of Engineers
324 West 7th Street
Mountain Home, AR 72653
Phone: 870-425-2700
District: Little Rock

Norfork Lake is just east of the Bull Shoals project and shares its Project Office. From Little Rock, go 135 miles north on US-65, then 50 miles east on US-62 to the Project Office where maps and information are available. Norfork consists of 32,195 land acres, 22,000 water acres and 380 shoreline miles.

Norfork provides both open breezy stretches for sailing and quiet secluded coves, which are ideal for water sports. Undeveloped shoreline allows for ample room to enjoy the hills and hollows. The Corps operates 8 camping areas with swimming beaches and boat launches located at most. ORVs/ATVs are prohibited. Several marinas provide boat rentals and related services. The Robinson Point National Recreation Trail and the Norfork section of the Ozark Trail enable nature observers and photographers to view the Ozark Mountains through the change of seasons.

Bidwell Point: May-Sep, 46 sites with electric hookups, 2 basic sites, $13–$17, drinking water, dump, restrooms, showers, playground, swimming. From Mountain Home, Arkansas, go 9 miles east on US-412/62, then 2 miles north on SR-101. Cross the lake on the 101 bridge and take the first access road to the right, follow signs. 870-467-5375.

Cranfield: Apr-Oct, 67 sites with electric hookups, $16, drinking water, dump, restrooms, showers, playground, canoeing, swimming, 35-foot RV length limit. From Mountain Home, Arkansas, east 5 miles on US-412/62, then left on Cranfield Road (CR-34) for 3 miles, follow signs. 870-492-4191.

Dam-Quarry: May-Sep, 24 sites with electric (50amp) and water hookups and 44 electric-only sites, $16–$19, drinking water, dump, restrooms, showers, playground, hiking trails. From Mountain Home, go 14 miles south on SR-5 to Salesville, then left on SR-177 for 2 miles. The campground is located below Norfork Dam, follow signs. 870-499-7216.

Gamaliel: May-Sep, 64 sites with electric hookups, $16, drinking water, dump, restrooms, showers playground, swimming, 35-foot RV length limit. From Mountain Home, go 9 miles east on Hwy-412/62, then 5 miles north on SR-101, then 3 miles southeast on CR-42, follow signs. 870-467-5680.

Henderson Park: Apr-Sep, 38 sites with electric hookups, $14, drinking water, dump, restrooms, showers, marina, 30-foot RV length limit, convenience store. From Mountain Home, go 10 miles east on US-412/62, cross the bridge, turn left at first access road, follow signs. 870-488-5282.

Jordan: Apr-Sep, 38 sites with electric hookups, 5 tent sites, $9–$15, drinking water, dump, restrooms, swimming, 35-foot RV length limit. From Mountain Home, take SR-5 south to Salesville, then left on SR-177 for 5 miles to Jordan Community, then north on CR-64 for 3 miles, follow signs. 870-499-7223.

Panther Bay: Apr-Sep, 15 sites with electric hookups, 13 basic sites, $9–$14, drinking water, dump, restrooms, swimming, playground, marina. From SR-201 in Mountain Home, go east on US-62 for 8.6 miles, then 1 mile north on SR-101, turn right at the first access road, follow signs. 870-492-4544.

Robinson Point: Apr-Oct, 102 sites with electric (some 50amp) hookups, $16–$17, drinking water, dump, restrooms, showers, playground, swimming hiking trails, 35-foot RV length limit. From Mountain Home, travel east 9 miles on US-412/62, turn right on CR-279 for 3 miles, follow signs. 870-492-6853.

16) OZARK LAKE

U.S. Army Corps of Engineers
6042 Lock & Dam Road
Ozark, AR 72949
Phone: 479-667-2129
District: Little Rock

Ozark Lake extends 36 miles along the Arkansas River. The project covers 10,600 acres of water and 6,349 land acres. The shoreline of the lake varies from steep bluffs and tree-lined banks to open farmlands and level fields. The lock and dam is on the Arkansas River, 1 mile southeast of Ozark (just south of I-40). The project office is immediately below the dam.

Recreation facilities are located on the shorelines of Ozark and Hammerschmidt Lakes. Fishing is abundant from boats or riverbanks and boat ramps are conveniently located. The lake is stocked with striped sea bass and walleyed pike. Year round fishing is good for catfish, bream, crappie, white and largemouth bass. A hiking trail begins high atop the bluffs overlooking Ozark Lake and winds through the forest floor. Six Corps-managed camping areas are at the lake.

Aux Arc: All year, 60 sites with electric (some 50amp) & water hookups, $17–$18, drinking water, dump, restrooms, showers, playground. From Ozark, Arkansas, take SR-23 south for 1.5 mile to SR-309. Turn left and follow signs. 479-968-5008.

Citadel Bluff: May-Sep, 25 sites with electric hookups, non-reservable, $6, drinking water, restrooms. From Cecil, Arkansas, go 1.6 miles north on SR-41. 479-667-2129.

Clear Creek: Mar-Oct, 25 RV/tent sites with electric hookups and 11 basic sites, $9–$16, drinking water, dump, restrooms, showers. From Alma, Arkansas, take SR-162 for 5.2 miles south, then left on the paved road for 3.6 miles, follow signs. 479-632-4882.

River Ridge: Apr-Sep, 18 sites, no hookups, non-reservable, free, no facilities. From Cecil, Arkansas, go 12 miles west on SR-96, then 1.5 miles northeast on Hoover's Ferry Rd. 479-667-2129.

Springhill: All year, 33 sites with electric (some 50amp) & water hookups, 9 electric-only sites and 3 basic sites, $9–$18, drinking water, dump, restrooms, showers. From Barling, AR, go 1.5 miles north on SR-59 to Lock & Dam Road in Fort Smith. 479-452-4598, (1700 Lock & Dam Rd, Barling, AR 72923).

Vine Prairie: All year, 1 full hookup site, 12 electric-only and 7 basic sites, non-reservable, $8-$15, drinking water, dump, restrooms, showers. From Mulberry, Arkansas, go 1.7 miles south on SR-917. 479-997-8122.

California

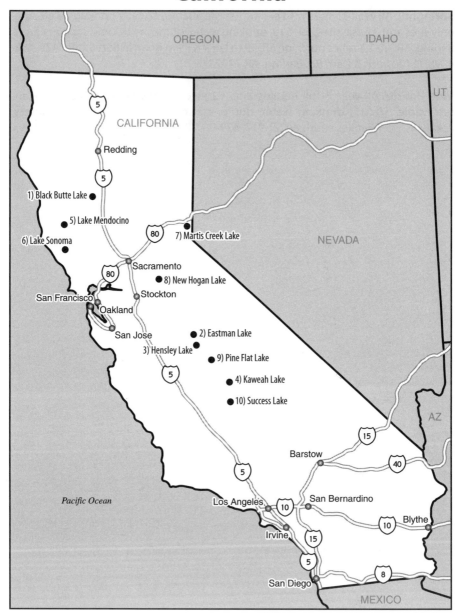

1) Black Butte Lake   7) Martis Creek Lake
2) Eastman Lake   8) New Hogan Lake
3) Hensley Lake   9) Pine Flat Lake
4) Kaweah Lake   10) Success Lake
5) Lake Mendocino
6) Lake Sonoma

Map #	Auto Touring	Biking	Boating	Climbing	Cultural / Historic Sites	Educational Programs	Camping	Groceries / Supplies	Fishing	Hiking	Horseback Riding	Hunting	Off Highway Vehicles	Lodging	Visitor Center	Page #
1		♦	♦				♦	♦	♦	♦	♦	♦			♦	41
2		♦	♦				♦	♦	♦		♦	♦			♦	42
3		♦	♦		♦		♦	♦	♦		♦	♦			♦	43
4			♦				♦	♦	♦	♦	♦				♦	43
5		♦	♦				♦	♦	♦		♦	♦			♦	44
6		♦	♦				♦		♦		♦	♦			♦	45
7		♦					♦	♦	♦		♦					46
8		♦	♦		♦	♦	♦	♦		♦	♦	♦	♦		♦	47
9		♦	♦				♦		♦	♦	♦	♦			♦	48
10			♦				♦	♦	♦	♦	♦	♦			♦	49

1) BLACK BUTTE LAKE

U.S. Army Corps of Engineers
19225 Newville Road
Orland, CA 95963
Phone: 530-865-4781
District: Sacramento

Black Butte Lake is located in the scenic foothills of north-central California about 100 miles north of Sacramento and 60 miles south of Redding. From I-5, take the Orland/Hwy-32 exit and go west 8 miles via CR-200/Newville Road, follow signs. The Black Butte project includes 6,199 land acres, 2,718 water acres and 28 shoreline miles.

The quiet lake, surrounded by beautiful, dark volcanic buttes, is best known for its warm-water fishing and is a popular destination for power boats and sailboats. Two Corps-managed campgrounds operate at the lake. Summer campfire programs are featured in the centrally located amphitheater. ATVs and ORVs are not permitted.

Buckhorn: All year, 65 sites, no hookups, $15, drinking water, dump, restrooms, showers. From I-5 take the Black Butte exit at Orland, then CR–200 (Newville Road) west for 14 miles, turn left at the campground. 530-865-4781.

Orland Buttes: Apr-Sep, 35 sites, no hookups, $15, drinking water, dump, restrooms, showers, interpretive trails, limited access to the lake due to steep cliffs. From I-5 Black Butte Lake exit at Orland, take CR-200 west for 6 miles, then left on CR-206 for 4 miles. 530-865-4781.

2) EASTMAN LAKE

U.S. Army Corps of Engineers
32175 Road 29
Raymond, CA 93653
Phone: 559-689-3255
District: Sacramento

Located 50 miles north of Fresno, Eastman Lake is 25 miles east of Chowchilla. The project encompasses 2,249 land acres, 1,070 water acres and 14 shoreline miles. Take Hwy-99 north to Avenue 15 east, follow to Road 26 east, then to Road 29 north. Turn left on Road 29 and travel 8 miles to the park entrance.

Tall grasses and scattered oak trees cover the rolling hills surrounding the lake. Wildlife is abundant. Eastman is a designated bass trophy lake, with fishing generally good throughout the year. Other popular activities include canoeing, swimming, water skiing and wildlife viewing. Campfire programs are presented in the amphitheater. The campground has equestrian sites and a group area.

Codorniz: All year, 65 sites with water hookups, 6 full hookup sites and 9 sites with electric and water hookups, some pull thrus, $14–$22, dump, restrooms, showers. From Hwy-99 at Chowchilla, east on Avenue 26, then north on Road 29, follow signs into the campground. Codorniz is 30 miles northeast of Madera, 25 miles east of Chowchilla and 50 miles north of Fresno. 559-689-3612

3) HENSLEY LAKE

U.S. Army Corps of Engineers
P.O. Box 85
Raymond, CA 93653
Phone: 559-673-5151
District: Sacramento

Hensley Lake is 17 miles northeast of Madera on CR-400. It is less than an hour's drive northeast of Fresno in the foothills of the Sierra Nevada en route to Yosemite National Park. The area that was once home to the Minok and Yokut Native Americans, ranchers and farmers now offers many outdoor enjoyment opportunities. Hensley consists of 1,860 land acres, 1,300 water acres and 22 shoreline miles.

Game fish abound at the lake and anglers can keep two bass over 15 inches in length. Popular activities include water skiing, swimming, trail riding and wildlife viewing. Campfire programs are presented in the campground amphitheater on Friday and Saturday evenings. Camp sites are located within walking distance to the lake.

Hidden View: All year, 55 sites (14 with electric hookups), some pull thrus, $16–$22, drinking water, dump, restrooms, showers, playground. From Hwy-99 in Fresno, take SR-41 north for 21 miles to SR-145, then west 8.4 miles to Road 33, north 1.1 miles to Road 400; northeast 7 miles to Road 603, west 1 mile to Road 407; turn right for 1.7 miles to the park. 559-673-5151, (25207 Road 407 Raymond, Raymond, CA 93653).

4) KAWEAH LAKE

U.S. Army Corps of Engineers
34443 Sierra Drive
Lemon Cove, CA 93244
Phone: 559-597-2301
District: Sacramento

Kaweah Lake is located on the Kaweah River 10 miles from Sequoia

National Park. From Visalia take Hwy-198 for 20 miles east to the park entrance. The project encompasses 2,006 land acres, 1,065 water acres and 22 shoreline miles. It is situated one hour southeast of Fresno.

Access to the shoreline may vary month to month. Every year from May-July the campground may be closed due to flooding. Visitors may call ahead to check on conditions.

There is both lake and stream fishing, and trout are abundant during the winter. The marina has camping supplies, tackle, boat rentals and fuel. Campers can enjoy bird-watching and wildflowers on interpretive trails. Ranger programs are presented at the campground on Saturday evenings from May to September. In peak season gates close at 10pm and off season at 9pm.

Horse Creek: All year, 80 sites, no hookups, some pull thrus, $16, drinking water, dump, restrooms, showers. From Visalia, California, take Hwy-198 for 20 miles east, follow signs to the campground. 559-597-2301.

5) LAKE MENDOCINO

U.S. Army Corps of Engineers
1160 Lake Mendocino Drive
Ukiah, CA 95482
Phone: 707-462-7581
Visitor Center: 707-485-8285
District: San Francisco

Lake Mendocino is located in the northern coast range of California, 3 miles northeast of Ukiah, where redwood forests meet the wine country. The project encompasses 3,550 land acres, 1,785 water acres and 15 shoreline miles. From Ukiah, travel 3 miles north on US-101, then exit on Lake Mendocino Dr. The Visitor Center, modeled after a Pomo round house, is operated jointly by the Corps of Engineers and the Coyote Valley Band of Pomo Indians; displays include information on the Pomo Indians, the Corps and Coyote Valley wildlife.

A hiking and horseback riding trail runs along the eastern shore of the lake and through the wildlife area. A hiking and bicycling trail follows the western shore of the lake. Off road vehicles are prohibited. Wildlife viewing is excellent; bald eagles often winter on the east side of the lake. Fishing is a popular activity; the lake has an abundance of bass, stripers, crappie, bluegill and catfish. Weekend programs are offered at campground amphitheaters.

Bushay: May-Sep, 160 sites, no hookups, 3 group areas, $20, drinking water, dump, restrooms, showers. From Ukiah, go 5 miles north on US-101, then Hwy-20 east for 2.75 miles. Cross Russian River Bridge, turn left, continue 1 mile to the top of the hill. 707-462-7581.

Chekaka: May-Sep, 20 sites, no hookups, $16, drinking water, restrooms, horse trail, 18-hole disc golf course in walking distance. From Hwy-101, 3 miles north of Ukiah, take the Lake Mendocino Drive exit, turn left at the North State Street traffic light and turn right (east) on Lake Mendocino Dr., follow signs. The campground is at the top of the hill, 2 miles from Hwy-101. 707-462-7581.

Kyen: Apr-Sep, 100 sites, no hookups, some pull thrus, $20–$22, drinking water, dump, restrooms, showers, walking distance to the lake, swim beach. From Ukiah, US-101 north 5 miles, then Hwy-20 east, right on Marina Dr. Continue past the north boat ramp to the campground entrance. 707-462-7581.

6) LAKE SONOMA

U.S. Army Corps of Engineers
3333 Skaggs Springs Road
Geyserville, CA 95441
Phone: 707-433-9483
District: San Francisco

Lake Sonoma is 2 hours north of San Francisco and 3 miles west of Geyserville. It is surrounded by world famous vineyards and land that is rich in history. Take Hwy-101 to Heraldsburg and exit at Dry Creek Road. Travel west for 11 miles to the park entrance and Visitor Center that features exhibits on the cultural and natural history of the Dry Creek Valley. A fish hatchery is located behind the Center. The lake extends westward for nine miles on Dry Creek and four miles on Warm Springs

Creek. It has 2,637 water acres and 53 shoreline miles. 14,441 land acres are included at the Sonoma project.

The lake is surrounded by 40 miles of trails for use by hikers, mountain bikers and horseback riders. A detailed brochure on the trail system is available at the visitor center. Liberty Glen Campground sits on a ridge with views of the Warm Springs arm of the lake, but the campground does not have access to the shoreline. It is the only camping area accessible by road. Campground gates close at 10pm.

Liberty Glen: All year, 97 sites, no hookups, $16. Presently, dump station, restrooms and shower facilities are closed. Campers need to pack their own water. Please call the project office for information about current water conditions. From US-101 in the town of Heraldsburg exit at Dry Creek Road, go 11 miles west to the park boundary, continue west another 4 miles, follow signs. 707-431-4533.

7) MARTIS CREEK LAKE

U.S. Army Corps of Engineers
P.O. Box 6
Smartville, CA 95977
Phone: 530-587-8113 (Apr-Nov)
District: Sacramento

Martis Creek Lake is set in the Sierra Nevada Mountains near Lake Tahoe in northeastern California. It has 1,820 land acres, 71 water acres and 3 shoreline miles. From I-80 at Truckee, take the Central Truckee exit and turn south on SR-267 for 6 miles. The area provides unique opportunities to spot wildlife on a recurring basis and is a great place for bird watching. The peaceful off-the-beaten-path campground features hiking, biking, canoeing and kayaking.

Anglers will find a variety of trout in the lake. A catch-and-release program is in effect. Anglers must use barbless hooks and artificial lures only. Live bait is not permitted. No fishing is allowed in the streams above the lake. No motorized (gas or electric) boats are allowed.

Alpine Meadows: May-Oct, 25 sites, no hookups, pull thrus, non-reservable, $12, drinking water, restrooms, 30-foot RV length limit. Weekend evening campfire programs in season. The campground is closed during winter months due to weather conditions. From I-80 at Truckee, take the Central Truckee exit and turn south on to SR-267 southeast for six miles.

8) NEW HOGAN LAKE

U.S. Army Corps of Engineers
2713 Hogan Dam Road
Valley Springs, CA 95252
Phone: 209-772-1343
District: Sacramento

Located an hour east of Stockton, New Hogan Lake is set against the foothills of the Sierra Nevada on the Calaveras River. The project includes 3,054 acres of land, 3,099 water acres and 50 miles on the shoreline. From Stockton, take SR-26 for 30 miles to Valley Springs. A mile before reaching town, turn right onto Hogan Dam Road and follow for 1.5 miles to the park entrance.

Water skiing is excellent along the entire 50-mile shoreline. The lake provides year-round fishing and fish cleaning facilities are available. Weekend camping is popular; early reservations are suggested. Campfire programs are featured on weekends in season. The south shore is a designated wildlife viewing area. Bald eagles may be viewed in the vicinity. Historic sites are nearby. A golf course is also nearby.

Acorn: All year, 132 sites, no hookups, $14, drinking water, dump, restrooms, showers, frisbee golf course. From Stockton, take Hwy-26 east for 30 miles, turn right on Hogan Dam Road for 1 mile, follow signs.

Oak Knoll: May-Sep, 47 sites, no hookups, $12, drinking water, dump, restrooms, showers, group camping facility. From Stockton, take Hwy-26 east for 30 miles, turn right on Hogan Dam Road (one-half mile before Valley Springs), go 1 mile, follow signs. 209-772-1343.

9) PINE FLAT LAKE

U.S. Army Corps of Engineers
P.O. Box 117
27295 Pine Flat Road
Piedra, CA 93649
Phone: 559-787-2589
District: Sacramento

Pine Flat Lake, within the Sierra and Sequoia National Forests, is 35 miles east of Fresno. The lake, with 4,422 water acres and 67 shoreline miles, is surrounded by 8,668 land acres. From Fresno, take Belmont Avenue east (becomes Trimmer Springs Road). The lake is about 3 miles past the town of Piedra on Trimmer Springs Road. To get to the Park Headquarters and the dam, turn right on Pine Flat Road from Trimmer Springs Road in Piedra.

The last two spotted bass world records came out of Pine Flat Lake. Two marinas have boat and slip rentals and fuel. The Blue Oak Nature Trail is located at Island Park that also has a Corps-managed campground. Camping is also available at Fresno County Parks and at RV parks and resorts around the lake.

Island Park: All year, 97 sites; no hookups, drinking water, $20, dump, restrooms, showers (fee), boat ramp, group camping area. Some campsites may be closed due to high water levels; call the Corps office for information. From Fresno, travel east on Belmont Avenue (turns into Timmer Springs Road) and follow signs to Island Park recreation area, turn right and follow signs to the campground.

10) SUCCESS LAKE

U.S. Army Corps of Engineers
29330 Highway 190
Porterville, CA 93258
Phone: 559-784-0215
District: Sacramento

Success Lake is located 8 miles east of Porterville at the southern end of the Central Valley. From Porterville, travel 5 miles east on Hwy-190 to the Project Office. There are 3,016 land acres, 1,142 water acres and 11 shoreline miles in the project.

The lake provides good habitat for bass, crappie, bluegill and catfish. In spring and summer months, high water covers shoreline vegetation creating superb shoreline angling. Success Marina offers fishing and boating supplies, boat rentals and fuel. Campfire programs are presented at Tule Campground on Saturdays from Memorial Day to Labor Day. Off road vehicles are not allowed. There is a golf course nearby.

Tule: All year, 103 sites (9 have electric and water hookups), some pull thrus, $16–$21, drinking water, dump, restrooms, showers. From Hwy-99 in central CA, take Hwy-190 east for 8 miles past Porterville, follow signs to the campground.

Connecticut

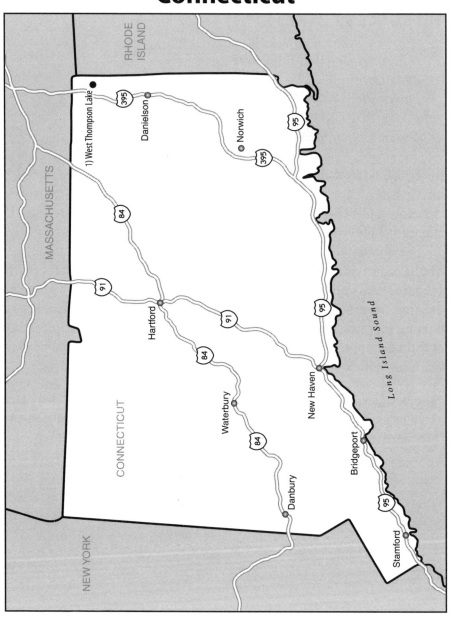

1)   West Thompson Lake

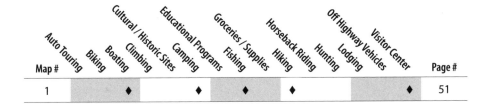

Map #															Page #
1		◆		◆		◆	◆						◆		51

1) WEST THOMPSON LAKE

U.S. Army Corps of Engineers
449 Readon Street
Thompson, CT 06255
Phone: 860-923-2982
District: New England

The 200-acre lake, located in the northeast corner of the state, is popular with anglers of all ages. The West Thompson project encompasses 1,857 acres of natural resources where many wildlife viewing areas are available. From I-395 exit 99, take SR-200 to SR-193, follow signs to the Visitor Center.

The rustic Corps-managed campground offers wooded sites. Hiking, interpretive trails, and an amphitheater are within the campground. A boat ramp gives boating and fishing enthusiasts access to the lake. Swimming is available at a nearby state park and there is a convenience store in the area. There is an 18-hole golf course nearby.

West Thompson: May-Sep, 11 sites with electric & water hookups, 11 basic sites, drinking water, $15–$30, dump, restrooms, showers, playground, frisbee golf. From I-395 exit 99, follow SR-200 to Thompson Center. Go 2 miles south on Rt-193. Cross Rt-12 at the traffic light. Turn right onto Reardon Road. Travel one-half mile, turn left for .2 mile, then right. 860-923-3121.

Florida

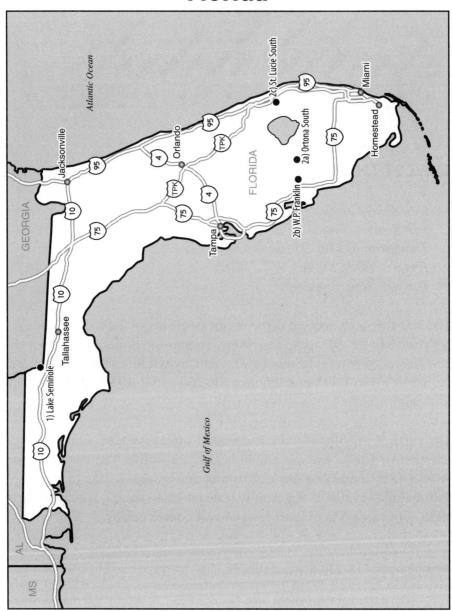

1) Lake Seminole
2) Okeechobee Waterway
   a) Ortona South
   b) W.P. Franklin
   c) St. Lucie South

Map #	Auto Touring	Biking	Boating	Climbing	Cultural / Historic Sites	Educational Programs	Camping	Fishing	Groceries / Supplies	Hiking	Horseback Riding	Hunting	Lodging	Off Highway Vehicles	Visitor Center	Page #
1			♦		♦	♦		♦		♦		♦			♦	53
2	♦		♦		♦	♦		♦	♦	♦					♦	54

1) LAKE SEMINOLE

U.S. Army Corps of Engineers
2382 Booster Club Road (P.O. Box 96)
Chatahoochee, FL 32324
Phone: 229-662-2001
District: Mobile

Lake Seminole has 37,000 acres of water and over 18,000 acres of surrounding land. From Tallahassee, Florida, travel west on US-90 to Chatahoochee, then north on Decatur Street. Decatur becomes Booster Club Road. The dam and Visitor Center are on the left at 2382 Booster Club Road. Lake Seminole waters extend into Georgia. Historic Bainbridge, GA is nearby.

The lake offers recreational opportunities; areas for wildlife viewing and bird-watching are abundant. Of the three Corps-managed campgrounds listed here, only Eastbank – near the Jim Woodruff Dam – has hookups.

Eastbank: All year, 69 sites with electric (some 50amp) & water hookups, $14–$18, drinking water, dump, restrooms, showers, laundry, boat ramp with courtesy dock. From I-10 exit 166, north on Hwy-269, then left on US-90 to Bolivar St (Booster Club Road). Turn right 1 mile, then left at East Bank Road. 229-662-9273.

Hales Landing: All year, 14 sites, no hookups, non-reservable, $10, drinking water, NO dump station, showers. From US-84, southwest on SR-253 for 3.8 miles, then Ten Mile Still Road 2 miles, follow signs. Located 12 miles south of Bainbridge, Georgia. 229-662-2001.

River Junction: All year, 16 sites, no hookups, non-reservable, $10, drinking water, NO dump station, restrooms, showers, group camping area, boat ramp. From I-10 exit 166, north on Hwy-269, then left at US-90 (in Chatahooochee, FL) to Bolivar Street (Booster Club Road). Turn right, 2 miles, then left at River Junction sign. 229-662-2001.

2) OKEECHOBEE WATERWAY

U.S. Army Corps of Engineers
525 Ridgelawn Road
Clewiston, FL 33440
Phone: 863-983-8101
District: Jacksonville

The Okeechobee Project Office is in Clewiston, on the south side of the lake. It is about 65 miles west of West Palm Beach. From I-95 exit 68, take US-98 west (becomes US-441 north). Take US-441 to SR-80 west (becomes US-27 north) into Clewiston. Okeechobee's lake, waterway and surrounding countryside has 26,377 land acres, 451,000 water acres and 402 shoreline miles. Lake Okeechobee is the largest lake in Florida and the second largest fresh water lake in the U.S. It is a popular fishing destination. Boat ramps are conveniently located throughout. Three marinas provide supplies and boating services. ATVs or ORVs are not allowed.

The Corps manages recreation areas at the lake and along the adjacent waterways. RV camping is available on waterways leading into the lake. Ortona and Franklin campgrounds are west of the lake and St. Lucie campground is east of the lake. Manatees can be observed at all locations. Ortona, on the Caloosahatchee River section of the waterway, offers a tranquil, serene country setting. Franklin camping area is just 15 minutes from Fort Myers where visitors will find flea markets, malls and the historic Edison Home. St. Lucie South is about 10 minutes from Stuart, FL. There are many state parks and private campgrounds near Lake Okeechobee.

2a) Ortona South

Ortona South: All year, 51 sites with electric (50amp) & water hookups, $24, dump, restrooms, showers, laundry, fishing piers, golf nearby. From La Belle, Florida, east on SR-80 for 8 miles to Dalton Lane, follow signs. 863-675-8400, (4330 Dalton Lane SW, Moore Haven, FL 33471).

2b) W.P. Franklin

W.P. Franklin: All year, 30 RV/tent sites with electric (50amp) & water hookups, some pull thrus, 8 sleep-on-boat sites with electric, $24, drinking water, dump, restrooms, showers, laundry, playground, fishing pier. From I-75 exit 141, follow SR-80 east 3 miles to SR-31 and go north 3 miles to River Rd then go east 5 miles to N Franklin Lock Road, follow signs. 239-694-8770, (17801 North Franklin Lock Rd, Alva, FL 33920).

2c) St. Lucie South

St. Lucie South: All year, 9 sites with electric (50amp) and water hookups, 3 tent sites, 8 sleep-on-boat sites with electric, $24, dump, restrooms, showers, laundry, playground. From I-95 exit 101 (Stuart/Indiantown), SR-76 west for one-half mile to Locks Road, then right, follow signs. 772-287-1382, (2170 SW Canal St, Stuart, FL 34997).

Georgia

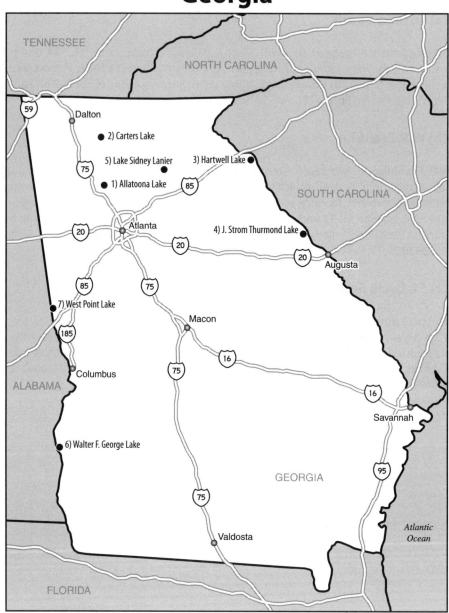

1) Allatoona Lake
2) Carters Lake
3) Hartwell Lake
4) J. Strom Thurmond Lake
5) Lake Sidney Lanier
6) Walter F. George Lake
7) West Point Lake

Map #	Auto Touring	Biking	Boating	Climbing	Cultural/Historic Sites	Educational Programs	Camping	Fishing	Groceries/Supplies	Hiking	Horseback Riding	Hunting	Off Highway Vehicles	Lodging	Visitor Center	Page #
1	♦		♦		♦	♦	♦	♦				♦		♦	♦	57
2		♦	♦			♦		♦	♦	♦		♦		♦	♦	59
3			♦			♦	♦	♦						♦	♦	60
4	♦	♦	♦		♦	♦	♦	♦	♦	♦	♦	♦	♦		♦	60
5	♦		♦		♦	♦		♦	♦	♦		♦			♦	62
6			♦			♦	♦	♦		♦		♦		♦	♦	64
7			♦			♦	♦	♦		♦					♦	64

1) ALLATOONA LAKE

U.S. Army Corps of Engineers
P.O. Box 487
1138 State Road Spur SE 20
Cartersville, GA 30120
Phone: 678-721-6700
District: Mobile

Allatoona Lake is located only 45 miles north of Atlanta, off I-75 and I-575 in the foothills of the Blue Ridge Mountains. From Atlanta, go 45 miles north on I-75 to exit 290, east on GA-20 for 50 yards (to the first traffic light) then south onto the GA-20 spur for 4 miles to the Visitor Center. The Center features video exhibits and displays about the area's history ranging from the time of early Indians to the gold mining and iron making days, from Civil War up to the present. The Allatoona project encompasses 26,738 land acres, 12,010 water acres and 270 shoreline miles. More than 13 million visitors enjoy recreation at Allatoona each year.

There are seven Corps-managed campgrounds at Allatoona Lake, with boat ramps, swimming and varied activities available. Wildlife viewing is abundant along the shores of the beautiful lake. Off road vehicles are prohibited. Other accommodations at the lake include Red Top Mountain State Park, private RV parks and cabin rentals. Shopping, museums and historic sites are in the area.

Clark Creek North: Apr-Sep, 24 sites with electric (some 50amp) & water hookups, $24-$26, some pull thrus, dump, restrooms, showers, laundry, swimming, 40-foot RV length limit. From I-75 exit 278, go north on Glade Road for 2 miles, cross the bridge, follow signs. 678-721-6700, (6100 Glade Rd SE, Acworth, GA 30102).

McKaskey Creek: Mar-Sep, 32 sites with electric & water hookups, 2 full hookup, 17 basic, $20–$24, drinking water, dump, restrooms, showers, laundry, swimming, 30-foot RV length limit. From I-75 exit 290, go east 50 yards and turn right on GA Spur 20 for 2 miles then left onto McKasky Creek Rd for 1 mile, follow signs. 678-721-6700, (McKaskey Rd SE, Cartersville, GA).

McKinney: All year, 150 sites with electric & water hookups, $20–$26, dump, restrooms, showers, laundry. From I-75 exit 278, go east on Glade Road for 3 miles, turn left at the second 4-way stop at King's Camp Road, go 1 mile to the road fork, take a left and follow signs. 678-721-6700, (Kings Camp Rd SE, Acworth, GA 30102).

Old Hwy 41 #3: Apr-Sep, 44 sites with electric & water hookups, $20–$26, dump, restrooms, showers, laundry. From I-75 exit 278 (Glade Road), go west .7 mile to stop light, then right onto GA-92 (Lake Acworth Dr) for .8 mile, crossing overpass, turn right and go to the bottom of the overpass, turn left, go 2.5 miles, follow signs. 678-721-6700.

Payne: Mar-Sep, 39 sites with electric (some 50amp) & water hookups, 2 full hookup sites and 19 basic sites, $20–$26, drinking water, dump, restrooms, showers, laundry swimming. From I-75 exit 277, east on Hwy-92 about 2 miles, then left on Old Alabama Road, then right on Kellogg Creek Road for 1.5 miles, follow signs. 678-721-6700.

Victoria: Mar-Oct, 70 sites with electric (some 50amp) & water hookups, 2 full hookup sites, $20–$24, dump, restrooms, showers, laundry, swimming. Follow I-75 north to I-575 north to exit 11 (Sixes Rd) left off the exit for 2.5 miles, then left on Bells Ferry Rd for 1.5 miles to Victoria Landing Dr, then right to the 3-way stop, then left to the 4-way stop, then right. 678-721-6700, (Victoria Landing Dr, Woodstock, GA 30189).

Sweetwater: Mar-Sep, 107 sites with electric (some 50amp) & water hookups, 2 full hookup sites and 42 basic, $20–$26, drinking water, dump, restrooms, showers, laundry, playground, swimming. From I-75 exit 290, go east on SR-20 for 12 miles, then right on Fields Chapel Road for 2 miles, follow signs. 678-721-6700.

2) CARTERS LAKE

U.S. Army Corps of Engineers
1850 Carters Dam Road - P.O. Box 96
Oakman, GA 30732
Phone: 706-334-2248
District: Mobile

Carters Lake is one of the most scenic lakes in the Southeast. It lies 70 miles north of Atlanta. From Atlanta take I-575 north to the Carters Lake exit and follow signs to the desired project location. Carters Lake has 4,250 surface acres and 76 miles of rugged, largely undeveloped shoreline.

The Amadahy Trail, a 3.5 mile loop with easy to moderately difficult terrain, is open to hikers and mountain bikers. Camping can be found in four Corps-managed areas. A motor bike trail is at Ridgeway. Campground amenities include boat ramps, fishing piers, playgrounds and swimming areas.

Doll Mountain: May-Sep, 39 sites with electric (50amp) and water hookups, some pull thrus, 27 tent sites, $16–$24, drinking water, dump, restrooms, showers, laundry, playground. From I-75 exit 293, take Hwy-411 north, then right on Hwy-136, then left on Hwy-382, then right into the access road (across from fire station). Located on the south side of the lake. Caution: Park access road has a steep downhill grade going into the campground. 706-276-4413.

Harris Branch: May-Sep, 10 sites, no hookups, non-reservable, $16, drinking water, restrooms, showers, laundry, playground, swimming. South side of the lake, three miles off Hwy-382. 706-276-4545.

Woodring Branch: Apr-Oct, 31 sites with electric & water hookups, 11 tent sites, $18–$20, drinking water, dump, restrooms, showers, laundry, swimming, playground, hiking trail. From I-75 exit 293, follow Hwy-411 north, then right on Hwy-136, follow signs. North side of the lake. 706-276-6050.

3) HARTWELL LAKE

U.S. Army Corps of Engineers
5625 Anderson Highway (Hwy-29)
Hartwell, GA 30643
Phone: 706-856-0300
District: Savannah

The Hartwell Lake project is located just off US-29 on the GA/SC border. The Operations Manager's Office and Visitor Center is one mile past the dam on the Georgia side, or 5 miles north of Hartwell, GA. The project includes 24,209 land acres, 55,950 water acres and 962 shoreline miles. Many lake access areas can easily be reached from I-85.

RV camping is available at 2 Corps-managed campgrounds on the Georgia side of the lake. There are also 4 campgrounds on the South Carolina side of the project (listed in the South Carolina section of this guide). Boat ramps and fishing piers are at all camping areas. A state park and a private resort also provide camping and lodging. Golf carts, ATVs and motorized scooters are prohibited.

Paynes Creek: May-Sep, 44 sites with electric (50amp) and water hookups, some pull thrus, $18-$20, dump, restrooms, showers, swimming, playground. 37 sites are waterfront. Located on the Togaloo River arm of Hartwell Lake. From I-85 exit 177, south on SR-77 for 5 miles, follow directional signs last 10 miles. 888-893-0678, (518 Ramp Rd, Hartwell, GA 30643).

Watsadler: All year, 51 lakefront sites with electric (50amp) and water hookups, $22, dump, restrooms, showers, playground. Located next to the Project Office adjacent to the dam. From I-85 exit 177, SR-77 toward Hartwell, then Hwy-29 north (toward Anderson, SC) for 4 miles, follow signs, entrance on left. 888-893-0678 (286 Watsadler Rd, Hartwell, GA 30643).

4) J. STROM THURMOND LAKE

U.S. Army Corps of Engineers
510 Clarks Hill Highway
Clarks Hill, SC 29821

Phone: 864-333-1100 or 800-533-3478
District: Savannah

Thurmond Lake's Visitor Center is located on the South Carolina side of the dam. From I-20 exit 183, the dam is north on US-221. The lake is a long, relatively narrow body of water that extends from the dam (just north of Augusta, GA) to 29 miles up the Savannah River, 46 miles up the Little River and 6 miles up the Broad River. With a shoreline of 1,200 miles and 71,000 acres of water, it straddles the SC/GA border.

Corps-managed campgrounds listed include 9 in Georgia and 4 in South Carolina. Campground amenities include boat ramps, fishing piers, fish cleaning stations, playgrounds and swimming. On the Georgia side of the lake, camping is also available at Bobby Brown State Park and Elijah Clark State Park. Historic sites are near many of the campgrounds.

Note: Four more campgrounds at the Thurmond project are listed in the South Carolina section of this book.

Big Hart: Apr-Oct, 24 shaded sites with electric & water hookups, some pull thrus, 7 basic sites, $18–$20, drinking water, dump, restrooms, showers. Adjacent to a recreation area with swim beach and playground. From I-20 exit 172 (Thomson/Hwy-78), north 8 miles on Hwy-78 to Russell Landing Road, then right 4 miles, follow signs. 706-595-8613 (5258 Washington Rd, Thomson, GA 30824).

Broad River: Mar-Sep, 31 sites with electric & water hookups, some pull thrus, $18–$20, dump, restrooms, showers. Double & triple sites ideal for family and friends traveling together. Campground is on the Broad River's south bank. From I-85 exit 173 (Hwy-17), go south 30 miles, then Hwy-72 (toward Calhoun Falls) for 11 miles, then right on Hwy-79 for 10 miles, cross Broad River, campground on right. 706-359-2053 (8181 Elberton Hwy, Tignall, GA 30668).

Bussey Point: All year, 10 basic sites, pump water, non-reservable, $6, rustic restrooms. From the Hwy-47 Little River Bridge in Lincoln Co., north 1.8 miles, right on Ashmore-Barden Road, 3 miles to stop sign, right on Double Branches Road, go 3 miles, pavement ends one-half mile before entrance. 864-333-1100.

Clay Hill: Apr-Sep, 10 sites with electric & water hookups, 7 basic sites, non-reservable, $12–$16, drinking water, dump, restrooms, showers. From I-20 exit 172, go 4 miles on US-78 to SR-43, continue to Amity Woodlawn Road, follow signs. 706-359-7495.

Hesters Ferry: Apr-Sep, 16 shaded sites with electric & water hookups, 9 basic sites, $16–$18, drinking water, dump, restrooms, showers, boat ramp, playground, all sites are waterfront, located on Fishing Creek. From Lincolnton, Georgia, go 12 miles north on Hwy-79, then east 2 miles on Rt-44, follow signs. 800-533-3478 or 706-359-2746 (1864 Graball Rd, Tignall, GA 30668).

Petersburg: All year, 93 sites with electric (50amp) and water hookups, some pull thrus, $16–$22, dump, restrooms, showers, laundry, swimming beaches, hiking trail. Closest to Augusta. From I-20 exit 183 (Appling), north 6 miles on Hwy-221. At 4-way stop continue another 2 miles, follow signs, entrance on left. 706-541-9464 (3998 Petersburg Rd, Appling, GA 30802).

Raysville: Mar-Oct, 55 sites with electric (50amp) and water hookups, some pull thrus, $20–$22, dump, restrooms, showers. On the Little River. From I-20 exit 172 (Thomson/Hwy-78), north 3 miles, then right on Hwy-43 for 6 miles, entrance on left. 706-595-6759 (6489 Lincolnton Rd NE, Thomson, GA 30824).

Ridge Road: Apr-Sep, 63 sites with electric (50amp) and water hookups, some pull thrus, 6 tent sites, $16–$22, dump, restrooms, showers, beautiful scenery. From I-20 exit 183 (Appling), north 6 miles on US-221. At 4-way stop, left on SR-47, then 5 miles, follow signs. 706-541-0282 (5886 Ridge Rd, Appling, GA 30802).

Winfield: Mar-Sep, 80 sites with electric (50amp) and water hookups, $22, dump, restrooms, showers, wildlife viewing. Many sites are waterfront. From I-20 exit 175, north 7 miles, then north on Hwy-150, left on Mistletoe Road, 2 miles, then left, follow signs. 706-541-0147 (7701 Winfield Rd, Appling, GA 30802).

5) LAKE SIDNEY LANIER

U.S. Army Corps of Engineers
1050 Buford Dam Road
Buford, GA 30518
Phone: 770-945-9531
District: Mobile

Lake Sidney Lanier is nestled in the foothills of the Georgia Blue Ridge Mountains just 35 minutes northeast of Atlanta. From I-985/Buford take SR-20 west (or from SR-400/Cumming take SR-20 east) to Suwanee Dam Road north 3 miles, then left on Buford Dam Road. The Visitor Center is one mile on the right. The project has 19,288 land acres, 38,000 water acres and 540 shoreline miles.

The lake is well known for its aqua-blue colored water and spectacular scenery. Shopping malls, outlet centers, restaurants and golf courses are nearby. Seasonal festivals and special events are featured in local towns. There are nine Corps-managed campgrounds at Lake Sidney Lanier; most have boat ramps, swimming areas and playgrounds. Gas, propane, marinas, restaurants and convenience stores are near the campgrounds.

Bald Ridge: Mar-Oct, 82 sites with electric (some 50amp) and water hookups, some pull thrus, $25-$27, dump, restrooms, showers, laundry. From Atlanta SR-400 north to exit 16, then right on Pilgrim Mill Road, then right on Sinclair Shoals Road, then left on Bald Ridge Road. 770-889-1591, (4100 Bald Ridge Rd, Cumming, GA 30041).

Bolding Mill: Apr-Sep, 88 sites with electric & water hookups, 9 tent sites, $25-$27, some pull thrus, dump, restrooms, showers, laundry. From Atlanta, take SR-400 north to exit 17, right onto SR-306, then right onto SR-53 and left onto Old Sardis Rd and left on Chestatee Rd. 770-534-6960, (4055 Chestatee Rd, Gainesville, GA 50506)

Duckett Mill: Apr-Sep, 97 sites with electric (some 50amp) and water hookups, some pull thrus, 14 tent sites, $17–$27, drinking water, dump, restrooms, showers, laundry. From SR-400 exit 17, turn right on SR-306, then right on SR-53, right on Duckett Mill Road. 770-532-9802, (3720 Duckett Mill Rd, Gainesville, GA 30506).

Old Federal: Mar-Oct, 59 sites with electric (some 50amp) and water hookups, 24 basic sites, $19–$27, drinking water, dump, restrooms, showers, laundry. From I-985 exit 8, turn left on Hwy-347/Friendship Road, turn right on McEver Road, then left on Jim Crow Road, follow signs. 770-967-6757, (6219 Old Federal Rd, Flowery Branch, GA 30542).

Sawnee: Apr-Sep, 44 sites with electric (some 50amp) and water hookups, 11 basic sites, $19–$27, drinking water, dump, restrooms, showers, laundry. From SR-400 exit 14, turn left on SR-20 east, then left on Sanders Road, at first stop sign go right on Buford Dam Road. 770-887-0592, (3200 Buford Dam Rd, Cumming, GA 30041).

Shady Grove: Apr-Sep, 76 sites with electric (some 50amp) and water hookups, some pull thrus, 42 basic sites, group camping areas, 8 tent sites, $17–$23, drinking water, dump, restrooms, showers, laundry. From SR-400, right on Hwy-369 (Browns Bridge Road), then right on Shady Grove Road. 770-887-2067.

Toto Creek: Apr-Sep, 10 sites, non-reservable, $17, drinking water, showers. From Cumming, travel north on SR-400, then right on SR-136 and right at the stop sign, turn left before crossing the bridge. 770-945-9531.

6) WALTER F. GEORGE LAKE

U.S. Army Corps of Engineers
427 Eufala Road
Fort Gaines, GA 39851
Phone: 229-768-2516
District: Mobile

W.F. George Lake, sometimes referred to as Lake Eufala, extends 85 miles along the Chatahoochee River and borders Alabama and Georgia. From Fort Gaines, Georgia, take Hwy-39 north for 2 miles; the W.F. George Resource Building is on the left. With 640 miles of shoreline, the lake offers plenty of room for water-related activities.

Corps-managed campgrounds include three on the Alabama side of the lake (see Alabama section) and one in Georgia, listed below. Gracious antebellum mansions are located in nearby historic towns, including Cuthbert, GA and Eufala, AL.

Cotton Hill: All year, 104 sites (94 have electric & water hookups), some pull thrus, some tent only sites, $18-$20, drinking water, dump, restrooms, showers, laundry, fish cleaning station, playground, boat ramp, swimming, interpretive trail. From Ft. Gaines, follow SR-39 north 7 miles, follow signs. 229-768-3061.

7) WEST POINT LAKE

U.S. Army Corps of Engineers
500 Resource Management Dr.
West Point, GA 31833
Phone: 706–645–2937
District: Mobile

West Point Lake straddles the AL/GA border, just north of Interstate 85. From Alabama, take I-85 north to Georgia exit 2 to US-29 north. The Visitor Center is on the left. Information and maps are available. The project includes 32,282 land acres, 26,864 water acres and 539 miles of shoreline. Surrounded by deep forests and rolling hills, West Point Lake extends along the Chattahoochee River. A wildlife management area of 10,000 acres is located at the upper end of the lake, providing a habitat for many kinds of game and non-game wildlife.

Fishing is the most popular activity at the lake. A dozen creeks and more than 40 square miles of lake provide plenty of good fishing spots. The lake abounds with bass, catfish, crappie and bream. Bank fishing is excellent at most locations. Personal watercraft and water safety courses are offered from February to September in the Visitor Center.

There are three Corps-managed campgrounds on the Georgia side of the lake, Holiday, Heard and Whitetail. The Amity campground is listed in the Alabama section. Among the campground amenities are boat ramps, fishing piers, playgrounds, ball fields and swimming.

Holiday: Feb-Sep, 143 sites (92 have electric & water hookups), $16–$22, drinking water, dump, restrooms, showers, laundry. From LaGrange, Georgia, west on Hwy-109, after crossing the First Lake Bridge across the lake, go one more mile, turn left on Thompson Road, at the next intersection bear left, follow signs. 706-884-6818 (954 Abbotsford Rd, Lagrange, West Point, GA 30240).

R. Shaefer Heard: All year, 117 sites with electric & water hookups, $22, dump, restrooms, showers, laundry, amphitheater. From West Point, Georgia, go 4 miles north on US-29, follow signs. 706-645-2404 (101 Shaefer Heard Park Rd, West Point, GA 31833) .

Whitetail Ridge: Mar-Nov, 58 sites with electric & water hookups, some pull thrus, $22, dump, restrooms, showers, laundry, hiking trails. From LaGrange, Georgia, west on Hwy-109, after crossing the first bridge across the lake, go 1 mile, then left on Thompson Road, follow signs. 706-884-8972 (565 Abbotsford Rd, Legrange, GA 30240).

Idaho

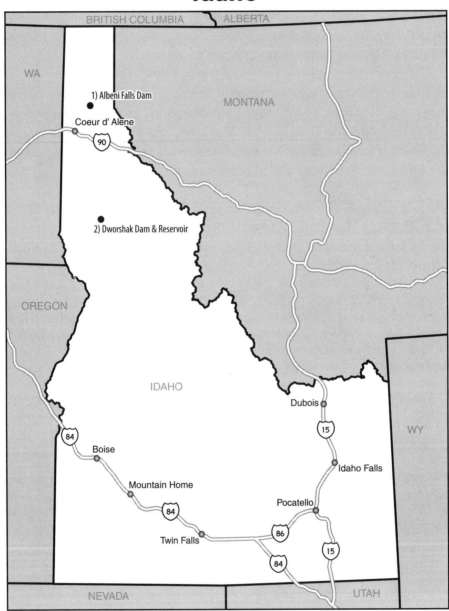

1) Aleni Falls Dam & Lake Pend Oreille
2) Dworshak Dam & Reservoir

Map #	Auto Touring	Biking	Boating	Climbing	Cultural/Historic Sites	Camping	Educational Programs	Fishing	Groceries/Supplies	Hiking	Horseback Riding	Hunting	Lodging	Off Highway Vehicles	Visitor Center	Page #
1	◆	◆	◆	◆		◆		◆	◆		◆		◆		◆	67
2		◆				◆		◆		◆		◆			◆	68

1) ALBENI FALLS DAM & LAKE PEND OREILLE

U.S. Army Corps of Engineers
2376 East Highway 2
Oldtown, ID 83822
Phone: 208-437-3133
District: Seattle

Located in the panhandle of Idaho, the Albeni project includes 4,844 land acres, 94,600 water acres and 226 shoreline miles. The Albeni Visitor Center is located 2 miles east of the WA/ID border on US-2. History and natural history exhibits are featured. The Center offers tours of the Albeni Falls Dam four times daily from Memorial Day to Labor Day.

Albeni Falls Dam sits on the Pend Oreille River. Behind the dam, the waters of the Pend Oreille stretch 65 miles through a glacially-carved valley that separates three mountain ranges. Rimmed by mountains that rise 6,500 feet, Lake Pend Oreille is one of the largest and deepest natural lakes in western U.S. Three Corps-managed areas offer RV camping. A popular day trip for visitors is the Pack River area to observe wildlife. Shopping, restaurants and a theme park are near Springy Point.

Priest River: May-Sep, 20 sites, no hookups, some pull thrus, $16, dump, restrooms, showers. One mile east of the town of Priest River on US-2. The park is also known as the "Mudhole." 208-437-3133.

Riley Creek: May-Sep, 67 sites with electric (50amp) & water hookups, some pull thrus, $16 (add $5 for electric), dump, restrooms, showers. Gates close at 10pm. From US-2 in Laclede, south on Riley Creek Road 1 mile. 208-437-3133.

Springy Point: May-Oct. 38 sites, no hookups, some pull thrus, $16, dump, restrooms, showers. Gates close at 10pm. From Sandpoint, south on US-95, across the Long Bridge, turn west onto Longshore Dr for 3 miles, then right in Springy Point. 208-437-3133)

2) DWORSHAK DAM AND RESERVOIR

U.S. Army Corps of Engineers
P.O. Box 48
Ahsahka, ID 83520
Phone: 208-476-1255
District: Walla Walla

Dworshak Reservoir is located in scenic forested and mountainous country in central Idaho. The Visitor Center is 5 miles west of Orofino on Hwy-7. After entering the project, follow signs to the Visitor Center, which is adjacent to the north dam abutment. The lake with 19,824 water acres and 54 shoreline miles is surrounded by abundant wildlife on 27,035 land acres. There is excellent wildlife viewing throughout. Lewis and Clark camped in this area, where they rested from their trip over the Bitterroot Range and built canoes for their trip on to the Pacific Ocean.

Fishing on the lake is excellent for salmon, trout and bass. The Dworshak National Fish Hatchery is the largest steelhead trout hatchery in the world. Additional camping is available at Dworshak State Park.

Dent Acres: May-Sep, 50 sites with full hookups, some pull thrus, $18, dump, restrooms, showers, fish cleaning station, playground, hiking trail, group camping facility. From Hwy-12, cross the bridge at Orofino and turn left onto Hwy-7. Travel 200 yards, turn right and go 19 miles, follow signs. The road into the campground has some sharp curves and steep grades. 208-476-9029.

Illinois

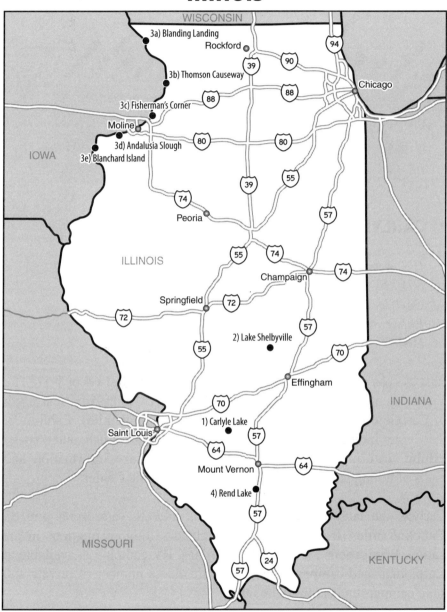

1) Carlyle Lake
2) Lake Shelbyville
3) Mississippi River Camping
      a) Blanding Landing
      b) Thomson Causeway

c) Fisherman's Corner
d) Andulsuia Slough
e) Blanchard Island
4) Rend Lake

Map #	Auto Touring	Biking	Boating	Climbing	Cultural / Historic Sites	Educational Programs	Camping	Groceries / Supplies	Fishing	Horseback Riding	Hiking	Hunting	Off Highway Vehicles	Lodging	Visitor Center	Page #
1		♦	♦				♦	♦	♦		♦	♦		♦		♦	70
2			♦				♦	♦	♦		♦			♦		♦	71
3	♦	♦	♦		♦	♦	♦	♦	♦		♦				♦	72
4	♦	♦	♦				♦	♦	♦	♦	♦	♦	♦	♦		♦	74

1) CARLYLE LAKE

U.S. Army Corps of Engineers
801 Lake Road
Carlyle, IL 62231
Phone: 618-594-2484
District: St. Louis

Easy access to Carlyle Lake can be found from I-70, I-64 or I-57. The Visitor Center is located in the Dam West Recreation Area just north of Carlyle on SR-127 (go east on William Road, 1 mile). Exhibits at the Center include a 215-gallon aquarium with native fish, and a snake exhibit featuring the massasauga rattlesnake. Lake information and maps of hiking and biking trails are available at the Center.

Carlyle, the largest lake in Illinois, has 24,988 water acres and 88 shoreline miles. It is one of the top inland sailing destinations in the nation. Boat rentals are offered at marinas. RV camping is available at Corps-managed campgrounds. There are also a number of private and state campgrounds around the lake.

Boulder: Apr-Sep, 76 sites with electric (some 50amp) hookups, 11 tent sites, $14–$28, drinking water, dump, restrooms, showers, laundry. From I-57 take Old US-50 west 19 miles to Boulder Road, then north 7 miles. 618-226-3586.

Coles Creek: May-Sep, 121 sites with electric hookups, 27 full hookup sites, $14–$28, drinking water, dump, restrooms, showers, laundry. From I-57 take Old US-50 for 19 miles west, then north on Boulder Road for 4 miles, then west on CR-1700N and continue until the road connects with CR-2400, continue to the campground. 618-226-3211.

Dam West: Apr-Nov, 89 sites with electric (50amp) hookups, 28 full hookup sites, some pull thrus, $12–$28, drinking water, dump, restrooms, showers, laundry. 618-594-4410.

2) LAKE SHELBYVILLE

U.S. Army Corps of Engineers
RR 4, Box 128B – 315 E. Main St.
Shebyville, IL 62565
Phone: 217-774-3951
District: St. Louis

Lake Shelbyville is located in the heart of central Illinois, 35 miles south of Decatur. The Visitor Center is on the east side of the dam (south side of the lake) just outside the town of Shelbyville. Maps and information are available. The project consists of 11,100 acres of water and 29,408 acres of land. Popular game fish species include crappie, largemouth bass, muskie, walleye, white bass and bluegill. In the Okaw Bluff Wetlands there are nine photo blinds, a viewing stand and a one-mile nature trail.

Throughout the season, park rangers present free weekend interpretive programs at the Visitor Center, campground amphitheaters and on beaches. RV camping may be found at five Corps-managed locations. A resort on the lake has lodging and an 18-hole golf course. Eagle Creek State Park has camping.

Bo Wood: Apr-Oct, 77 sites with electric (50amp) hookups, some pull thrus, $18-$22, drinking water, dump, restrooms, showers, laundry, boat ramp, playground. From Sullivan, go 2 miles south on SR-32, then right, follow sign. 217-774-3951.

Coon Creek: Apr-Oct, 207 sites with electric (some 50amp) hookups, 8 full hookup sites, $18-$22, drinking water, dump, restrooms, showers, laundry, playground, swimming beach, interpretive trail. From Shelbyville, 4.5 miles north on SR-128 to CR-1750N, then .9 mile east to CR-1900E, then north .35 mile to CR-1785N, then east 1.75 miles to CR-2075E, then south 1.75 miles. 217-774-3951.

Lithia Springs: Apr-Oct, 113 sites with electric (50amp) hookups, $18–$22, drinking water, dump, restrooms, showers, laundry, playground, swimming beach. Located on the east side of the lake. From Shelbyville, go 3 miles east on SR-16, then north 2 miles on CR-2200E, then west 1.4 miles on CR-1500N. 217-774-3951.

Lone Point: May-Sep, 63 sites with electric hookups, 2 full hookup sites, 7 tent sites, $16, drinking water, dump, restrooms, showers, playground. Located on the west side of the lake. From Shelbyville go 4.5 miles north on SR-128 to CR-1750, then .9 mile east to CR-1900, then north .35 mile to CR-1785, then east 2.5 miles to CR-2150, then south .7 mile to CR-1725N, then east .25 mile to CR-2175E, then south .7 mile to the campground. 217-774-3951.

Opossum Creek: May-Sep, 51 sites with electric hookups, 22 tent sites, $16, drinking water, dump, restrooms, showers, playground. On the west side of the lake. From Shelbyville 3.5 miles north on SR-128 to CR-1650N, then .9 mile east to CR-1880E, then south .5 mile to CR-1600N, then east 1 mile. 217-774-3951.

3) MISSISSIPPI RIVER CAMPING

U.S. Army Corps of Engineers
P.O. Box 2004
Rock Island, IL 61204
Phone: 309-794-5338
District: Rock Island

The Mississippi River Project of the Corps' Rock Island District maintains public recreation areas along a 314-mile stretch of the River. The Illinois portion of the project runs from the Wisconsin state line south to Lock & Dam 22 (near I-72). The Mississippi River Visitor Center is located on Rock Island which can be accessed from I-74 in Illinois (River Dr or 7th Ave exit). The Center offers the best view of "locking through," where visitors can watch pilots as they skillfully maneuver tons of cargo through. Up to 2,500 bald eagles winter along the Mississippi near the locks and dams…they can be seen from mid-December through early March.

Note: Another interesting Mississippi River location is the National Great Rivers Museum, located just north of St. Louis in East Alton, IL.

The modern museum, visited by millions of travelers each year, tells the story of the great river, its history and impact on the nation. From I-270 exit 34 (north of St. Louis and two miles east of the river in Illinois), take SR-3 north for about 11 miles to SR-143. The museum is just off SR-143 at Melvin Price Lock & Dam. The facility is operated by the Corps St. Louis District. For more information call 877-462-6979.

There are five Corps-managed campgrounds along the river in Hanover, Thomson and Hampton, IL and in the Quad Cities area. Watching river traffic is a popular pastime. Historic sites can be found along the river as well as scenic drives.

3a) Blanding Landing

Blanding Landing: May-Oct, 30 sites with electric (50amp) hookups, 7 tent sites, $10–$14, drinking water, dump, restrooms, showers, playground. From Hanover, Illinois, on US-84, turn west on Fulton Street next to Apple River Bridge, follow signs 8 miles. 563-582-0881 (South River Rd, Hanover, IL 61041).

3b) Thomson Causeway

Thomson Causeway: Apr-Oct, 126 sites with electric (50amp) hookups, 5 tent sites, $10–$16, drinking water, dump, restrooms, showers, playground, interpretive trail. Located on an island on the Mississippi River. From Thomson, IL on US-84 turn west onto Main Street, then south on Lewis Ave, follow signs. 815-259-3628 (Lewis Ave, Thomson, IL 61285).

3c) Fisherman's Corner

Fisherman's Corner: Apr-Oct, 28 sites with electric (50amp) hookups, some pull thrus, 6 tent sites, $10–$16, drinking water, dump, restrooms, showers, playground, bike trail. On US-84 just north of Hampton, close to Rock Island. 309-496-2720 (Route 84 No, Hampton, IL 61256).

3d) Andalusia Slough

Andalusia Slough: May-Oct, 16 sites, some pull thrus, non-reservable, $4, drinking water, restrooms, dump, laundry. Across the river from Davenport, Iowa, 2 miles west on SR-92. 563-263-7913.

3e) Blanchard Island

Blanchard Island: May-Oct, 34 sites, non-reservable, $4, drinking water, dump, restrooms. From Muscatine, IA bridge, 1.5 miles east on SR-92, south 4 miles, second right past Copperas Creek Bridge. 563-263-7913.

4) REND LAKE

U.S. Army Corps of Engineers
12220 Rend City Road
Benton, IL 62812
Phone: 618-724-2493
Visitor Center: 618-439-7430
District: St. Louis

Located in the heart of southern Illinois, Rend Lake is a haven for wildlife and a recreational haven for visitors. It consists of 18,900 acres of water, 162 shoreline miles and 21,962 acres of land. The Visitor Center, located at the south side of the lake, has educational programs throughout the warm weather months and maps for hiking and biking trails.

A wildlife viewing adventure awaits visitors on any of the nature trails and quiet early risers will see deer as they feed at the forest edge. Abundant nature viewing is featured at the Wildlife Refuge. The Rend Lake Demonstration Garden has interesting exhibits on local plants and animals. Rend Lake is one of the best areas for birding.

Four Corps-managed campgrounds welcome RV and tent campers. Ranger-led programs are held at campgrounds in season. Campgrounds also have playgrounds, ball fields, basketball and tennis courts. Trap shooting and sporting clays are available near the campgrounds. Horseback riding and trail riding are available at Wayne Fitzgerrel State Park. There is a marina at Rend Lake. Other attractions include the 27-hole championship Rend Lake Golf Course and Southern Illinois Artisans Shop.

618 724-2498 Exit 77
R-
on left

04/06/2013

Gun Creek: Apr-Oct, 100 sites with electric hookups, some pull thrus, $16, drinking water, dump, restrooms, showers, swimming beach. From I-57 exit 77, west on SR-154 for .25 mile, then left on Gun Creek Trail, south .25 mile, then right on Golf Course Road, 1/2 mile. 618-629-2338.

North Sandusky: Apr-Oct, 103 sites with electric hookups, 15 full hookup sites, $16–$22, drinking water, dump, restrooms, showers, playground, swimming beach. From I-57 exit 77, west 4.5 miles on SR-154 to Rend City Road, then south 1 mile to stop sign. Park entrance is on the south side of the intersection. 618-625-6115.

South Marcum: Apr-Oct, 147 sites with electric (50amp) hookups, 14 tent sites, $12–$16, drinking water, dump, restrooms, showers, playground, hiking trail. From I-57 exit 71, west for 3 miles on SR-14, then north on Rend City Road. Turn right onto Main Dam and go 3 miles to the park entrance on left. 618-435-3549.

South Sandusky: Apr-Oct, 121 sites with electric hookups, 18 full hookup sites, some pull thrus, 8 tent sites, $12–$22, drinking water, dump, restrooms, showers, interpretive trail, bicycle trails. From I-57 exit 71, go west on SR-14 for 3 miles to Rend City Road for 6 miles, park entrance on right. 618-625-3011.

Iowa

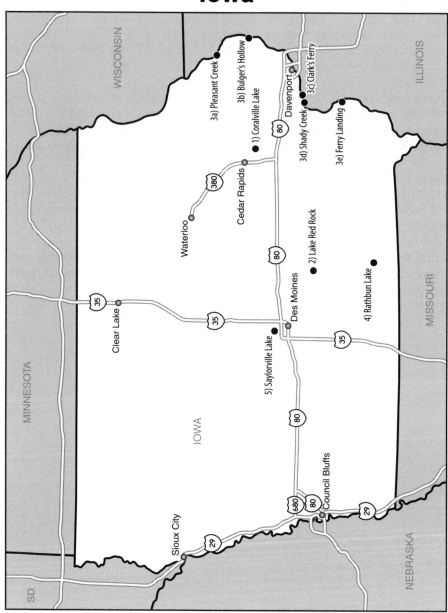

1) Coralville Lake
2) Lake Red Rock
3) Mississippi River Camping
   a) Pleasant Creek
   b) Bulger's Hollow
   c) Clark's Ferry

d) Shady Creek
e) Ferry Landing
4) Rathbun Lake
5) Saylorville Lake

Map #	Auto Touring	Biking	Boating	Climbing	Cultural/Historic Sites	Educational Programs	Camping	Fishing	Groceries/Supplies	Hiking	Horseback Riding	Hunting	Lodging	Off Highway Vehicles	Visitor Center	Page #
1	♦	♦	♦				♦		♦	♦	♦	♦				77
2	♦	♦	♦				♦	♦	♦	♦	♦	♦			♦	78
3			♦				♦		♦	♦					♦	79
4		♦	♦				♦		♦	♦	♦	♦				80
5		♦	♦				♦	♦	♦	♦	♦	♦			♦	81

1) CORALVILLE LAKE

U.S. Army Corps of Engineers
2850 Prairie De Chien Road NE
Iowa City, IA 52240
Phone: 319-338-3543
District: Rock Island

The 5,430-acre Coralville Lake is six miles north of Iowa City on the Iowa River with easy access from Interstates 80 and 380. From I-80 exit 244 (Dubuque Street) go north 3 miles to West Overlook Road, then one-quarter mile to the park areas.

Corps-managed camping is available in three areas. Advance reservations are recommended for summer weekends. Camping is also available at nearby Lake McBride State Park. Boat ramps are conveniently located throughout and there are three marinas. Public golf courses are nearby as is the state's largest shopping mall in Iowa City. Other local attractions include the Herbert Hoover Presidential Library, the Amana Colonies and Devonian Fossil Gorge.

Dam Complex: Apr 15-Oct 15, 136 wooded sites with electric hookups, 9 full hookup sites, 36 tent sites, $12–$24, drinking water, dump, restrooms, showers. From I-80 exit 244, take Dubuque Street north 3 miles to West Overlook Road, then 1/4 mile to the park. 319-338-3543 (2850 Prairie De Chien Rd NE, Iowa City, IA 52240).

Sandy Beach: May-Sep, 48 sites with electric hookups, 2 full hookup sites, 10 tent sites, $12–$22, drinking water, dump, restrooms, showers. From I-380 exit 10, east onto 120th Street then south on Curtis Bridge Road, then east on Sandy Beach Road. 319-338-3543 (3369 Sandy Beach Rd NE, Solon, IA 52333).

Sugar Bottom: May-Sep, 214 sites with electric (50amp) hookups, 12 full hookup sites, some pull thrus, 17 tent sites, $12–$24, drinking water, dump, restrooms, showers. From I-380 exit 4, east on Penn Street to N Front Street (turns into Mehaffey Bridge Road). After crossing the bridge go south into the campground. 319-338-3543 (2192 Mehaffey Bridge Rd, Solon, IA 52333).

2) LAKE RED ROCK

U.S. Army Corps of Engineers
1105 Highway T15
Knoxville, IA 50138
Phone: 641-828-7522
District: Rock Island

The 19,000-acre Lake Red Rock, Iowa's largest lake, has 100 shoreline miles surrounded by more than 60,000 land acres. The project is located about 30 miles southeast of Des Moines and 4 miles southwest of Pella on CR-T15. Red Rock's Visitor Center, open daily in season, has wildlife exhibits and a gift shop.

Large numbers of deer can be seen throughout the lake area. White pelicans migrate through the area every spring and fall. Large numbers of Bald Eagles can be observed during winter months. There is a 13-mile paved hiking and biking trail at the lake and equestrian trails are at the South Elk Rock Park area. RV camping is offered at five areas. Interpretive programs are featured Memorial Day through Labor Day at the amphitheater. Nearby towns include: Pella, Iowa, known for its Dutch heritage and Knoxville, Iowa, the Sprint Car Capital of the World. Visitors will find shopping malls, museums, zoo and many other attractions in Des Moines, Iowa's capital.

Howell Station: Mar-Oct, 143 sites with electric (some 50amp) hookups, $20, drinking water, dump, restrooms, showers. From Pella, IA take Hwy-T15 southwest for 5 miles, then east on Idaho Dr to 198th Pl, south to the campground. 641-828-7522, (1081 198th Pl, Pella, IA 50138).

North Overlook: Apr-Sep, 46 wooded sites with electric (50amp) hookups, 1 full hookup site, 9 tent sites, $8–$16, drinking water, dump, restrooms, showers, playground, amphitheater. From Pella, Iowa, go 3 miles southwest on CR–T15. 641-828-7522, (1007 Highway T15, Pella, IA 50219).

Wallashuck: Apr-Oct, 80 sites with electric (some 50amp) hookups, 1 full hookup site, $16, drinking water, dump, restrooms, showers, playground. From Pella, Iowa, go 4 miles west on CR-G28, then south on 190th Ave. 641-828-7522, (890 190th Ave, Pella, IA 50219).

Whitebreast: Apr-Sep, 113 sites with electric (some 50amp) hookups, some pull thrus, $16, drinking water, dump, restrooms, showers, 2 group camping areas, fish cleaning station, playground, swimming beach, amphitheater. From Knoxville, IA go 8 miles northeast on CR-T15, then north 2 miles on CR-S71. 641-828-7522, (971 Highway S71, Knoxville, IA 50138).

3) MISSISSIPPI RIVER CAMPING

U.S. Army Corps of Engineers
PO Box 2004
Rock Island, IL 61204
Phone: 309-794-5338
District: Rock Island

Fifteen campgrounds dot the shoreline along the Upper Mississippi River Project. Five of these are in Iowa, from the Dubuque area to south of the Quad Cities area. Please check in with the campground manager upon arrival. Clark's Ferry has an amphitheater for ranger programs. There is an observation deck at the Visitor Center (Lock & Dam #15) in Rock Island. The riverfront area has an abundance of wildlife including songbirds, turkeys, herons, eagles, woodpeckers and deer. Fishing is a popular activity. All campgrounds have boat launches and many have playgrounds. Shady Creek has hiking and a golf course nearby.

3a) Pleasant Creek

Pleasant Creek: May-Oct, 60 sites, non-reservable, $4, drinking water, dump. From Dubuque, 24 miles south on US-52, follow signs to Lock & Dam #12. 563-582-0881.

3b) Bulger's Hollow

Bulger's Hollow: May-Sep, 26 sites (9 tent-only), non-reservable, $4, drinking water, dump, restrooms. From Clinton, 3 miles north on US-67, then 1 mile east on 170th Street. 563-582-0881.

3c) Clark's Ferry

Clark's Ferry: Apr-Oct, 27 sites with electric (50amp) hookups, $16–$18, drinking water, dump, restrooms, showers, boat launch, playground, horseshoe. From Davenport, Hwy-22 west about 15 miles, turn at Clarks Ferry sign in Montpelier, follow signs. 563-381-4043 or 563-263-7913, (3860 Sunset Beach, Montpelier, IA 52759).

3d) Shady Creek

Shady Creek: May-Oct, 53 sites with electric (50amp) hookups, $16–$18, drinking water, dump, restrooms showers. From Davenport, west about 17 miles on Hwy-22, turn at Shady Creek sign. 563-263-7913 (3550 Hwy 22, Muscatine, IA 52761).

3e) Ferry Landing

Ferry Landing: Open all year, non-reservable, 20 free sites, drinking water, dump. From Muscatine, south on US-61, east on SR-99, follow signs to Lock & Dam #17. 563-263-7913.

4) RATHBUN LAKE

U.S. Army Corps of Engineers
20112 Highway J–5T
Centerville, IA 52544
Phone: 641-647-2464
District: Kansas City

The 11,013-acre lake is located in the rolling hills of southern Iowa. Rathbun Lake, also known as "Iowa's ocean," has 155 shoreline miles and is surrounded by 24,925 land acres. From Des Moines, go 85 miles southeast on SR-5. Five Corps-managed areas provide RV camping. Additional camping can be found at Honey Creek State Park and at private campgrounds at the lake.

Bridge View: May-Sep, 103 sites with electric (some 50amp) hookups, 11 basic sites, $12–$18, some pull thrus, drinking water, dump, restrooms, showers. ATV park nearby. From Moravia, 10 miles west on Hwy-J18, follow signs. 641-647-2464, (11456 Bridgeview Pl, Melrose, IA 52569).

Buck Creek: May-Sep, 42 sites with electric (some 50amp) hookups, $16–$18, drinking water, dump, restrooms, showers. From Centerville, 5 miles north on Hwy-5 to Hwy-J29, then 4 miles northwest to Hwy-J5T, north 2 miles, follow signs. 641-724-3206, (13796 Crappie Circle, Moravia, IA 52571).

Island View: May-Sep, 194 sites with electric (some 50amp) hookups, $16–$28, drinking water, dump, restrooms, showers. From Centerville, 2.5 miles on Hwy-5, then 4 miles northwest on Hwy-J29, then .1 mile north on Hwy-J5T. 641-647-2079, (19357 Island View Pl, Centerville, IA 52544).

Prairie Ridge: May-Sep, 54 sites with electric (50amp) hookups, $18, drinking water, dump, showers. From Moravia, 4 miles west on Hwy-J18, then south 2.5 miles on 200th Ave (gravel), follow signs. 641-724-3103, (12755 200th Ave, Moravia, IA 52571).

Rolling Cove: May-Sep, 32 sites, no hookups, $12, drinking water, dump, restrooms, showers, marina nearby. From Centerville, 2 miles west on Hwy-2, then north on Hwy-T14 for 5.5 miles, then west on Hwy-J5T for 2 miles, then north on 160th Ave for 1.5 miles, follow signs. 641-647-2464, (16017 Ranger Circle, Mystic, IA 52574).

5) SAYLORVILLE LAKE

U.S. Army Corps of Engineers
5600 NW 78th Avenue
Johnston, IA 50131
Phone: 515–276–4656
Visitor Center: 515-964-0672
District: Rock Island

The Saylorville Lake Project covers 26,000 acres and stretches for over 50 miles up the Des Moines River Valley, northwest of Des Moines. From I-35/80 exit 127 in Des Moines take Hwy-141 north for about 6 miles to Hwy-415 (NW Saylorville Dr). The Visitor Center, located on the east side of the dam, features exhibits on the history and natural resources of the area. Maps and brochures are available and there is a gift shop.

The 24-mile paved, multi-purpose Neal Smith Trail runs from Des Moines to Big Creek State Park and connects the campgrounds to all recreation areas on the east side of the lake. It is used for biking, hiking, jogging, walking and in-line skating (no motor vehicles allowed). Bob Shetler, Cherry Glen and Prairie Flower camping areas are on the east side of the lake near the trail. Bob Shetler is the campground of choice for many shore fishermen. The Des Moines River is within easy walking distance. Saylorville Lake is also popular with travelers as it is just 5 miles from the interstate. Interpretive programs are presented in season. There are golf courses nearby. Other nearby activities include frisbee disc golf course, accessible fishing pier and swimming.

Acorn Valley campground is on the heavily wooded west side of the lake. Equestrian trails are in Jester County Park on the northwest shore.

Acorn Valley: May-Sep, 29 RV sites with electric hookups, 79 walk-in, tent only sites, $12–$22, drinking water, dump, restrooms, showers. From Interstate 35/80 exit 131 (Johnston/Saylorville Lake) north on Merle Hay Road through Johnston for 2.8 miles. At 4-way stop, turn left on NW Beaver Dr for 3.7 miles. At National Weather Service Bldg, turn right on NW Coryden Dr, then right into campground. Gate is closed 10pm to 6am. 515-276-0429, (9615 NW Beaver Dr, Johnston, IA 50131).

Bob Shetler: May-Sep, 67 sites with electric (some 50amp) hookups, 1 full hookup site, $16–$22, drinking water, dump, restrooms, showers. From I–35/80 exit 131 go 2.8 miles north on Merle Hay Road through Johnson. At 4-way stop, turn left and go 1 mile northwest on Beaver Dr. At the large concrete water storage tank on right, go .8 mile northwest (right) on 78th Ave. Turn right at the T-intersection. 515-276-0873, (5200 NW 78th Ave, Johnston, IA 50131).

Cherry Glen: Apr-Oct, 125 sites with electric hookups, 3 full hookup sites. $18–$24, drinking water, dump, restrooms, showers, 38-foot RV length limit. From I-35 exit 90 (Ankeny Industrial Pkwy), take Hwy-160 west for 2.4 miles (it becomes Hwy-415). Take Hwy-415 north for 4.1 miles. At the campground sign, get into the left lane and take NW 94th Ave for one-half mile. 515-964-8792, (4586 NW 94 Ave, Polk City, IA 50325).

Prairie Flower Group Area: Apr-Oct, a large, open 60-acre campground with 248 sites, electric, water, $16–$24, dump. Many of the family sites in the south offer a pleasant view of the lake, while the north is mostly for group camping in circle-the-wagon style. Bike rentals, firewood. From I-35 exit 90 (Ankeny Industrial Pkwy) take Hwy-160 west for 2.4 miles (it becomes Hwy-415), continue on Hwy-415 for 5.6 miles. At the campground sign, get into the left turn lane and take NW Lake Dr for .2 mile. 515-984-6925, (10370 NW Lake Dr, Polk City, IA 50325).

Kansas

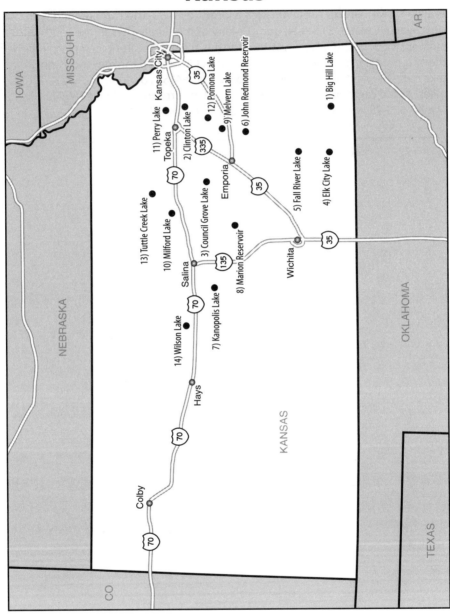

1) Big Hill Lake
2) Clinton Lake
3) Council Grove Lake
4) Elk City Lake
5) Fall River Lake
6) John Redmond Reservoir
7) Kanapolis Lake
8) Marion Reservoir
9) Melvern Lake
10) Milford Lake
11) Perry Lake
12) Pomona Lake
13) Tuttle Creek Lake
14) Wilson Lake

Map #	Auto Touring	Biking	Boating	Climbing	Cultural / Historic Sites	Educational Programs	Camping	Fishing	Groceries / Supplies	Hiking	Horseback Riding	Hunting	Off Highway Vehicles	Lodging	Visitor Center	Page #
1			♦				♦	♦		♦	♦	♦	♦			85
2	♦	♦	♦			♦	♦	♦		♦	♦	♦			♦	86
3	♦		♦			♦	♦	♦		♦		♦		♦		87
4			♦				♦	♦		♦		♦				88
5			♦				♦	♦	♦	♦		♦				89
6	♦	♦	♦				♦	♦		♦	♦	♦		♦	♦	90
7	♦	♦	♦			♦	♦	♦	♦	♦	♦	♦		♦		91
8			♦				♦	♦		♦		♦				92
9			♦				♦	♦	♦	♦	♦	♦			♦	93
10		♦	♦				♦	♦	♦	♦		♦	♦	♦	♦	94
11			♦				♦	♦		♦	♦	♦		♦	♦	95
12		♦	♦		♦	♦	♦	♦		♦	♦	♦		♦	♦	96
13		♦	♦				♦	♦		♦	♦	♦		♦	♦	97
14		♦	♦				♦	♦		♦	♦	♦			♦	98

1) BIG HILL LAKE

U.S. Army Corps of Engineers
P.O. Box 426
Cherryvale, KS 67335
Phone: 620-336-2741
District: Tulsa

From Independence, travel 7 miles east on US-160, then 4 miles north on KS-169, then 5 miles east on the county road. The project office is on the west side of the dam. The project has 1,404 land acres, 1,204 water acres and 20 shoreline miles. The Corps manages three campgrounds.

Big Hill Lake is a productive, popular fishing spot. Big Hill Lake Horse Trail, 17 miles long with varied terrain, is also popular.

Cherryvale Park: All year, 24 sites with electric hookups, some pull thrus, $16–$18, drinking water, dump, restrooms, showers, playground. From US-169 at Cherryvale, Kansas, go east on Main Street through Cherryvale. At the end of Main Street, turn south onto Olive Street, go one-half block and turn east onto CR-5000. Follow paved road 4.5 miles, follows signs. Located on the west side of the dam, north of the project office. 620-336-2741.

Mound Valley: Apr-Oct, 72 sites with electric hookups, 2 with sewer, 8 basic sites, $10–$17, drinking water, dump, restrooms, showers, swimming. Located on the east side of the lake. Exit off US-169 at Cherryvale, then go east through Cherryvale on Main Street, turn south at the end of Main Street onto Olive Street, go one-half block (follow sign), turn east onto CR-5000 and follow the paved road for 4.5 miles. 620-336-2741.

Timber Hill: Apr-Oct, 20 sites, no hookups, some pull thrus, non-reservable, $10, drinking water, dump, restrooms, showers. From the east side of the dam, go 3 miles north, then west on the gravel road. 620-336-2741.

2) CLINTON LAKE

U.S. Army Corps of Engineers
872 N 1402 Road
Lawrence, KS 66049
Phone: 785-843-7665
District: Kansas City

From Lawrence, travel one mile west on Clinton Parkway. The project has 16,361 land acres, 7,000 water acres and 85 shoreline miles.

RV camping is found at Corps-managed campgrounds and Clinton State Park where there is also a swimming beach. There is a marina on the north shore. A golf course, model plane airport and the Clinton Lake Historical Society Museum are nearby. The University of Kansas is in Lawrence.

Cedar Ridge: Apr-Oct, 100 sites with electric (some 50amp) and water hookups, $18, drinking water, dump, restrooms, showers, laundry. From Lawrence take Hwy-40 (6th Street) west 4 miles, then left on CR-442, go west 5 miles to Stull. Go left onto CR-1023, go south about 6 miles to CR-6, turn left, 3.5 miles. 785-843-7665, (1205 E 700 Rd, Lawrence, KS 66047).

Hickory/Walnut: May-Sep, 220 sites (94 have electric hookups), 16 shoreline boat-in sites, $10–$16, drinking water, dump, restrooms, showers, laundry. From Lawrence, take Hwy-40 (6th Street) west 4 miles, then left onto CR-442 and go 5 miles to Stull, then left on CR-1023, go 6 miles to CR-6, turn left and go 4 miles through Clinton. The park is next to town, follow signs. 785-843-7665, (1184 E 700 Rd, Lawrence, KS 66047).

Rockhaven: Apr-Oct, 50 sites, no hookups, non-reservable, $6–$8, drinking water, restrooms, horse/mule camping. From Stull, 6 miles south on SR-1023, then 3 miles east on SR-458, then .8 mile north on CR-700E (gravel). 785-843-7665, (1050 E 700 Rd, Lawrence, KS 66047).

3) COUNCIL GROVE LAKE

U.S. Army Corps of Engineers
945 Lake Road
Council Grove, KS 66846
Phone: 620-767-5195
District: Tulsa

Located about 30 miles southwest of Topeka. From the Kansas Turnpike (I-335) go west 26 miles on US-56 to Council Grove. In the famous Flint Hills region of Kansas, the project is on the Neosho River with over 3,310 acres of water, 40 shoreline miles and 5,887 land acres. The lake is named for the town of Council Grove where the Osage Indians signed a treaty to establish the Old Santa Fe Trail. A marker in town indicates the place where the treaty was signed.

Camping areas at the project are all managed by the Corps. Boat ramps are located throughout. An ATV area is below the dam in Outlet Channel East. Sightseeing is in the nearby historic town of Council Grove.

Canning Creek: All year, 38 sites with electric (50amp) and water hookups, 3 basic sites, $11–$20, dump, restrooms, showers, playground. Located 1.5 miles north of Council Grove on SR-177. Go west across Dam Road at the west end of the dam, turn right on to City Lake Road and travel 2 miles west. 620-767-6745, (City Lake Rd, Council Grove, KS 66846).

Kit Carson Cove: Mar-Nov, 14 sites with electric & water, 1 basic site, non-reservable, $8–$14, restrooms. From US-56 in Council Grove, 2 miles north on SR-177, then west. 620-767-5195.

Marina Cove: All year, 3 sites with electric hookups, 1 basic site, non-reservable, $8–$14, restrooms. From Council Grove, 1.5 miles north on SR-177, then 1 mile west on Dam Road, 1.5 miles west on right. 620-767-5195.

Neosho: All year, 8 sites with electric hookups, non-reservable, $12–$14, drinking water, restrooms. From Council Grove, 1.5 miles north on SR-177, 1 mile west on Dam Road, right on City Lake Road 1 mile, then .3 mile west on right. 620-767-5195, (City Lake Rd, Council Grove, KS 66846).

Richey Cove: Apr-Oct, 33 sites with electric (some 50amp) and water hookups, 16 electric-only, $11–$20, dump, restrooms, showers, playground, swimming, hiking trail. From Council Grove go 3 miles north on SR-177, entrance on west side of highway. 620-767-5800.

Santa Fe Trail: Apr-Oct, 30 sites with electric & water hookups, 1 full hookup, 5 electric-only, $11–$18, dump, restrooms, showers, playground. From Council Grove go north 1.5 miles on SR-177, then west on Dam Road 1 mile to City Lake Road, turn right and go 1 mile west to the campground. 620-767-7125.

4) ELK CITY LAKE

U.S. Army Corps of Engineers
P.O. Box 426
Cherryvale, KS 67335
Phone: 620-336-2741
District: Tulsa

Located 127 miles east of Wichita in southern Kansas, 5 miles northwest of the town of Independence. From Independence, go 7 miles north on US-75, then 4 miles west and 2 miles south on county road. The project includes 15,336 land acres, 3,122 water acres and 50 miles of shoreline.

Elk City Lake features six scenic hiking trails through colorful forests and through some of the most interesting rock formations in the state. Elk City State Park is nearby. The State of Kansas uses 11,680 acres of project lands for wildlife management and public hunting.

Card Creek: All year, 16 sites with electric hookups, 4 basic, some pull thrus, non-reservable, $12–$14, drinking water, dump, restrooms, showers. From Elk City junction SR-39, go 7 miles southeast on US-160, then 1.3 miles north and 1.7 miles northwest. 620-336-2741.

Outlet Channel: Apr-Oct, 15 sites, no hookups, non-reservable, $8, drinking water, dump, restrooms. From Elk City, go 7 miles northwest of Independence on the county road below the dam. Sites are located on the west side of the spillway. 620-336-2741.

5) FALL RIVER LAKE

U.S. Army Corps of Engineers
RR 1 Box 243E
Fall River, KS 67047
Phone: 620-658-4445
District: Tulsa

Fall River Lake is located 70 miles east of Wichita and 4 miles west of the town of Fall River just off US-400. From junction US-77/US-400 (east of Wichita) go east on US-400 to mile marker 344 (250 Road), then northeast. The project office is on the west side of the dam. The lake is about a mile wide at the dam site and stretches up the picturesque Fall River for 15 miles.

Flowers, birds and game enhance the project situated in rolling prairie country. There is good wildlife viewing. The 10,900-acre Fall River Game Management Area is located within the project. **Note**: There are some low water crossings in some areas.

Damsite: Apr-Oct, 18 full hookup sites (some 50amp), 10 electric-only sites, 5 basic, $13–$21, drinking water, dump, restrooms, showers, laundry. From US-400 turn north at mile marker 344 (250 Road), then turn east for 2.4 miles, turn south at the park entrance, follow signs. 620-658-4445.

Rock Ridge Cove North: 25 sites with electric hookups, 19 basic sites, non-reservable, $9–$16, drinking water, dump, restrooms. From junction US-400 & Hwy-99, go 7.8 miles east, 1.7 miles north and 1.5 miles west. Low water crossing. 620-658-4445.

Whitehall Bay: Apr-Oct, 9 full hookup sites (50amp), 15 electric-only sites, $13–$21, drinking water, dump, restrooms, showers, laundry. From US-400 turn north at mile marker 344 and go about 1 mile, then turn east and go 2.8 miles across the dam, turn north .8 mile, then west .7 mile, then north 1.8 miles across the low water crossing, west .4 mile, then south 1 mile to campground. 620-658-4445.

6) JOHN REDMOND RESERVOIR

U.S. Army Corps of Engineers
1565 Embankment Road SW
Burlington, KS 66839
Phone: 620-364-8613
District: Tulsa

John Redmond Reservoir is located in the broad Neosho River Valley. From I-35 exit 155, go south on US-75 to Embankment Road (3.5 miles north of Burlington), travel west and follow signs to the Dam area and Visitor Center. The project includes 30,693 land acres, 9,710 water acres and 69 shoreline miles.

Corps-managed camping areas include Riverside East and West for individual camping and Damsite for group camping only. The spillway area, a popular place for fishing, can be accessed from Riverside East. The multi-use Hickory Creek Trail is open to hikers, horseback riders and mountain bikers. There are 140 acres of trails for ATVs and dirt bikes. Numerous wildlife viewing areas are located around the reservoir. Sightseers will enjoy the Flint Hills Wildlife Refuge or wandering the old Indian grounds.

Riverside East: Apr-Oct, 53 sites with electric & water hookups, some pull thrus, $15, dump, restrooms, showers. On the east bank of the Neosho River. Good wildlife viewing from the hiking trail. From Burlington, travel 3.5 miles north on US-75, then 1.5 miles west on Embankment Road, follow signs. 620-364-8613.

Riverside West: May-Sep, 37 sites with electric & water hookups, 6 basic, $8–$15, drinking water, dump, restrooms, showers, playground, interpretive trail. On the west bank of the Neosho River. From Burlington, travel 3.5 miles north on US-75, then 2.5 miles west on Embankment Road, follow signs. 620-364-8613.

7) KANOPOLIS LAKE

U.S. Army Corps of Engineers
105 Riverside Drive
Marquette, KS 67464
Phone: 785-546-2294
District: Kansas City

From Salina, go 20 miles southwest on KS-140, then 10 miles south on KS-141. Kanopolis Lake is located on the Smoky Hill River and is one of the oldest lakes in Kansas. The project has 18,580 land acres, 3,427 water acres and 41 shoreline miles.

Two Corps-managed campgrounds include Riverside on the southeast end of the dam and Venango at the northwest end of the dam. Horse Thief and Langly State Parks also have camping as well as horseback riding and mountain biking. Nearby, the Fort Hanker Museum at Kanapolis and the Rogers Art Gallery and Museum at Ellsworth portray the settlement of the American West.

Riverside: Apr-Oct, 9 sites with electric hookups and 31 basic sites, $12–$18, drinking water, dump, restrooms, showers, playground. River access for fishing. From Salina, west on Hwy-140 for 19 miles to Hwy-141, then 14 miles south to the end of the dam to Riverside Dr. Follow for .5 mile east. Caution: Steep river banks may be dangerous for unattended children. 785-546-2294.

Venango: All year, 32 sites with electric & water hookups, 102 electric-only sites and 70 basic sites, some pull thrus, $12–$18, drinking water, dump, restrooms, showers, playground, swimming. From Salina, go west for 19 miles on Hwy-140, then 12 miles south on Hwy-141, then .5 mile west, follow signs. 785-546-2294.

8) MARION RESERVOIR

U.S. Army Corps of Engineers
2105 North Pawnee
Marion, KS 66861
Phone: 620-382-2101
District: Tulsa

Marion Reservoir is 46 miles northeast of Wichita. From I-135 east in Newton, 24 miles north on KS-15, then 12 miles east on US-56. The reservoir encompasses 6,200 acres of water surrounded by another 6,000 acres of public lands.

RV camping is available at four parks, with boat ramps located throughout. Wildlife observers will enjoy the Willow Walk Nature Trail located at Cottonwood Point.

Cottonwood Point: Mar-Nov, 45 sites with electric (some 50amp) and water hookups, 59 electric-only, some pull thrus, $15–$18, drinking water, dump, restrooms, showers, interpretive trail, playground, swimming. Located 4 miles northwest of Marion, KS off US-56, turn north on Old Mill Road and go 2.8 miles north. Follow signs. 620-382-2101.

French Creek Cove: Mar-Nov, 20 sites with electric hookups, drinking water, non-reservable, $10. From Marion, go 7 miles west on US-56, then 1 mile north on KS-15 and 1 mile east on 210th Street. 620-382-2101.

Hillsboro Cove: Mar-Nov, 30 sites with electric & water hookups, 21 electric-only, some pull thrus, $15-$17, drinking water, dump, restrooms, showers. From Marion, go 5 miles northwest on US-56, turn north on Night Hawk, then east, follow signs. 620-382-2101.

Marion Cove: All year, 6 basic sites, $7, non-reservable, drinking water, restrooms. From Marion, go 3 miles west on US-56, then 1 mile north on Pawnee past the project office on left. 620-382-2101, (2125 North Pawnee Rd, Marion, KS 66861).

9) MELVERN LAKE

U.S. Army Corps of Engineers
31051 Melvern Lake Parkway
Melvern, KS 66510
Phone: 785-549-3318
District: Kansas City

From Topeka, go 40 miles south on US-75. The Project Information Center is located 1/4 mile west of the KS-31 exit off US-75 at the south end of the dam. Exhibits, brochures and pamphlets are available. Melvern Lake project is situated on the eastern edge of the Kansas Flint Hills Region and covers 6,900 acres of water and 18,000 acres of land open for public use.

There are fish cleaning stations and playgrounds at all four Corps-managed campgrounds. Coeur D'Alene and Outlet have swimming beaches. There is a stocked fishing pond at the Outlet campground and a marina at Coeur D'Alene. Eisenhower State Park has camping and horseback riding.

Arrow Rock: May-Sep, 24 sites with electric & water hookups, 5 electric-only sites, 16 basic sites, $12–$17, drinking water, dump, restrooms, showers, laundry. From US-75, Olivet exit, go 1 mile west on KS-276 to South Fairlawn Road, then 1 mile north to Arrow Rock Parkway, then west 1 mile. 785-549-3318.

Coeur D'Alene: May-Sep, 33 sites with electric (50amp) & water hookups, 1 full hookup site, 26 basic sites, $12–$16, drinking water, dump, restrooms, showers, laundry. From US-75, Melvern exit, go 2 miles south on Melvern Lake Parkway, then 1 mile northwest on Coeur D'Alene Parkway. 785-549-3318.

Outlet: Apr-Oct, 61 sites with electric & water hookups, 89 full hookup sites, $17–$20, drinking water, dump, restrooms, showers. From US-75 Melvern exit, go 1/4 mile west on Melvern Lake Parkway to cut off road, then 1/4 mile west to River Road Pkwy, then 1/2 mile north. 785-549-3318.

Turkey Point: May-Sep, 50 sites with electric (some 50amp) and water hookups, $12–$17, drinking water, dump, restrooms, showers, laundry. From Osage City, go south on KS-170 to 301st St, then 2 miles east, then 1 mile south on Indian Hills Road to Turkey Point Parkway, then 1/2 mile south. 785-549-3318.

10) MILFORD LAKE

U.S. Army Corps of Engineers
4020 West KS-57 Highway
Junction City, KS 66441
Phone: 785-238-5714
District: Kansas City

Milford Lake is located just north of I-70, about 65 miles west of Topeka. From I-70 exit 295, go north on US-77 for 4 miles, then left on KS-57, then left and 1.5 miles to the Milford Lake Information Center where displays and exhibits are featured and maps and directions are available. The lake has 163 shoreline miles and the project encompasses 15,600 water acres and 32,263 land acres.

The Milford Nature Center is located at the project. ATV areas at School Creek and Timber Creek are for vehicles less than 50" wide only. Corps-managed campgrounds include Curtis Creek and West Rolling Hills on the southwest side of the lake, School Creek on the west side and Timber Creek on the east side. In addition, a county park, state park, city park and private campground all have RV camping. Restaurants are in the nearby town of Milford.

Curtis Creek: Apr-Sep, 81 sites with electric & water hookups, 8 tent sites, $12–$18, dump, restrooms, showers, playground, boat ramp, pier. From I-70 exit 290, go north 5 miles, then west on 837 for 6 miles. 785-238-4636, (6902 Curtis Creek Rd, Junction City, KS 66441).

School Creek: Apr-Oct, 44 sites, no hookups, primitive camping, drinking water, non-reservable, $8, restrooms, boat launch, pier, off-road/ATV area. From Wakefield, 1 mile west on SR-82. 785-238-5714.

Timber Creek: Apr-Oct, 45 sites, no hookups, drinking water, non-reservable, $8, restrooms, boat launch, playground, off-road/ATV area. From Wakefield, 1 mile east on SR-82. 785-238-5714.

West Rolling Hills: Apr-Sep, 56 sites with electric & water hookups, 6 basic sites, 3 pull thrus, tent area adjacent to beach, $12–$19, dump, restrooms, showers, swimming, marina. From I-70 exit 290, go 5 miles to 244, then east .5 mile. 785-238-4636, (5028 West Rolling Hills Rd, Junction City, KS 66441).

11) PERRY LAKE

U.S. Army Corps of Engineers
10419 Perry Park Drive
Perry, KS 66073
Phone: 785-597-5144
District: Kansas City

From Topeka take US-24 east for 17 miles to Perry. Turn left on Ferguson Road north of Perry for about 2 miles. Turn left at 39th Street (Spillway Road) and travel about a mile, then turn right on Perry Park Dr. The brick building on the right is the Corps information center. The project has 31,641 land acres, 11,148 water acres and 160 miles of shoreline.

A 30-mile National Recreation Trail follows the eastern shoreline of Perry Lake. Four Corps-managed campgrounds, as well as Horse Trail State Park (with a 25-mile equestrian trail) and Perry State Park (with a mountain bike trail), are located at the lake.

Long View: May-Sep, 26 wooded sites with electric hookups, 13 basic sites and 6 tent sites, $12–$16, drinking water, dump, restrooms, showers. From Oskaloosa, go 6 miles west on KS-92, then 2 miles south on Ferguson Road, then 2 miles west on 86th Street. 785-597-5144, (7752 Longview Park Rd, Ozawkie, KS 66070).

Old Town: May-Sep, 33 shaded sites with electric hookups, 46 basic, some pull thrus, $12–$16, drinking water, dump, restrooms, showers. From Ozawkie, travel 1.5 miles east on KS-92, follow signs. 785-597-5144, (9952 Old Town Trail, Ozawkie, KS 66070).

Rock Creek: Apr-Oct, 64 sites with electric (some 50amp) hookups, 55 basic and 25 tent sites, $12–$18, drinking water, dump, restrooms, showers. From Hwy-24 west of the town of Perry, travel 3 miles north on KS-237, then east on Rock Creek Park Road. 785-597-5144.

Slough Creek: Apr-Oct, 85 sites with electric (some 50amp) and water hookups, 121 sites with no hookups, some pull thrus, 18 tent sites, $12–$18, drinking water, dump, restrooms, showers, group camping area. From Perry, junction Hwy-24, go 7 miles north on Ferguson Road, then 1 mile southwest on Slough Creek Road. 785-597-5144.

12) POMONA LAKE

U.S. Army Corps of Engineers
5260 Pomona Dam Road
Vassar, KS 66524
Phone: 785-453-2201
District: Kansas City

From Topeka, go 24 miles south on US-75, then 7 miles east on KS-268. The Project Information & Visitor Center has displays about the lake and the environment and maps and brochures. Pomona has 4,000 water acres, 52 miles of shoreline and 8,025 land acres.

Located near the Santa Fe Trail, the lake has scenic beauty as well as an abundance of wildlife. Excellent fishing can be found at the lake's many bank fishing areas. Power boating and sailing are also popular at the lake. Two marinas provide fuel and boating services and supplies. Designated swimming beaches are at Michigan Valley and Pomona State Park. Camping is available at Corps-managed parks and at Pomona State Park.

Carbolyn Park: May-Sep, 32 sites with electric (some 50amp) & water hookups, $16, drinking water, dump, restrooms, showers, playground. Lots of shade in a secluded location, 25 miles south of Topeka on US-75. Park entrance is 4.5 miles south of Lyndon, on the east side of the highway, follow signs. 785-453-2201.

Cedar: All year, 8 primitive sites, free, non-reservable, restrooms. From Michigan Valley, 2 miles west on East 213th St, 1 mile on South Shawnee Heights Road. 785-453-2201.

Michigan Valley: May-Sep, 95 sites with electric & water hookups, $12–$18, dump, restrooms, showers, playground, swimming. From US-75, east on KS-268 for 7 miles to Pomona Dam Road, then north for 2.5 miles across the dam, turn west on Wolf Creek Parkway for 500 feet, then south to the park entrance. 785-453-2201.

Outlet Park: All year, 36 sites with electric & water hookups, $10-$16, dump, restrooms, showers, laundry, playground, nature trail. Located along 110 Mile Creek. From US-75, go east on KS-268 for 7 miles, turn north on Pomona Dam Road and go .5 mile to 229th Street (just before the dam), turn east to the park entrance. 785-453-2201.

Wolf Creek: Apr-Oct, 87 sites with electric & water hookups, $12–$16, dump, restrooms, showers, playground, ball field, group camping area. From US-75, go east on KS-268 for 7 miles to Pomona Dam Road, then north 2.5 miles across the dam. Turn west on Wolf Creek Parkway for 1.2 miles. 785-453-2201.

13) TUTTLE CREEK LAKE

U.S. Army Corps of Engineers
5020 Tuttle Creek Blvd.
Manhattan, KS 66502
Phone: 785-539-8511
District: Kansas City

Tuttle Creek Lake is situated some 55 miles northwest of Topeka. From I-70 exit 313, go 9 miles north on KS-177, then 5 miles north on US-24 to the dam project office. The lake's long narrow shoreline stretches for 100 miles and the entire project has 12,500 surface acres of water and 16,000 acres of land. Tuttle, the second largest lake in Kansas, is located in the scenic Flint Hills.

The Corps manages two campgrounds, both on the west side of the lake. There are four state parks, the River Pond unit of Tuttle Creek State Park is the most popular for RV camping. The county operates a primitive campground. Random camping elsewhere is prohibited. The off road vehicle area is just below the east end of the dam with access from Dyer Road.

Stockdale: Apr-Sep, 12 sites, no hookups, 3 pull thrus, 14 tent sites, $8–$12, drinking water, dump, restrooms, showers. From junction US-24/KS-13 at the west end of the dam, travel north and west 5 miles, then right on Riley County Rd (CR-895), then two miles, right on CR-396, then 2.5 miles to the campground. Entrance road is minimally maintained and can be flooded. Tuttle Creek State Park is nearby. 785-539-8511.

Tuttle Creek Cove: Apr-Oct, lakefront sites, 44 with electric (some 50amp) hookups and 11 basic sites, some pull thrus, $12–$18, limited availability of drinking water, dump, restrooms, showers. From junction US-24/KS-13, east on KS-13 for 200 yards, then north on Tuttle Creek Road, 3 miles. 785-539-8511, (6000 Tuttle Creek Cove Rd, Manhattan, KS 66503).

14) WILSON LAKE

U.S. Army Corps of Engineers
4860 Outlet Road
Sylvan Grove, KS 67481
Phone: 785-658-2551
District: Kansas City

From Salina, go west on I-70 to the Wilson exit (#206), then 7 miles north on SR-232 to the Visitor Center. Located in the Post Rock Country of north-central Kansas, the lake has 9,000 water acres and 100 shoreline miles. There are 25,574 land acres in the project.

Three Corps-managed camping areas include Minooka on the south side of the lake, Sylvan Park located below the dam near the administration building and Lucas Park on the north side of the lake. Wildlife viewing is excellent from the Burr Creek Nature Trail at Sylvan Park, especially at dawn and dusk. Wilson State Park and a golf course are nearby.

Lucas Park: Apr-Oct, 16 sites with electric (some 50amp) and water hookups, 54 electric-only sites, 16 basic sites, $12–$24, some pull thrus, drinking water, dump, restrooms, showers. From I-70 exit 206, go 9 miles north on SR-232, park is on left. 785-658-2551.

Minooka: Apr-Oct, 102 sites with electric (some 50amp), 2 sites with electric & water hookups, 39 basic sites, some pull thrus, $12–$24, drinking water, dump, restrooms, showers. From I-70 exit 199, go north on Dorrance Road 7 miles. 785-658-2551.

Sylvan Park: All year, 27 sites with electric hookups, some pull thrus, $12–$18, drinking water, dump, restrooms, showers. From I-70 exit 206, go 8 miles north on SR-232, before crossing the dam turn right at KS-181, go east 100 yards, then turn left, follow the road past the Visitor Center. 785-658-2551.

Kentucky

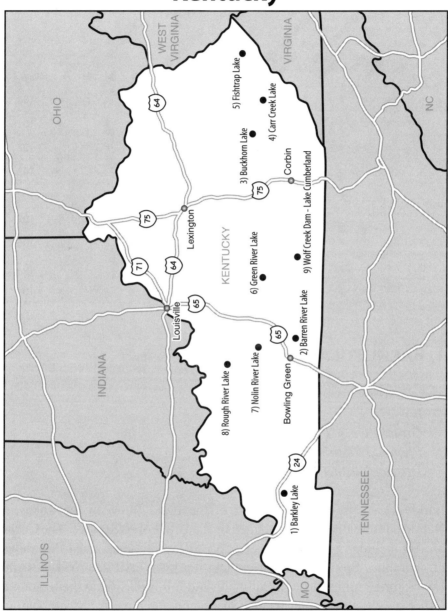

1) Barkley Lake
2) Barren River Lake
3) Buckhorn Lake
4) Carr Creek Lake
5) Fishtrap Lake

6) Green River Lake
7) Nolin River Lake
8) Rough River Lake
9) Wolf Creek Dam - Lake Cumberland

Map #	Auto Touring	Biking	Boating	Climbing	Cultural / Historic Sites	Educational Programs	Camping	Fishing	Groceries / Supplies	Hiking	Horseback Riding	Hunting	Lodging	Off Highway Vehicles	Visitor Center	Page #
1	♦	♦	♦		♦	♦	♦	♦		♦	♦	♦	♦		♦	100
2	♦		♦		♦	♦		♦	♦	♦		♦	♦		♦	101
3	♦	♦	♦		♦	♦		♦	♦	♦		♦	♦			102
4			♦			♦		♦		♦		♦				103
5		♦	♦			♦		♦	♦			♦				104
6			♦			♦		♦		♦		♦			♦	105
7	♦		♦		♦	♦		♦		♦	♦	♦	♦			106
8	♦		♦		♦	♦		♦		♦		♦			♦	107
9		♦	♦		♦	♦		♦	♦	♦		♦			♦	108

1) BARKLEY LAKE

U.S. Army Corps of Engineers
Box 218
Grand Rivers, KY 42045
Phone: 270-362-4236
District: Nashville

Barkley Lake is the eastern part of the Land Between the Lakes, a National Recreation Area managed by the U.S. Forest Service. The Corps project includes 51,043 land acres, 57,920 water acres and 1,004 miles of shoreline. From Western Kentucky Parkway exit 4, travel west on US-62 for 13 miles through Eddyville and follow US-62 to the Resource Office and Visitor Center located just below the dam. A "Steamboating on the Cumberland" exhibit is featured at the Visitor Center. Maps and brochures are available.

Corps-managed camping areas include one in Tennessee and 3 in Kentucky. Other camping is available at the state park and private marinas and resorts on the lake. Local points of interest include a Civil War Monument and historic relics. Good wildlife viewing can be found throughout the project. Full service marinas, restaurants and golf are nearby. Fort Donelson National Military Park is on Lake Barkley's western shore.

Bumpus Mills: Apr-Sep, 15 sites with electric & water hookups, non-reservable, $16-$17, dump, restrooms, showers, laundry, swimming. Located in Tennessee. From I-24 exit 65 (Cadiz), travel south on Hwy-139 (turns into SR-120). Go through Bumpus Mills, then west on Tobaccoport Road, follow signs, go 1 mile on gravel road, continue straight at the "Y" and follow signs. (20 miles from Clarksville, TN.) 931-232-8831.

Canal: Apr-Oct, 97 sites with electric (some 50amp) & water hookups, 17 full hookup sites (some 50amp), some pull thrus, $16–$29, dump, restrooms, showers, laundry, playground, swimming. From I-24 exit 31, south on Hwy-453 for 2 miles. 270-362-4840.

Eureka: Apr-Sep, 23 sites with electric & water hookups, $15–$20, dump, restrooms, showers, laundry, playground, swimming, water skiing. From I-24 exit 40 (Kuttawa) go west on Hwy-62/641, then south on Hwy-810, then west on SR-1271, follow signs. 270-388-9459.

Hurricane Creek: Apr-Sep, 45 sites with electric (some 50amp) & water hookups, 6 tent sites, some pull thrus, $12–$22, dump, restrooms, showers, laundry, playground, swimming. From I-24 exit 45, turn right on Hwy-293 west for .3 mile. Turn left on Hwy-93 south for 5.3 miles. Turn right on Hwy-274 south for 5.7 miles, then right on Hurricane Camp Road. (12 miles from Cadiz.) 270-522-8821.

2) BARREN RIVER LAKE

U.S. Army Corps of Engineers
1088 Finney Road
Glasgow, KY 42141
Phone: 270-646-2055
District: Louisville

The project, some 20 miles southeast of Bowling Green and about 15 miles southwest of Glasgow, encompasses 14,667 land acres, 10,000 water acres and 140 shoreline miles. From I-65 exit 53 (Cave City), travel 10 miles south on KY-90 to Glasgow, then 5 miles south on US-

31 to KY-252 for 9 miles to the dam. The project office and Visitor Center are located on the north end of the dam. Maps, brochures and information on area attractions are available.

Three Corps-managed campgrounds have accommodations suitable for RVs. Playgrounds, hiking and interpretive trails can be found in the campgrounds. Off road vehicles are prohibited. Boat ramps are located throughout. Swimming areas are available at Bailey's Point and The Narrows. Cool water near the dam provides for good fishing for hybrid striped bass and rainbow trout when stocked.

Barren River State Park on US-31 also has camping plus lodging, marina and golf. Area attractions include Mammoth Caves National Park and many federally protected Native American villages and burial sites.

Bailey's Point: Apr-Oct, 175 sites with electric (some 50amp) and water hookups, 40 basic sites, $14–$21, drinking water, dump, restrooms, showers, laundry. Largest Corps campground, scenic views of the lake. From Glasgow, Kentucky, take US-31E south for 15 miles to Hwy-252. Turn right and go 1.5 miles to Hwy-517, turn right, follow signs. 270-622-6959.

Tailwater: Apr-Sep, 48 sites with electric (50amp) & water hookups, some pull thrus, $17, restrooms. From Glasgow, Kentucky, take US-31E south for 4 miles, turn right on SR-252 which will cross the dam in 8 miles. Tailwater entrance road is at the south end of the dam, follow signs. (Approximately 19 miles from Bowling Green KY.) 270-622-7732.

The Narrows: Apr-Sep, 92 gravel sites with electric (50amp) & water hookups, $21, restrooms, showers, laundry, playground, swimming area. From Glasgow KY, take US-31E south for 10 miles, turn right on Hwy-1318, follow signs (about 14 miles southwest of Glasgow). 270-646-3094.

3) BUCKHORN LAKE

U.S. Army Corps of Engineers
804 Buckhorn Dam Road
Buckhorn, KY 41721
Phone: 606-398-7251
District: Louisville

The Buckhorn project encompasses 4,646 land acres, 1,230 water acres and 65 shoreline miles. From Hazard, Kentucky, travel 9 miles north on KY-15, then 20 miles east on KY-28. Maps and brochures are available at the Corps office located near the town of Buckhorn (north side of the lake).

Buckhorn offers the scenic beauty of the Appalachian Mountain Range. Two Corps-managed campgrounds have boat ramps and other amenities. Attractions in the area include Daniel Boone National Forest, Red River Gorge Geological Area and Buckhorn State Resort where there is lodging, dining and an 18-hole golf course. Restaurants and miniature golf are nearby.

Buckhorn: Apr-Oct, 30 sites with electric (50amp) and water hookups, 15 boat-in tent sites (primitive) and 4 primitive walk-in sites. $12–$20, cable TV, dump, restrooms, showers, laundry. From I-64 exit 98 take Mountain Parkway to exit 33 at Slade, then KY-11S through Beattyville. Continue on KY-11 to Boonville, go straight past the courthouse to KY-28W. Follow KY-28 about 23 miles to Buckhorn. 606-398-7220, (104 Tailwater Camp Rd, Buckhorn, KY 41721).

Trace Branch: May-Sep, 14 sites with electric (some 50amp) & water hookups, $12-$20, dump, restrooms, showers. From I-75 exit 41 (London) or exit 38, take Daniel Boone Parkway east for 44 miles to Hyden Spur, exit to Tim Couch Pass and immediate left toward Thousandsticks onto Bull Creek Road, 2.5 miles to KY-257, then north for 5 miles to Dryhill, go right across Dryhill Bridge, then left on Toulouse Road for 5 miles to Mosley Bend Road intersection, continue straight .5 mile to Trace Branch area on left. 606-398-7251.

4) CARR CREEK LAKE

U.S. Army Corps of Engineers
843 Sassafras Creek Road
Sassafras, KY 41759
Phone: 606-642-3308
District: Louisville

Carr Creek is located in the mountainous region of southeastern Kentucky, 16 miles east of Hazard and 18 miles north of Whitesburg. From Hazard, travel 16 miles south on KY-15, then 1 mile north on KY-

1089. The project office is located below the dam, behind the Little Dove Church at Sassafras. Information and maps are available. The project includes 3,196 land acres, 710 water acres and 24 shoreline miles.

Fishing and boating are primary activities at the lake. Camping is available at the Corps-managed Littcarr Campground. Carr Creek State Park on Hwy-15 also has camping. Nearby attractions include the Daniel Boone National Forest and Buckhorn Lake.

Littcarr: Apr-Oct, 45 sites with electric (50amp) & water hookups and 6 basic sites, $20, dump, restrooms, showers, laundry, playground, horseshoes, shuffleboard, nature trail. From I-75 exit 38 (SR-192) east to Daniel Boone Pkwy (DBP.) Follow DBP to SR-15, then south on SR-15 to SR-160. Turn north and follow for 4 miles. 606-642-3052.

5) FISHTRAP LAKE

U.S. Army Corps of Engineers
2204 Fishtrap Road
Shelbiana, KY 41562
Phone: 606-437-7496
District: Huntington

There are 14,858 land acres, 1,131 water acres and 43 shoreline miles at Fishtrap. From Pikeville, travel 12 miles east on US-460, then 2 miles east on SR-1789 to the project office located just downstream of the dam.

Located in rich coalfield country, near the Virginia state line, steep mountains surround the project area. Boat ramps and a marina are at the lake. A mountain biking trail is popular. The one Corps-managed camping area opens on Memorial Day and closes on Labor Day.

Grapevine: May-Sep, 10 sites with electric and water, 18 basic sites, non-reservable, $8–$12, dump, restrooms, showers, playground. From the town of Phyllis (north of the lake), go .5 mile west on SR-194. 606-835-4564.

6) GREEN RIVER LAKE

U.S. Army Corps of Engineers
544 Lake Road
Campbellsville, KY 42718
Phone: 270-465-4463
District: Louisville

The Green River project has 25,583 land acres, 8,210 water acres and 147 miles of shoreline. From I-65 exit 43, go east on the Cumberland Pkwy toward Glasgow/Somerset. Stay on Cumberland/Louie Nunn Pkwy (portions toll) to exit 49. Take KY-55 toward Columbia. Turn left onto KY-55/Jamestown Street and follow KY-55. Turn right onto KY-1061/Lake Road to the Visitor Center. The Center features interpretive exhibits.

Three Corps-managed areas have RV camping. Off road vehicles are prohibited.

Holmes Bend: Apr-Oct, 42 sites with electric & water hookups, 60 electric-only sites, 23 basic, $17–$21, drinking water, dump, restrooms, showers, laundry. From Columbia, Kentucky, take exit 49 off the Cumberland Pkwy, then go north on KY-55 for 1.5 miles, turn right on KY-551 and continue 1 mile, turn left on Holmes Bend Road, follow signs. 270-384-4623, (Holmes Bend Rd/KY-682, Columbia, KY 42728).

Pikes Ridge: Apr-Sep, 20 sites with electric (50amp) & water hookups, 1 full hookup site and 39 basic, $15–$19, drinking water, dump, restrooms. From Campellsville KY, take KY-70 east for 4 miles, turn right on KY-76 and continue for 4.8 miles, turn right on Pikes Ridge Road, follow signs. 270-465-6488.

Smith Ridge: Apr-Sep, 31 sites with electric (50amp) & water hookups, 31 electric-only sites and 18 basic, some pull thrus, $17–$21, drinking water, dump, restrooms, showers. From Campbellsville, Kentucky, take KY-70 east for 1 mile, turn right on KY-372 and continue 3 miles, turn right on County Park Road, follow signs. 270-789-2743, (1500 County Park Rd, Campbellsville, KY 42719).

7) NOLIN RIVER LAKE

U.S. Army Corps of Engineers
2150 Nolin Dam Road
Bee Spring, KY 42207
Phone: 270-286-4511
District: Louisville

Located north of Bowling Green, the lake is accessible from I-65 or from the Western Kentucky Parkway. Known for its blue-green water, the lake has 5,795 water acres and 172 miles of shoreline. There are 12,155 land acres in the project. From I-65 exit 53, go west into Brownsville, then north for 5 miles on KY-259, then right on KY-728, follow signs.

Portions of Nolin River path are within Mammoth Cave National Park, making it scenic for canoe trips. Canoe rentals are available locally. Three Corps-managed camping areas welcome RVs. Nolin Lake State Park also has camping. Golf and riding stables are nearby.

Dog Creek: Apr-Sep, 24 sites with electric & water hookups, 46 basic sites, $15–$22, drinking water, dump, restrooms, playground, swimming area. From Louisville take I-65 exit 76 at Upton, then Hwy-224 west for 9 miles to Millerstown, turn left on Hwy-479, go 8 miles to Hwy-88, turn left and go 2.1 miles, then right on Hwy-1015, then 1.1 miles. 270-524-5454, (890 Dog Creek Rd, Cub Run, KY 42729).

Moutadier: Apr-Oct, 81 sites with electric (some 50amp) & water hookups, 86 basic sites, $15–$22, drinking water, dump, restrooms, showers. From Louisville, take I-65 south to the Western Kentucky Pkwy (WKP). Take WKP west for about 30 miles to Hwy-259 at Leitchfield, KY. Take Hwy-259 south for about 12 miles to Hwy-2067, turn left on Hwy-2067, follow signs. 270-286-4230, (1343 Moutadier Rd/KY-2067, Leitchfield, KY 42754).

Wax: Apr-Sep, 56 sites with electric (some 50amp) & water hookups, 54 basic sites, some pull thrus, $15–$22, drinking water, dump, restrooms, showers. From Louisville, take I-65 south to exit 76 at Upton, then Hwy-224W to Millerstown 9 miles. Turn left on Hwy-479 and go 8 miles to Hwy-88, turn left for .5 mile. 270-242-7578, (14069 Peonia Rd, Clarkson, KY 42726).

8) ROUGH RIVER LAKE

U.S. Army Corps of Engineers
14500 Falls of Rough Road
Falls of Rough, KY 40119
Phone: 270-257-2061
District: Louisville

Located 51 miles north of Bowling Green, the Rough River project encompasses 8,974 land acres, 4,860 water acres and has 220 miles of shoreline. From Louisville, travel west on US-60 to Harned, then south for 10 miles on KY-79 to the project office/Visitor Center, which is on KY-79. Information, maps and brochures are available.

There are four Corps-managed campgrounds with a large number of lakefront sites. Camping is also available at Rough River Dam State Park, where visitors will also find 18-hole and 9-hole golf courses and miniature golf. Local attractions include the historic Green Farm and Pine Knob Theater featuring outdoor dramas based on folklore of the area, June through September. There are many caves in the area including the Mammoth Caves, the longest cave system in the world.

Axtel: Apr-Sep, 42 sites with 50amp electric & water hookups, 1 full hookup site and 115 basic sites, $15–$22, drinking water, dump, restrooms, showers, playground, swimming area. From Louisville, take US-60 to Harned, then south on Hwy-259. Travel 9 miles and turn west on Hwy-79 for .5 mile. 270-257-2584.

Cave Creek: Apr-Sep, 16 sites with 50amp electric & water hookups, 70 basic sites, $10–$14, drinking water, dump, restrooms, showers, playground, 35-foot RV length limit. From Elizabethtown, Kentucky, take Western Kentucky Pkwy to the Leitchfield exit (#107), then north to Hwy-259 to Hwy-54, travel west on Hwy-54 for 11 miles, then 6 miles on Hwy-79, then east on Hwy-736 for 2 miles. 502-879-4304.

Laurel Branch: Apr-Sep, 25 sites with electric (50amp) & water hookups and 52 basic sites, $14–$19, drinking water, dump, restrooms, playground. From Louisville, take US-60 to Harned, then 10 miles west on Hwy-79, then east on Hwy-259 for .5 mile to Hwy-110, then west on Hwy-110 for 1 mile, follow signs. 270-257-8839.

North Fork: Apr-Sep, 50 sites with electric (50amp) & water hookups, 1 full hookup site and 56 basic sites, some pull thrus, $17–$22, drinking water, dump, restrooms, showers, playground, swimming. From Louisville, take US-60 to Harned, then take Hwy-79 west for 9 miles. 502-257-8139.

9) WOLF CREEK DAM – LAKE CUMBERLAND

U.S. Army Corps of Engineers
855 Boat Dock Road
Somerset, KY 42501
Phone: 606-679-6337
District: Nashville

The Cumberland project is located south of Lexington near the Tennessee state line and south of the Cumberland Parkway. It encompasses 48,580 land acres, 50,250 water acres and 1,085 shoreline miles. The Lake Cumberland Visitor Center is located at the Resource Manager's office on Boat Dock Road, about 4 miles south of Somerset on US-27 at red light #29. A self-guided study in nature overlooks the lake at the Visitor Center. Tours of the dam are available in summer and the educational fish hatchery is next door.

During the recreation season, the Corps conducts an interpretive demonstration of a 1877 grist mill, which is on the National Register of Historic Places. Other places of interest nearby include the Mill Springs National Historical Landmark, Natural Arch, Yahoo Falls and Big Fork National River and Recreation Area. Five Corps-managed areas provide camping at Cumberland. Other campgrounds can be found at Burnside State Park and at marinas and private resorts around the lake.

Cumberland Point: Apr-Sep, 30 sites with electric & water hookups, $17–$23, dump, restrooms, showers, laundry, playground. From Nancy, Kentucky, take Hwy-235 south for 1 mile, then right onto Hwy-761 and go 9 miles. 606-871-7886, (1000 Highway 761, Nancy, KY 42544).

Fall Creek: Apr-Oct, 10 sites, non-reservable, $18, drinking water, dump, restrooms, showers. Located off Hwy-2393 about 4 miles from Conley Bottom Resort. 606-348-6042.

Fishing Creek: Apr-Sep, 27 sites with electric & water hookups (some family tent sites) and 20 electric-only sites, $17–$24, drinking water, dump, restrooms, showers, laundry, playground, swimming, convenience store. From Somerset, Kentucky, take Hwy-80 west for 5 miles, turn right on Hwy-1248 and follow for 2 miles. Entrance is on the left at the bottom of the hill. 606-679-5174 or 606-679-6337, (1611 Highway 1248, Somerset, KY 42501).

Kendall: All year, 102 sites with electric (50amp) & water hookups, 6 tent sites, $14–$24, dump, restrooms, showers, laundry, playground, hiking and bike trails. From Jamestown, KY take US-127 south for 10 miles, turn right on Kendell Road, just before crossing the dam, follow signs. 270-343-4660, (80 Kendall Rd, Jamestown, KY 42629).

Waitsboro: Apr-Oct, 25 sites with electric & water hookups, 1 full hookup site and 4 tent sites, $14–$24, drinking water, dump, restrooms, showers, laundry, playground. From Somerset, Kentucky, take US-27 south for 5 miles, turn right on Waitsboro Road, follow signs. 606-561-5513, (500 Waitsboro Dr, Somerset, KY 42501).

Minnesota

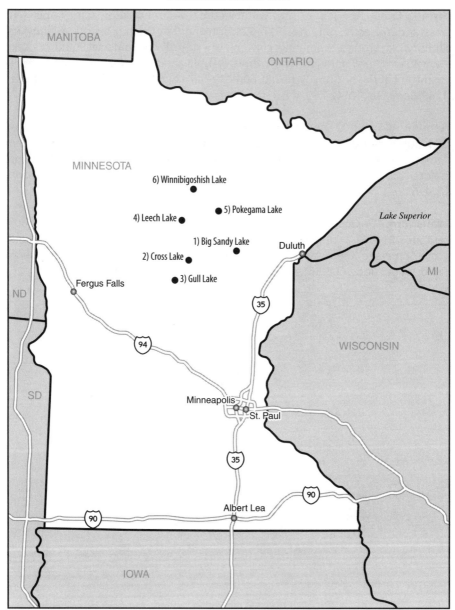

1) Big Sandy Lake
2) Cross Lake
3) Gull Lake

4) Leech Lake
5) Pokegama Lake
6) Winnibigoshish Lake

Map #	Auto Touring	Biking	Boating	Climbing	Cultural / Historic Sites	Camping	Educational Programs	Fishing	Groceries / Supplies	Hiking	Horseback Riding	Hunting	Lodging	Off Highway Vehicles	Visitor Center	Page #
1			♦		♦	♦		♦		♦		♦			♦	111
2		♦	♦			♦		♦		♦		♦				112
3			♦		♦	♦		♦		♦		♦			♦	112
4			♦			♦	♦	♦		♦		♦				113
5			♦			♦		♦				♦				114
6			♦			♦		♦				♦				115

1) BIG SANDY LAKE

U.S. Army Corps of Engineers
22205 531st Lane
McGregor, MN 55760
Phone: 218-426-3482
District: St. Paul

Located 120 miles north of St. Paul, on the canoe route that once linked Lake Superior and the Mississippi River, Big Sandy Lake is a part of the Corps' Mississippi River Headwaters Project. The dams that created the lakes were constructed in the 1800's. When the dam at Big Sandy was built, it included a lock to pass boat traffic through. It was the northernmost lock on the Mississippi River and was the site of an early trading post. Today the lockhouse has been renovated to display interpretive exhibits and artifacts at the Visitor Center. From MN-65 travel to the north entrance of Big Sandy Lake and follow signs to the Visitor Center located at the dam.

At the Corps-managed campground, about half of the campsites are located near the shoreline of Big Sandy Lake and the Sandy River. Other amenities at the campground include boat ramps, swimming, horseshoes, a nature trail and a multi-use court.

Sandy Lake: May-Sep, 43 sites with electric hookups, some pull thrus, 8 walk-in tent sites, $16–$24, drinking water, dump, restrooms, showers, laundry. Take MN-65 north of McGregor and follow south entrance signs to the campground. 218-426-3482.

2) CROSS LAKE

U.S. Army Corps of Engineers
35507 County Road 66
Crosslake, MN 56442
Phone: 218-692-2025
District: St. Paul

Located 22 miles north of Brainerd, Minnesota, Cross Lake is in the Whitefish chain of lakes. It has 13,660 water acres and 119 miles of scenic shoreline. From Hwy-25 north, turn right on CR-3, then north to Crosslake, Minnesota. The Corps-managed campground is in a wooded setting, with some lakefront sites.

Fishing and hunting are popular sporting activities within the project. Other amenities available at the campground include a boat ramp, playground, swimming beach and biking.

Cross Lake: May-Sep, 69 sites with electric hookups and 50 basic sites, $18-$24, drinking water, dump, restrooms, showers, laundry. From Brainerd, Minnesota, on Hwy-25, turn right on CR-3 and travel north to Crosslake. Entrance is on the left directly across from junction of CR-3 & CR-66. 218-692-2025.

3) GULL LAKE

U.S. Army Corps of Engineers
10867 East Gull Lake Drive NW
Brainerd, Minnesota 56401
Phone: 218-829-3334
District: St. Paul

The Gull Lake project is located 130 miles north of St. Paul and 10 miles northwest of Brainerd. Take SR-210 west to SR-371, then north on SR-371 for about 6 miles, turn left at the Federal Recreation Area sign. The project office is on the southeast side of the lake; information is available. The original 7-room dam tender's house is listed on the National Register of Historic Places; prehistoric archaeology of the dam site is also significant with Aboriginal burial mounds on the National Register. An interpretive exhibit is featured at the Visitor Center.

The Corps-managed campground is in a wooded setting and has interpretive hiking trails through the forested areas. It also has a swimming beach and playground. ORVs/ATVs are prohibited. Boat and canoe rentals are available in the area. Nearby attractions include golf, shopping, restaurants and an amusement park.

Gull Lake: Apr-Oct, 39 sites with electric (some 50amp) hookups, $12–$26, drinking water, dump, restrooms, showers. From junction MN-210 & MN-371 in Baxter, travel north on MN-371 for 5.8 miles. Turn left onto CR-125 (Gull Dam Road), follow signs, about 3 miles. 218-829-3334.

4) LEECH LAKE

U.S. Army Corps of Engineers
1217 Federal Dam Drive NE
Federal Dam, MN 56641
Phone: 218-654-3145
District: St. Paul

The 126,000-acre lake is located in the middle of the Chippewa National Forest, 200 miles northwest of Minneapolis. From Grand Rapids, Minnesota, take US-2 west for 33 miles to Bena, Minnesota, then CR-8 for 8 miles to Federal Dam, Minnesota.

The lake is well known for its excellent perch, walleye and muskie fishery. The Leech Lake Indian Reservation is nearby.

The Corps-managed campground is located in a wooded setting and offers a variety of recreation in the campground as well as nature trails and a marina and fish cleaning stations. Ranger programs are presented in season. Other amenities at the campground include a playground, horseshoes, shuffleboard, volleyball and badminton. Firewood is available for a fee.

Leech Lake: 68 sites with electric (some 50amp) hookups, 5 full hookup sites and 4 tent sites, $10–$22, drinking water, dump, restrooms, showers, laundry. From Grand Rapids, Minnesota, take US-2 west for 33 miles to Bena, Minnesota, then CR-8 south for 8 miles. 218-654-3145.

5) POKEGAMA LAKE

U.S. Army Corps of Engineers
34385 US Hwy-2
Grand Rapids, MN 55744
Phone: 218-326-6128
District: St.Paul

The 16,000-acre lake is near Grand Rapids just south of US-2. From Grand Rapids, travel west on US-2 for 2 miles, then south at sign.

Located at the headwaters, the Corps-managed campground is situated next to the river with good shoreline fishing. The campground is nestled in a scenic area and wildlife viewing is excellent. Birders enjoy seeing bald eagles, loons, duck, geese and many other species. The Forest History Center is nearby.

Pokegama Dam: Apr-Oct, 19 sites with electric (50amp) hookups and 2 tent-only sites, $12–$24, drinking water, dump, restrooms, showers, playground. From Grand Rapids, west on US-2 for 2 miles, turn left at sign. 218-326-6128.

6) WINNIBIGOSHISH LAKE

U.S. Army Corps of Engineers
22205 531st Ln.
McGregor, MN 55760
Phone: 218-426-3482
District: St. Paul

Winnibigoshish is 102 miles northwest of Duluth. Situated in the Chippewa National Forest, the lake is located northwest of Deer River and north of US-2. The lake is 67,000 acres in size and has 141 miles of shoreline. It was formed by a huge ice block left behind by a receding glacier. From Deer River, Minnesota, go 2 miles west on US-2, then turn right on MN-46 and go 12 miles north. Turn left on Itasca CR-9 and go two miles, follow signs.

The area has nesting bald eagles and is home to many other birds and mammals including black bear. Winnibigoshish is considered a world-class fishery. The camping area is east of the Mississippi River and the dam. There is one boat ramp that leads into the river and a fish cleaning station. There is a playground within the campground.

Winnie Dam: May-Oct, 22 sites with electric (some 50amp) hookups, $18, drinking water, dump, restrooms, no showers. From Deer River, Minnesota, west on US-2, for 1 mile, then turn right on MN-46 for 12 miles, turn left on CR-9, follow signs, 2 miles. 218-326-6128 (34385 US Hwy 2, Grand Rapids, MN 55744).

Mississippi

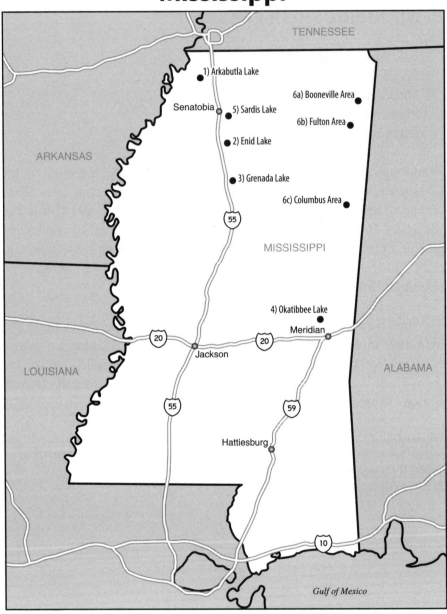

1) Arkabutla Lake
6a) Booneville Area
Senatobia
5) Sardis Lake
6b) Fulton Area
2) Enid Lake
3) Grenada Lake
6c) Columbus Area
55
MISSISSIPPI
4) Okatibbee Lake
Meridian
20
20
Jackson
LOUISIANA
ALABAMA
55
59
Hattiesburg
10
Gulf of Mexico

1) Arkabutla Lake	6) Tennessee-Tombigbee Waterway
2) Enid Lake	a) Booneville Area
3) Grenada Lake	b) Fulton Area
4) Okatibbee Lake	c) Columbus Area
5) Sardis Lake	

Map #	Auto Touring	Biking	Boating	Climbing	Cultural/Historic Sites	Educational Programs	Camping	Fishing	Groceries/Supplies	Hiking	Horseback Riding	Hunting	Lodging	Off Highway Vehicles	Visitor Center	Page #
1		♦	♦				♦	♦		♦		♦				117
2		♦	♦				♦	♦		♦	♦	♦	♦	♦		118
3			♦	♦	♦		♦	♦		♦		♦	♦	♦	♦	119
4	♦	♦	♦				♦	♦		♦		♦			♦	119
5			♦				♦	♦		♦		♦	♦			120
6			♦	♦	♦	♦	♦	♦		♦		♦			♦	121

1) ARKABUTLA LAKE

U.S. Army Corps of Engineers
3905 Arkabutla Dam Road
Coldwater, MS 38618
Phone: 662-562-6261
District: Vicksburg

Located in northern Mississippi, 30 miles south of Memphis, Tennessee, the project includes 44,520 land acres, 12,730 water acres and 134 shoreline miles. From I-55 exit 280 (Hernando), travel 13 miles west on Scenic Loop 304 to the project.

On the Coldwater River, the lake is known for its large crappie and excellent sailing conditions. Corps campgrounds at the lake include Dub Patton on the north end of the dam near the town of Eudora and Hernando Point on the east side of the lake.

Dub Patton: Mar-Oct, 66 sites with electric (50amp) & water hookups, $16–$20, drinking water, dump, restrooms, showers, hiking. From I-55 exit 280 (Hernando) travel west on Scenic Route 304, follow signs. 662-562-6261.

Hernando Point: All year, 83 sites with electric (50amp) & water hookups, $16–$20, drinking water, dump, restrooms, showers, playground, swimming. From I-55 exit

280 (Hernando) travel west to US-51, then south on US-51 to area sign, then west on Wheeler Road and follow signs. 662-562-6261, (788 Wheeler Rd, Hernando, MS 38632).

2) ENID LAKE

U.S. Army Corps of Engineers
264 CR-39
Enid, MS 38927
Phone: 662-563-4571
District: Vicksburg

Enid Lake is 65 miles south of Memphis, Tennessee, and 26 miles north of Grenada. The project spans 28,476 land acres, 15,560 water acres and has 125 shoreline miles. From I-55 exit 233, travel east on CR-36/Enid Dam Road to the Project Office where information is available.

Located in the Hills region of the state, about 140 miles north of Jackson, the lake is noted for its fishing, with several world records posted at the lake. It is also recognized for its family camping facilities. George P. Cossar State Park also has camping.

Chickasaw Hill: All year, 36 sites with electric (some 50amp) & water hookups and 15 tent sites, $10–$14, drinking water, dump, restrooms, showers. From I-55 exit 233, take CR-36 (Enid Dam Road) east for 1 mile to the Enid Lake Field Office, then north for 3 miles on Chapel Hill Road, then east on Pope Water Valley Road for 7 miles, then south on Chickasaw Road for 1.5 miles. 662-563-4571.

Persimmon Hill: All year, 72 sites with electric & water hookups, $16-$18, drinking water, dump, restrooms, showers. From I-55 exit 233, go 1 mile on Enid Dam Road (CR-36) east, then south across the top of the dam 2 miles, follow signs. 662-563-4571.

Wallace Creek: All year, 99 sites with electric (50amp) & water hookups, $16–$18, drinking water, dump, restrooms, showers. From I-55 exit 233, travel east on Enid Dam Road (CR-36) about 2.5 miles, follow signs. 662-563-4571.

Water Valley Landing: Mar-Oct, 29 sites with electric (50amp) & water hookups, $14, drinking water, dump, restrooms, showers. On the south side of the reservoir. From I-55 exit 227, go 17 miles east on SR-32, then 2 miles on CR-53, follow signs. 662-563-4571.

3) GRENADA LAKE

U.S. Army Corps of Engineers
P.O. Box 903
Grenada, MS 38902
Phone: 662-226-5911
District: Vicksburg

Grenada Lake, about 100 miles south of Memphis, Tennessee, has 35,820 water acres, 148 shoreline miles and 54,559 land acres. From I-55 exit 206 (Grenada), travel 4 miles east on MS-8, then follow Scenic Loop Drive 333 to the dam area. The Visitor Center, at the south end of the dam, features a film presentation and a multi media touch screen to access information about the lake. The Center also has a variety of exhibits and an observation deck overlooking the lake.

Grenada Lake is home to the "Thunder On Water" festival held annually in June. Civil War redoubts are located on project lands and Civil War Reenactments are held. RV camping, with many lakefront sites, is available at the Corps facilities and at Hugh White State Park. Golf is nearby.

North Abutment: All year, 56 sites with electric (50amp) & water hookups, some pull thrus, $18, drinking water, dump, restrooms, showers. Amphitheater overlooks the lake. From I-55 exit 206, take Hwy-8 east through the city of Grenada for 3 miles, then left on Scenic Loop 333 across the dam and take the second road to the right. 662-226-1679.

North Graysport: All year, 51 sites with electric (50amp) & water hookups, some pull thrus, $10, drinking water, dump, restrooms, showers. Amphitheater overlooks the lake. From I-55 exit 206, take Hwy-8 east for 4 miles across the lake, follow signs. 662-226-1679.

4) OKATIBBEE LAKE

U.S. Army Corps of Engineers
8604 Okatibbee Dam Road
Collinsville, MS 39325

Phone: 601-626-8431
District: Mobile

Okatibbee Lake is located 8 miles north of Meridian, Mississippi, along SR-19. The project encompasses 7,494 land acres, 3,800 water acres and 28 shoreline miles. The Visitor Center is near the north end of the dam. Boating and fishing are popular. Anglers will find large populations of bass, crappie and catfish. The fishing platform at the tailrace below the dam is a popular place to drop in a line.

Sightseeing, golf and restaurants are available in nearby Meridian. A water park is on the east side of the lake. There are five beaches and swimming areas around the lake. Camping is available at the Corps-managed facility listed below and at a park operated by the Harrison Waterway District.

Twiltley Branch: All year, 50 sites with electric (50amp) & water hookups and 11 sites with water only, $18–$20, dump, restrooms, showers, laundry, playground, swimming, hiking trail, group camping area. From Meridian, take SR-19 north for 8 miles, follow signs. 601-626-8068, (9200 Hamrick Rd No, Collinsville, MS 39325).

5) SARDIS LAKE

U.S. Army Corps of Engineers
29049 Hwy-315
Sardis, MS 38666
Phone: 662-563-4531
District: Vicksburg

The Sardis Lake project has 32,100 water acres and spans 163 shoreline miles. Surrounding project land encompasses 66,257 acres. The lake is 8 miles north of Oxford, Mississippi. From I-55 exit 252 (Sardis), travel 10 miles east on MS-315 – or – From I-55 exit 246 (Batesville) travel 10 miles east on MS-35.

Located on the Tallahatchie River, Sardis Lake is known for its sand beaches and fishing for its abundant bass and crappie. Camping is found at the Corps-operated campgrounds and at John Kyle State Park. Golf is nearby. Rental cabins are also available at the state park.

Clear Creek: All year, 52 sites with electric & water hookups, $10, drinking water, dump, restrooms, showers, playground. From I-55 exit 243A in Batesville, travel 21 miles east on MS-6 toward Oxford. Turn left at the West Oxford exit onto West Jackson Ave. Go about 3 miles, then left onto MS-315 and travel about 13 miles. 662-563-4531.

Oak Grove: All year, 82 sites with electric & water hookups, non-reservable, $16, drinking water, dump, restrooms. From I-55 exit 246, travel east on SR-35 to below the dam. 662-563-4531.

6) TENNESSEE-TOMBIGBEE WATERWAY

6a) Booneville Area

> *Bay Springs Visitor Center*
> *82 Bay Springs Resource Road*
> *Dennis, MS 38838*
> *Phone: 662-423-1287*
> *District: Mobile*

The Visitor Center features 8,000 square feet of exhibits and artifacts of the Tenn-Tom project, the natural resources of the area and the history of the waterway. There are a number of films for visitors to view and rangers present programs on water safety. From Dennis, Mississippi, take Hwy-4 west for 5 miles to the Center, on the east side of the lake in Tishomingo County. The area around the building includes a nature trail, dogtrot cabin and an overlook.

Piney Grove: Mar-Nov, 144 sites with electric (50amp) & water hookups, $18–$20, drinking water, dump, restrooms, showers, laundry, playground, swimming. From Booneville, Mississippi, take SR-30 east for 11 miles to Burton, turn right on CR-3501 for 3 miles, follow signs. 662-728-1134, (CR 3550, New Site, MS 38859).

6b) Fulton Area   Stayed 04/05/2013

Jamie L. Whitten Historic Center
100 Campground Road
Fulton, MS 38843
Phone: 662-862-5414
District: Mobile

The Visitor Center at Fulton features exhibits from the federal agencies that were involved in the economic development of northeast Mississippi. Outside the center, picnic areas and a long pier provide excellent views and vistas of the Tenn-Tom Waterway. The Center is 4.2 miles north of the junction of MS-25 & US-78 on the South Access Road.

Whitten Park: All year, 61 sites with electric & water hookups, some pull thrus, $18–$20, drinking water, dump, restrooms, showers, laundry. From US-78 exit 104 (Fulton exit), go north 200 yards, turn left on Access Road at the first traffic light, go north 4 miles. Campground is on the left side of the road within the Whitten Historical area. 662-862-5414, (100 Campground Rd, Fulton, MS 38843) .

662-862-7072

6c) Columbus Area

Waterway Management Center
3606 West Plymouth Road
Columbus, MS 39701
Phone: 662-327-2142
District: Mobile

Information about the Tenn-Tom Waterway is available at the Corps Office in Columbus—from US-82 exit at US-45/Plymouth Bluff Access Rd & travel north, turn left on Old West Point Rd for 1 mile, right on Right Bank Access Rd & right on West Plymouth Rd.

Blue Bluff: All year, 92 shady sites with electric & water hookups, $16–$18, drinking water, dump, restrooms, showers, 24-hour gate attendants. From junction of Hwy-145 and Meridian Street (downtown Aberdeen) travel north 2 miles on Meridian Street; turn right on Lock & Dam Road. Entrance road on the left. 662-369-2832, (20051 Blue Bluff Rd, Aberdeen, MS 39730).

DeWayne Hayes: All year, 100 sites with electric & water hookups, 10 basic sites, $16–$20, drinking water, dump, restrooms, showers, laundry. From Columbus, Mississippi, take US-45 north to junction US-373/50N. Turn left and follow US-373 for 1.5 miles to Stenson Creek Road, left on Stenson Creek, follow brown signs. Travel 2 miles to Barton's Ferry Road and turn left 1/2 mile. 662-434-6939.

Town Creek: All year, 100 sites with electric & water hookups, 10 basic sites, $16–$20, drinking water, dump, restrooms, showers, laundry. From Columbus, Mississippi, take US-45 north to Hwy-50. Turn left and follow Hwy-50 west past the Hwy-50 Waterway bridge. About 2 miles west of the bridge, turn north, follow signs. 662-494-4885, (10690 Witherspoon Rd, West Point, MS 39773).

Missouri

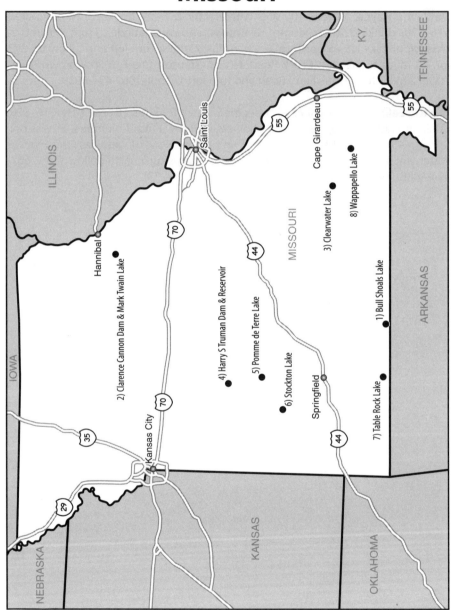

1) Bull Shoals Lake
2) Clarence Cannon Dam & Mark Twain Lake
3) Clearwater Lake
4) Harry S. Truman Dam & Reservoir

5) Pomme De Terre Lake
6) Stockton Lake
7) Table Rock Lake
8) Wappapello Lake

Map #	Auto Touring	Biking	Boating	Climbing	Cultural/Historic Sites	Educational Programs	Camping	Groceries/Supplies	Fishing	Hiking	Horseback Riding	Hunting	Lodging	Off Highway Vehicles	Visitor Center	Page #
1			♦				♦		♦	♦		♦				125
2	♦	♦	♦			♦	♦		♦		♦	♦	♦			126
3			♦				♦		♦	♦		♦				127
4	♦		♦			♦	♦	♦	♦		♦	♦	♦	♦	♦	128
5			♦				♦		♦	♦		♦				130
6			♦				♦		♦	♦	♦	♦	♦	♦		131
7	♦		♦			♦	♦	♦	♦	♦		♦	♦		♦	132
8	♦	♦	♦			♦	♦	♦	♦	♦	♦	♦	♦	♦	♦	134

1) BULL SHOALS LAKE

U.S. Army Corps of Engineers
324 West 7th Street
Mountain Home, AR 72653
Phone: 870-425-2700
District: Little Rock

Bull Shoals Lake is located 135 miles north of Little Rock, Arkansas, south of Branson near the MO/AR state line. From Little Rock, Arkansas, take US-65 north to junction US-62, then 50 miles east to Flippin and 4 miles north to the lake. Maps and information can be obtained at the Project Office in Arkansas. Bull Shoals has 62,326 land acres, 45,440 water acres and 740 shoreline miles. Its extensive area straddles the states of Arkansas and Missouri. In the beautiful Ozark Mountains, the lake is known for its exceptional water quality and outstanding fisheries. Bull Shoals has hundreds of lake arms and coves, perfect for boating, fishing, swimming and water sports of all kinds.

The area also has great appeal to bird-watchers, naturalists and hikers. Fall is a popular season at Bull Shoals when visitors are attracted to the spectacular Autumn foliage in the Ozarks.

Of the 11 Corps-managed campgrounds, 4 are in Missouri and 7 in Arkansas. They are included in their respective state sections. Most campgrounds at Bull Shoals have playgrounds, boat launches and public marinas. ORVs/ATVs are prohibited.

Beaver Creek: Mar-Oct, 37 sites with electric & water hookups, $12–$16, drinking water, dump, restrooms, showers, laundry. From Mountain Home, Arkansas, go north on SR-5 for 24 miles, then west for 42 miles on US-160 to Kissee Mills, Missouri, then left on Hwy-O, follow signs. 417-546-3708.

Pontiac Park: Apr-Sep, 30 sites with electric & water hookups, 5 basic sites, $12–$16, drinking water, dump, restrooms, showers. From Mountain Home, Arkansas, go north on SR-5 for 20 miles to junction of Hwy-W, then 7 miles west to Pontiac, Missouri, and southwest .3 mile to the access road, follow signs. 417-679-2222.

River Run: Mar-Oct, 32 sites with electric & water hookups, 5 basic sites, $16, drinking water, dump, restrooms, showers. From junction US-160 & US-76 in Forsyth, Missouri, take US-76 south for .5 mile to River Run access road, follow signs. 417-546-3646.

Theodosia: Apr-Sep, 31 sites with electric (some 50amp) and water hookups, $13–$17, drinking water, dump, restrooms, showers, laundry, marina, convenience store. From Mountain Home, Arkansas, go north on SR-5 for 24 miles to US-160. Follow US-160 for 12 miles to the park access road, follow signs. 417-273-4626.

2) CLARENCE CANNON DAM & MARK TWAIN LAKE

U.S. Army Corps of Engineers
20642 Highway J
Monroe City, MO 63456
Phone: 573-735-4097
District: St. Louis

Located in northeast Missouri, the project spans the Salt River Valley and includes 18,000 water acres, 285 shoreline miles and 45,881 land acres. It is 28 miles southwest of Hannibal and 120 miles northwest of

St. Louis. From Hannibal, take US-36 west for 17 miles, then Hwy-J south.

Three Corps campgrounds welcome RVs and Mark Twain State Park also has camping. Equestrian camping is available at Russell campground with easy access to the Joanna Multi-Use Trail. A shooting range is located below the dam in the W.G. See South Spillway. Local attractions include the Mark Twain birthplace, shopping, sightseeing and restaurants in nearby towns.

Frank Russell: Apr-Oct, 65 sites with electric hookups, $16, drinking water, dump, restrooms, showers, shaded horse stalls. From Hannibal, Missouri, take US-36 west for 17 miles to Hwy-J, then south for 9 miles. 573-735-4097.

Indian Creek: May-Nov, 65 full hookup sites,148 electric-only (some 50amp) and 20 tent sites, $16–$24, drinking water, dump, restrooms, showers. From Hannibal, Missouri, take US-36 west for 20 miles, then southwest on US-24 for 6 miles, then south on Hwy-HH for 2 miles, east on Monroe CR-581 for 3 miles. 573-735-4097.

Ray Behrens: Mar-Nov, 40 full hookup sites (50amp) and 122 electric only (50amp), $16–$24, drinking water, dump, restrooms, showers, amphitheater, playground, hiking trails. From Hannibal, Missouri, take US-36 west for 17 miles, turn south on Hwy-J and go 12 miles to the campground. 573-735-4097.

3) CLEARWATER LAKE

U.S. Army Corps of Engineers
RR 3 Box 3559-D
Piedmont, MO 63957
Phone: 573-223-7777
District: Little Rock

The project, 120 miles south of St. Louis, has 17,089 land acres, 1,630 water acres and 27 shoreline miles. Clearwater is located 7 miles west of Piedmont. From St. Louis go south on I-55 to exit 174, then continue south on US-67 to MO-34 west through the town of Piedmont to the lake. Clearwater Lake is noted for the grandeur of its hills and natural springs.

RV camping is available at Corps-managed parks and at state parks nearby. Wildlife viewing is excellent from numerous walking and hiking trails. Historic sites, restaurants and sightseeing may be found in nearby towns.

Bluff View: May-Sep, 20 sites with electric & water hookups, 41 basic sites, $12–$20, drinking water, dump, restrooms, showers. Located 8 miles west of Piedmont, Missouri. From Hwy-34 turn right on Hwy-49 and go 1 mile, then left on Hwy-AA for 7 miles. 573-223-7777.

Highway K: Apr-Oct, 21 sites with electric & water hookups and 61 basic sites, $12–$20, drinking water, dump, restrooms, showers. Located 5 miles southwest of Annapolis, Missouri, follow Hwy-49 south to the center of Annapolis. Turn right on Hwy-K for 5 miles, park entrance on left. If you cross the big bridge, you've gone too far. 573-223-7777.

Piedmont Park: Apr-Sep, 78 sites with electric (some 50amp) hookups and 20 basic sites, $12–$20, drinking water, dump, restrooms, showers. From Piedmont, Missouri, follow Hwy-34 for 7 miles, southwest to Hwy-HH, then 5 miles on HH to the dam, follow signs. 573-223-7777.

River Road: May-Sep, 97 sites with electric, drinking water, dump, showers. $12–$20, From Piedmont, Missouri, follow Hwy-34 southwest for 6 miles to Hwy-HH. Turn right and go 5.5 miles. The park is located below the dam. 573-223-7777.

4) HARRY S. TRUMAN DAM & RESERVOIR

U.S. Army Corps of Engineers
15968 Truman Road
Warsaw, MO 65355
Phone: 660-438-7317
District: Kansas City

The project encompasses 55,600 water acres, 212,913 land acres and 958 shoreline miles. From Kansas City go 19 miles south on US-71, then 75 miles east on MO-7 to Warsaw, then 1 mile north. The Harry S. Truman Visitor Center sits atop Kaysinger Bluff and provides a spectacular view of the dam and reservoir. Exhibits feature information about the rich history of the Osage River Valley from pre-civilization to modern day. There is good wildlife viewing from the observation deck.

Nine Corps camping areas are located at the project, with boat ramps and public marinas throughout. Area attractions include Benton County Museum in Warsaw, Henry County Museum in Clinton and the Lost Valley Hatchery & Aquarium just outside of Warsaw.

Berry Bend: Apr-Oct, 113 sites with electric hookups and 78 basic sites, $12–$18, drinking water, dump, restrooms, showers, laundry, swimming. Located on the Osage arm of the reservoir, 9 miles southwest of Warsaw. From Warsaw travel 4.4 miles west on MO-7, then 3 miles west on Hwy-Z, then 1.8 miles on paved access road. 660-438-3872.

Berry Bend Equestrian: All year, 24 sites with electric hookups and 65 basic sites, $12–$18, equestrian use only, drinking water, restrooms, showers, laundry. Located in Benton County about 10 miles west of Warsaw. From Hwy-Z, travel 2 miles south on Berry Bend access road. 660-438-7317.

Bucksaw Park: Apr-Oct, 12 sites with electric (some 50amp) & water hookups. 1 full hookup, 114 electric only and 181 basic sites, $12–$24, a few pull thrus, drinking water, dump, restrooms, showers, laundry, playground, swimming. From Clinton, Missouri, go 8 miles east on MO-7, then 3 miles south on Hwy-U, turn left at SE 803 road, stay on the paved road, follow signs. 660-477-3402, (673 SE 803 Rd, Clinton, MO 64735).

Long Shoal Park: Apr-Oct, 2 full hookup sites, 97 electric-only and 27 basic, $12–$18, drinking water, dump, restrooms, showers, laundry. From Warsaw, Missouri, go 4.4 miles west on MO-7, follow signs. 660-438-2342, (12733 Long Shoal Park Rd, Warsaw, MO 65355).

Osage Bluff: Apr-Oct, 41 electric only sites and 27 basic, $14-$18, drinking water, dump, restrooms, showers, laundry. Located 8 miles south of Warsaw. From Hwy-83 travel about 1 mile on Hwy-295, follow signs. 660-438-3873.

Sparrowfoot: Apr-Oct, 80 electric-only sites and 36 basic, $12-$18, drinking water, dump, restrooms, showers, laundry. Located in Henry County about 4 miles southeast of Clinton. From Hwy-13 travel about 1 mile east on SE 450 Rd, follow signs. 660-885-7546, (150 SE450, Clinton, MO 64735).

Talley Bend: Apr-Sep, 108 electric-only sites and 6 basic, $12-$18, drinking water, dump, restrooms, showers, laundry. Located in Saint Clair County about 13 miles northeast of Osceola. From Hwy-13 travel east on Hwy-C for 6 miles, follow signs. 417-644-2446.

Thibaut Point: Apr-Sep, 1 full hookup site, 25 electric-only sites and 25 basic, $12-$18, drinking water, dump, restrooms, showers, laundry, swimming. Located in Benton County 8 miles north of Warsaw. From Hwy-65 travel west on Hwy-T for 3 miles, turn south on Road 218 (gravel), follow 1 mile. 660-438-2767.

Windsor Crossing: Apr-Sep, 47 basic sites, $8, drinking water, restrooms, swimming. Located in Henry County 20 miles west of Warsaw and 18 miles east of Clinton. From MO-7 travel north on Hwy-PP for 4 miles, follow signs. 660-477-9275.

5) POMME DE TERRE LAKE

U.S. Army Corps of Engineers
Route 2, Box 2160
Hermitage, MO 65668
Phone: 417-745-6411
District: Kansas City

Located 60 miles north of Springfield, the lake is in the rugged, tree-covered hills of the west-central Missouri Ozarks. The project includes 7,790 water acres, 113 shoreline miles and 12,699 land acres. From Springfield, Missouri, go 53 miles north on US-65, then 5 miles west on US-54 and 4 miles south on MO-254. The project office is on the north side of the lake.

RV camping can be found at numerous Corps-managed areas and at two state parks on the lake. Playgrounds are located at all campgrounds. Swimming beaches are at Nemo Landing and Wheatland as well as both state parks. Fishing is a popular activity. The cool, clear spring waters make this lake an attractive destination for water recreation.

Damsite Park: All year, 39 sites with electric (some 50amp) & water hookups, 24 electric only sites, 65 basic, some pull thrus, $12–$22, drinking water, dump, restrooms, showers, laundry. From Springfield, Missouri, take US-65 north for 60 miles to Preston, Missouri, then US-54 west to Hermitage, then Hwy-254/64 south to Carsons Corner, then Hwy-254 west toward the dam. 417-745-2244.

Lightfoot Landing: Apr-Oct, 29 sites with electric & water hookups, 6 basic and 5 tent sites, $14–$20, drinking water, dump, restrooms, showers, laundry. From Springfield, Missouri, take Hwy-13 north to Bolivar, then Hwy-83 north to RB Hwy east to the campground. 417-282-6890.

Nemo Landing: All year, 11 sites with electric & water hookups, 48 electric-only sites and 61 basic, $12-$20, drinking water, dump, restrooms, showers, laundry. From Springfield, Missouri, take US-65 north past Louisburg to Hwy-NN west to Nemo. Turn west at the 4-way stop, follow signs. 417-993-5529.

Outlet Park: Apr-Oct, 14 sites with electric (some 50amp) & water hookups, 14 basic, $12-$20, drinking water, restrooms. Harbor Marina nearby. From Springfield, Missouri, take US-65 north to Preston, take Hwy-54 west to Hermitage, then south on Hwy-254/64 about 4 miles to Carson Corner. Turn west toward Pomme de Terre dam. Cross the dam and turn north on the paved road at the far end of the dam and follow the road to the park below the dam. 417-745-2290.

Wheatland Park: Apr-Oct, 41 sites with electric (some 50amp) & water hookups, 26 electric-only, 10 basic and 9 tent-only sites, $12–$20, drinking water, dump, restrooms, showers. From Springfield, Missouri, take Hwy-13 north to Bolivar, then travel north on Hwy-83 past Elkton to Hwy-254. Follow Hwy-254 to The Triangle and take CR-205 south, follow signs. 417-282-5267.

6) STOCKTON LAKE

U.S. Army Corps of Engineers
16435 East Stockton Lake Drive
Stockton, MO 65785
Phone: 417-276-3113
District: Kansas City

Located 50 miles north of Springfield in the scenic Missouri Ozarks, the project covers 36,415 land acres and has 24,632 water acres and 298 shoreline miles. From Springfield travel 29 miles north on MO-13 and 22 miles west on MO-32.

Camping is available at several Corps-managed areas and at Stockton State Park. Boating services and supplies and a restaurant can be found at three marinas on the lake. Camping cabins are available at the state park. Swimming beaches are located at Masters, Orleans Trail, Ruark Bluff and Stockton campgrounds. Equestrian trails are at Hawker Point and Orleans Trail. Stockton is popular for sailing, boating and scuba diving.

Cedar Ridge: Apr-Sep, 21 sites with electric hookups, 21 basic and 12 tent-only sites, $12–$18, drinking water, dump, restrooms, showers. From Bona, Missouri, take Hwy-245 north for 1/2 mile to Hwy-RA, turn left (north) on Hwy-RA for .7 mile. 417-995-2045, (Hwy RA, Dadeville, MO 65635).

Crabtree Cove: Apr-Sep, 31 sites with electric hookups, 27 basic and 4 tent-only sites, $12–$18, drinking water, dump, restrooms, showers. On the northeast corner of the lake. From Stockton take Hwy-32 for 3.5 miles, then south on the access road. 417-276-6799.

Hawker Point: Apr-Sep, 30 sites with electric hookups, 32 basic, $12–$18, drinking water, dump, restrooms, showers. On the northern end of Big Sac Arm of the lake. From Stockton, take Hwy-39 south for 6.2 miles, turn left on Hwy-H and continue for 5.2 miles. 417-276-7266.

Masters: May-Sep, 65 sites, no hookups, $10–$14, drinking water, dump, restrooms, showers, primitive group camp area. Located on the Little Sac Arm of the lake. From Fair Play, Missouri, take Hwy-32 west for 5 miles, then south on Hwy-RA, follow for 4 miles, then west onto the park access road. 417-276-6847 or 417-276-3113 (20291 S Hwy RA, Fair Play, MO 65649).

Orleans Trail: May-Sep, 118 sites, no hookups, $12, drinking water, dump, restrooms, showers, group camp area with electric. On the northeast part of the lake, just outside the town of Stockton. From Stockton, Missouri, take Hwy-39 south for 1/2 mile, then RB Road east 1/2 mile, then right on Blake Street. 417-276-6948, (Blake St, Stockton, MO 65785).

Ruark Bluff: Apr-Sep, 28 sites with electric hookups, 57 basic sites, 6 tent only sites, $10–$16, drinking water, dump, restrooms, showers. On the Big Sac Arm of the Sac River. From Greenfield, Missouri, take Hwy-H north for 6.4 miles, then east on the park access road, follow signs. 417-637-5303, (E Hwy H, Stockton, MO 65661).

7) TABLE ROCK LAKE

U.S. Army Corps of Engineers
4600 State Highway 165
Branson, MO 65616
Phone: 417-334-4101
District: Little Rock

The project, just 4 miles southwest of Branson, includes 24,846 land acres, 43,100 water acres and 745 shoreline miles. From Springfield,

Missouri, go 40 miles south on US-65 to Branson, then take US-165 west for 7 miles to Table Rock Dam. The Dewey Short Visitor Center features exhibits and audio-visual presentations. Located in the Ozark Mountains, the area provides extensive wildlife viewing. Twelve Corps campgrounds have RV accommodations. Table Rock State Park, as well as marinas and resorts on the lake also have camping. Nearby attractions include cave tours, shopping, restaurants and a theme park. Five commercial boat cruises operate seasonally at the lake.

Aunt's Creek: May-Oct, 52 sites with electric (some 50amp) hookups, $18, some pull thrus, drinking water, dump, restrooms, showers. From Branson West, junction of Hwy-76, travel 3.9 miles south on Hwy-13, then 2.7 miles west on Hwy-OO. 417-739-2792 (2837 State Hwy OO, Reed Springs, MO 65737).

Baxter: Apr-Sep, 25 sites with electric hookups,16 basic and 3 tent sites, $14-$18, drinking water, dump, restrooms, showers. From Lampe, Missouri, at junction of Hwy-13, travel 4.8 miles west on Hwy-H. 417-779-5370 (6431 State Hwy H, Lampe, MO 65616).

Big M: Apr-Sep, 14 full hookup sites, 4 electric-only and 35 basic sites, $14–$20, drinking water, dump, restrooms, showers. From Cassville, travel east on SR-76 for 9 miles, then Hwy-M to the access road, follow signs. 417-271-3190

Campbell Point: Apr-Sep, 38 sites with electric (some 50amp) hookups and 38 basic sites, $14–$19, a few pull thrus, drinking water, dump, restrooms, showers. Located east of Cassville, travel east on SR-76 to SR-39 southeast to Hwy-YY to the access road. 417-858-3903, (4600 State Hwy 165, Branson, MO 65616).

Cape Fair: Apr-Oct, 36 sites with electric (some 50amp) & water hookups, 33 electric-only and 13 basic sites, $14–$19, drinking water, dump, restrooms, showers. From Reeds Spring/junction SR-248, go south on Hwy-13 for 1.4 miles, then 8 miles west on Hwy-76 to Cape Fair, then southwest on Lake Road 76-82, follow signs, 417-538-2220, (1092 Shadrack Rd, Cape Fair, MO 65624).

Eagle Rock: Apr-Oct, 1 full hookup site, 25 sites with electric (some 50amp) hookups and 31 basic sites, $14–$18, some pull thrus, drinking water, dump, restrooms, showers. From Cassville, Missouri, take US-86 southeast for 4 miles to Eagle Rock Community, follow signs. 417-271-3215 .

Indian Point: Apr-Oct, 54 sites with electric (some 50amp) and water hookups and 23 electric-only sites, $18–$19, drinking water, dump, restrooms, showers. Close to Silver Dollar City Theme Park. From Branson, Missouri, take Hwy-76 west for 3 miles to Indian Point Road, then south for 2 miles. 417-338-2121, (3125 Indian Point Rd, Branson, MO 65616).

Long Creek: Apr-Oct, 13 sites with electric (some 50amp) & water hookups and 24 electric-only (some 50amp) sites and 10 basic, $14–$19, drinking water, dump, restrooms, showers. From Branson, Missouri, take US-65 south for 5 miles to Hwy-86 west for 3 miles to Long Creek Road, follow signs. 417-334-8427, (1036 Long Creek Rd, Ridgedale, MO 65739).

Old Highway 86: Apr-Oct, 23 sites with electric (some 50amp) & water hookups, 40 electric-only sites and 8 basic sites, $12–$19, drinking water, dump, restrooms, showers. From Branson, south on US-65 to Hwy-86 (near the Arkansas state line). Take Hwy-86 for 6 miles west, then north on Hwy-UU and follow to the campground. 417-779-5376, (1791 State Hwy UU, Blue Eye, MO 65611).

Viney Creek: May-Sep, 24 sites with electric (some 50amp) & water hookups and 22 basic, $14–$19, drinking water, dump, restrooms, showers. From Cassville, Missouri, travel southeast on Hwy-39 for 7 miles to Hwy-39/48, then west to the campground. 417-271-3860

Viola: Apr-Sep, 22 sites with electric (some 50amp) & water hookups and 15 electric only sites, $14–$19, drinking water, dump, restrooms, showers. From Shell Knob, Missouri, travel south on Hwy-39 for 7 miles to Hwy-39/48, then west to the campground. 417-858-3904, (RR5 Box 5210, Shell Knob, MO 65747).

8) WAPPAPELLO LAKE

U.S. Army Corps of Engineers
10992 Highway T
Wappapello, MO 63966
Phone: 573-222-8562
Visitor Center: 573-222-8773
District: St. Louis

This project, located in southeast Missouri, encompasses 36,120 land acres, 8,400 water acres and 180 shoreline miles. From St. Louis, travel south for 32 miles on I-55 to exit 174, take US-67 south for 88 miles to Greenville, turn left at Hwy-D and travel south 20 miles. The Bill Emerson Memorial Visitor Center has exhibits and various programs that focus on the natural beauty found in southeastern Missouri. The lake is near Mark Twain National Forest and the Mingo National Wildlife Refuge. RV camping is available at Corps-managed areas and at Lake Wappapello State Park. Camping cabins are also available in the state park.

Greenville: All year, 106 sites with electric hookups, 5 basic sites, $16–$20, drinking water, dump, restrooms, showers, river access. From US-67 in Greenville, continue 1 mile south, follow signs. 573-224-3884.

Peoples Creek: All year, 19 full hookup sites with electric (50amp), 38 electric-only sites $16–$20, drinking water, dump, restrooms, showers. The campground consists of two separate sections: 37 lakefront sites in the lower section and 20 sites in the upper. Reservations must be made at least 4 days in advance. From St. Louis, take I-55 south to US-67, then south on US-67 to Hwy-D near Greenville, south about 15 miles, follow signs. From Poplar Bluff, east on US-60, north on SR-51, west on Hwy-T to campground. 573-222-8234.

Redman Creek: All year, 108 full hookup sites (50amp) and 6 boat-in sites, $16–$20, drinking water, dump, restrooms, showers. From Poplar Bluff, take US-60 east to Hwy-T, travel north on Hwy-T, follow signs, 573-222-8233, (10270 Hwy T, Wappapello, MO 63966).

Montana

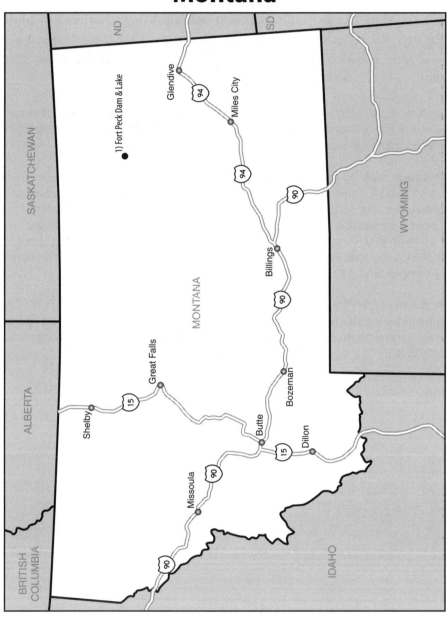

1)   Fort Peck Dam & Lake

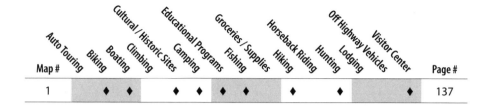

Map #	Auto Touring	Biking	Boating	Climbing	Cultural/Historic Sites	Camping	Educational Programs	Fishing	Groceries/Supplies	Hiking	Horseback Riding	Hunting	Lodging	Off Highway Vehicles	Visitor Center	Page #
1		♦	♦			♦	♦	♦	♦		♦		♦		♦	137

1) FORT PECK DAM & LAKE

U.S. Army Corps of Engineers
P.O. Box 208
Fort Peck, MT 59223
Phone: 406-526-3411
District: Omaha

The Fort Peck project, located in northeast Montana south of US-2, has 240,000 water acres, 1,520 shoreline miles and 168,591 land acres. From I-94 exit 211, follow SR-200(S) west for 76.5 miles then SR-24N for 56 miles. The Interpretive Center & Museum on site includes wildlife dioramas, aquariums, dinosaur fossils and the dam's construction history. The museum is open daily, Memorial Day to Labor Day. Powerhouse tours are also given.

Fort Peck Dam is the largest embankment dam in the United States, with the 5th largest man-made reservoir. The vast size of the project, plus its remote location, make it an ideal destination for a high-quality outdoor experience.

Down Stream: Apr-Oct, 73 sites with electric (some 50amp) hookups and 3 tent sites, $16–$18, some pull thrus, drinking water, dump, restrooms, showers. From Glasgow, Montana, go south on SR-24 for 18 miles to the dam. 406-526-3224.

Nelson Creek: All year, 16 basic sites, non-reservable, free, boat ramp, 40-foot RV length limit. From Fort Peck go 44 miles southeast on SR-24, then 7 miles west on the gravel road. 406-526-3411.

West End: May-Sep, 13 sites with electric hookups, non-reservable, $10–$16, drinking water, restrooms, showers, 35-foot RV length limit. On the west side of the dam. 406-526-3411.

Nebraska

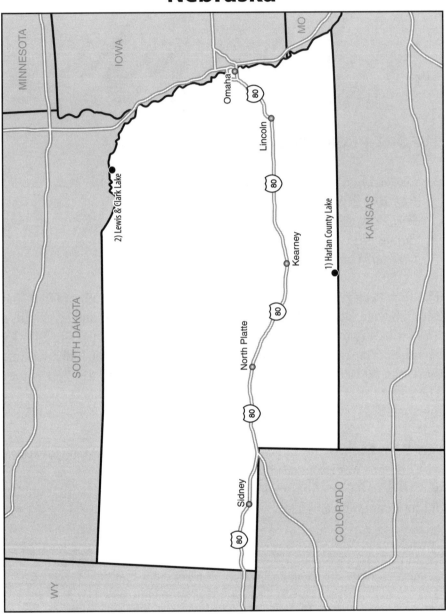

1)   Harlen County Lake
2)   Lewis & Clark Lake

Map #	Auto Touring	Biking	Boating	Climbing	Cultural/Historic Sites	Camping	Educational Programs	Fishing	Groceries/Supplies	Hiking	Horseback Riding	Hunting	Lodging	Off Highway Vehicles	Visitor Center	Page #
1	♦		♦			♦		♦		♦					♦	139
2	♦	♦	♦			♦	♦	♦	♦			♦			♦ ♦	140

1) HARLAN COUNTY LAKE

U.S. Army Corps of Engineers
70788 Corps Road A
Republican City, NE 68971
Phone: 308-799-2105
District: Kansas City

Harlan County Lake, the state's second largest lake, is located just north of the Kansas state line. It has 18,217 land acres, 13,240 water acres and 75 shoreline miles. From I-80 exit 257, travel 41 miles south on US-183 to the lake.

Four Corps camping areas are conveniently located around the lake. Shopping and restaurants can be found in two nearby towns.

Gremlin Cove: All year, 70 basic sites, non-reservable, $8-$10, drinking water, restrooms, showers. From US-136 in Republican City, go 1.2 miles south on Hwy-A (Berrigan Road) to the dam, north side. 308-799-2105.

Hunter Cove: Apr-Nov, 7 sites with electric (some 50amp) & water hookups, 77 electric-only and 76 basic sites, some pull thrus, $10-$18, drinking water, dump, restrooms, showers, laundry. Located on the east end of the lake. From Republican City (on US-136), turn south on Berrigan Road and travel 1.25 miles to Road B, then west 1 mile to the park. 308-799-2105.

Methodist Cove: Apr-Nov, 49 sites with electric hookups, 106 basic sites, some pull thrus, $10-$16, drinking water, dump, restrooms, showers. From Alma, NE on US-183, turn east on South Street and travel 2.5 miles to the park entrance. 308-799-2105.

North & South Outlet: All year, 60 sites, no hookups, non-reservable, $6, drinking water and restrooms. From Republican City on US-136 travel on Hwy-A – Go 2 miles south to the North Outlet –or– Go 1 mile north to the South Outlet. Campsites are on the north and south sides of the Republican River below the dam. 308-799-2105.

2) LEWIS & CLARK LAKE

U.S. Army Corps of Engineers
NE Highway 121
Yankton, SD 57078
Phone: 402-667-7873
District: Omaha

Lewis and Clark Lake is formed behind the Gavins Point Dam. The lake is 25 miles long and has 90 miles of shoreline. The entire project, with 17,126 land acres around the lock and dam, straddles the NE/SD border just west of Yankton, SD. The Visitor Center is located atop Calumet Bluff just downstream from the Gavins Point Powerplant. The Center provides a spectacular view of the lake, the dam and the Missouri River. Exhibits highlight the geology, exploration, early navigation, settlement and early history of the Missouri River. From Crofton, Nebraska, travel 13 miles north on Hwy-121 – or – From Yankton, South Dakota: From US-81 (near milepost 214 about 2 miles south of Yankton) go west on NE-121 for 4 miles. At fork in the road, Tailwater camping area is to the right & Visitor Center/Project Office is to the left. Powerplant tours are given on weekends and holidays.

Cottonwood: Apr-Oct, 75 sites with electric hookups, $14–$16, drinking water, dump, restrooms, showers. The campground is at the west side of Lake Yankton, a small lake below Gavins Point Dam. From Yankton, South Dakota, travel 4 miles west on SD-52, then south on Dam Toe Road, follow signs. 402-667-7873.

Nebraska Tailwaters: May-Oct, 32 sites with electric hookups and 11 basic sites, $12–$14, drinking water, dump, restrooms, showers. The campground is on the bank of the Missouri River and provides good shore fishing. From Yankton, South Dakota, travel south on US-81 for 2 miles, then west on Hwy-121 for 4 miles. 402-667-7873.

New Mexico

1) Abiquiu Dam & Reservoir
2) Cochiti Lake

Map #	Auto Touring	Biking	Boating	Climbing	Cultural/Historic Sites	Camping	Educational Programs	Fishing	Groceries/Supplies	Horseback Riding	Hiking	Hunting	Off Highway Vehicles	Lodging	Visitor Center	Page #
1	♦	♦	♦			♦	♦		♦		♦				♦	142
2	♦		♦			♦	♦		♦		♦				♦	143

1) ABIQUIU DAM & RESERVOIR

U.S. Army Corps of Engineers
4631 State Highway 96
Albiquiu, NM 87510
Phone: 505-685-4371
District: Albuquerque

From Santa Fe, travel 61 miles north on US-84 to SR-96 west. The project is located on SR-96 at the intersection of US-84. Abiquiu has 2,104 land acres, 7,489 water acres and 51 shoreline miles. The lake is located on the Rio Chama, a tributary of the Rio Grande. The reservoir offers some of the finest fishing in northern New Mexico.

The dam area provides a panoramic view of the Cerro Pedernal (Flint Mountain). It is surrounded by red sandstone formations. Reptile fossils 200 million years old have been found in the area. Nearby attractions include Ghost Ranch, Georgia O'Keefe Museum, San Pedro Wilderness and sightseeing in Santa Fe.

Riana: Apr-Oct, 13 sites with electric (some 50amp) & water hookups, 24 basic and 15 tent sites, $10–$14, drinking water, dump, restrooms, showers, playground. From Espanol, New Mexico, travel 30 miles north on US-84. Turn west on SR-96 and continue 1 mile. The campground is located on a 150-foot rock bluff overlooking the lake. 505-685-4561.

2) COCHITI LAKE

U.S. Army Corps of Engineers
82 Dam Crest Road
Pena Blanca, NM 87041
Phone: 505-465-0307
District: Albuquerque

From I-25 exit 259, travel northwest on NM-22 through Pena Blanca to the project office and Visitor Center. The project consists of 12,490 land acres, 1,200 water acres and 28 shoreline miles. Cochiti Dam is one of the largest earthfill dams in the U.S.

Cochiti Lake is located within the boundaries of the Pueblo de Cochiti Indian Reservation on the Rio Grande about halfway between Albuquerque and Santa Fe. Visitors are asked to observe and obey all Pueblo regulations. Good wildlife viewing can be found throughout the project including four osprey nesting platforms around the lake. Wind surfing is a popular activity. Cochiti is a no-wake lake. Sightseeing, shopping and restaurants are nearby. Campground gates close at 10 pm. ATVs and ORVs are prohibited.

Cochiti: All year, 18 sites with electric (some 50amp) & water hookups, 16 electric-only sites and 21 basic, $8–$14, some pull thrus, drinking water, dump, restrooms, showers, playground, swimming, interpretive trail. On the west side of the lake. From I-25 exit 259, go west on NM-22 through Pena Blanca to the project office, follow signs. 505-465-0307.

Tetilla Peak: Apr-Oct, 45 sites with electric (some 50amp) & water hookups and 7 tent sites, some pull-thrus, $8-$12 drinking water, dump, restrooms, showers, hiking trail. On the east side of the lake. From I-25 exit 264, travel west on SR-16 to the Tetilla area, follow signs. 505-465-0307.

North Carolina

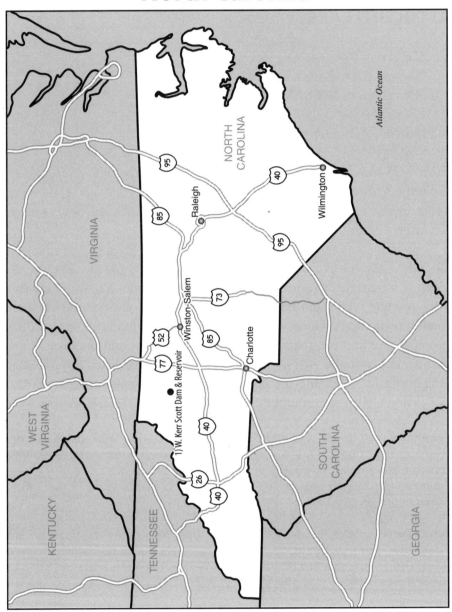

1)   W. Kerr Scott Dam and Reservoir

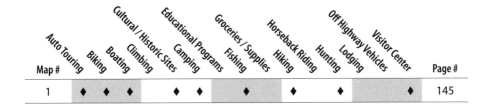

Map #	Auto Touring	Biking	Boating	Climbing	Cultural/Historic Sites	Educational Programs	Camping	Fishing	Groceries/Supplies	Hiking	Horseback Riding	Hunting	Off Highway Vehicles	Lodging	Visitor Center	Page #
1	♦	♦	♦			♦	♦		♦		♦		♦		♦	145

1) W. KERR SCOTT DAM AND RESERVOIR

U.S. Army Corps of Engineers
499 Reservoir Road
Wilkesboro, NC 28697
Phone: 336-921-3750/3390
District: Wilmington

The W. Kerr Scott Reservoir is located in the Yadkin River Valley northwest of Charlotte, and west of Winston-Salem. The project includes 4,305 land acres, 1,470 water acres and 66 shoreline miles. From Winston-Salem go northwest on US-421 to Wilkesboro, then 5 miles west on NC-268. Information is available from the Visitor Center. Turn right off NC-268 onto Reservoir Road at the W. Kerr Scott Dam sign and travel .25 mile, then turn left beside the Shady Grove Baptist Church to the Visitor Center. Three Corps-managed campgrounds have playgrounds, swimming and hiking trails.

Bandits Roost: Apr-Oct, 80 sites with electric (50amp) & water hookups, 20 tent sites, $16–$20, some pull thrus, drinking water, dump, restrooms, showers. Located on the south side of the lake. From Winston-Salem, take US-421 west to Wilkesboro, then SR-268 west 6 miles to Goshen Volunteer Fire Dept. on SR-1141. Turn right on Jess Walsh Road, 1/2 mile, follow signs. 336-921-3190.

Fort Hamby Park: Apr-Oct, 26 sites with electric (50amp) & water, 8 tent sites, $20, a few pull thrus, drinking water, dump, restrooms, showers. Located on the north side of the lake. From Winston-Salem, take US-421 west to Wilkesboro, about 5 miles past Wilkesboro, turn left on South Recreation Road, travel 1.5 miles. 336-973-0104, (1534 Recreation Rd, Wilkesboro, NC 28697).

Warrior Creek: Apr-Oct, 51 sites with electric hookups, 10 tent sites, $16–$20, drinking water, dump, restrooms, showers. Located on the south side of the lake. From Winston-Salem, take US-421 west to Wilkesboro, then SR-268 west 8 miles. After crossing the SR-268 bridge, turn right at the first road, follow signs. 336-921-2177.

North Dakota

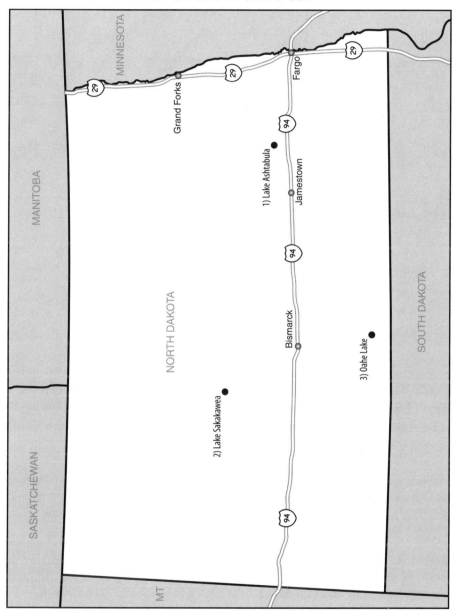

1)   Lake Ashtabula
2)   Lake Sakakawea
3)   Oahe Lake & Dam

Map #	Auto Touring	Biking	Boating	Climbing	Cultural/Historic Sites	Educational Programs	Camping	Groceries/Supplies	Fishing	Hiking	Horseback Riding	Hunting	Lodging	Off Highway Vehicles	Visitor Center	Page #
1		♦	♦				♦		♦		♦					148
2		♦	♦				♦		♦		♦		♦		♦	149
3		♦	♦				♦		♦		♦		♦		♦	150

1) LAKE ASHTABULA

U.S. Army Corps of Engineers
2630-114th Avenue SE
Valley City, ND 58072
Phone: 701-845-2970
District: St. Paul

Lake Ashtabula, in eastern North Dakota, has 3,053 land acres, 6,430 water acres and 78 shoreline miles. It is located northwest of Fargo. From I-94 exit 292, follow signs to CR-19 and travel northeast for about 12 miles. Year-round recreational opportunities are offered and wildlife viewing is excellent throughout the project.

Ashtabula Crossing East: May-Sep, 33 sites with electric hookups and 5 tent sites, $16, drinking water, dump, restrooms, showers, playground, swimming. From I-94 exit 292, go north through Valley City and 14 miles north on CR-21, follow signs. 790-845-2970.

Ashtabula Crossing West: May-Sep, 41 sites with electric hookups, non-reservable, $12–$14, drinking water, dump, restrooms, showers. From I-94 exit 292, go north through Valley City and 14 miles north on CR-21, follow signs. 790-845-2970.

Eggerts Landing: May-Sep, 36 sites with electric hookups and 4 tent sites, $16, drinking water, dump, restrooms, showers, playground, swimming, fish cleaning station. From I-94 exit 292, go north through Valley City and continue 14 miles north on CR-21, follow signs. 790-845-2970.

Mel Reiman: May-Sep, 10 sites with electric hookups and 9 tent sites, $12–$16, drinking water, dump, restrooms, showers, playground, swimming, fish cleaning station. From I-94 exit 292, go north through Valley City and north on CR-19 along the valley for 12 miles, follow signs. 790-845-2970.

2) LAKE SAKAKAWEA

U.S. Army Corps of Engineers
P.O. Box 527
Riverdale, ND 58565
Phone: 701-654-7411
District: Omaha

The project, located on the Missouri River 75 miles upstream from Bismarck, spans 121,574 land miles, 368,000 water acres and 1,884 shoreline miles. From Bismarck, travel 70 miles north via US-83 and ND-200. The dam and power plant are in Riverdale, 10 miles west on ND-200. Exhibits in the plant lobby display the construction and operation of Garrison Dam. Plant tours are given daily during summer months. The lake is an important resting spot for migrating whooping cranes.

There are 35 recreation areas around the large lake, including two Corps-managed campgrounds. Downstream is adjacent to a wooded wildlife management area and a National Fish Hatchery.

Downstream: May-Sep, 101 sites with electric (some 50amp) hookups and 17 tent sites, $10–$14, drinking water, dump, restrooms, showers. From Riverdale, take Hwy-200 west to the dam. After crossing the Spillway Bridge, take the Tow Road down the face of the dam. At the intersection at the bottom, turn left and go .25 mile east and turn right onto the campground access road. The campground is 1 mile south of the paved road. 701-654-7440.

East Totten Trail: May-Sep, 30 sites with electric hookups and 10 basic sites, non-reservable, $14, drinking water, dump, restrooms, boat ramp. From Garrison, go 6 miles east on SR-37 and then 2.5 miles south on US-83. Campground is on east side of highway. 701-654-7411.

3) OAHE LAKE

U.S. Army Corps of Engineers
28563 Powerhouse Road
Pierre, SD 57501
Phone: 605-224-5862
District: Omaha

The vast Oahe Lake's 2,250 shoreline miles are located between Pierre, South Dakota and Bismarck, North Dakota. It has some 53 recreation areas...most are managed by private concessionaires.

The project's Visitor Center is located in South Dakota and is situated on the east crest, providing an excellent view of the lake. The Center provides information about the history of the area, early navigation, settlement and natural history of the lake and Missouri River. Programs highlight the Lewis and Clark expedition and the fish of the area. The Center is open Memorial Day to Labor Day. Powerplant tours are given. To get to the Visitor Center from Pierre, South Dakota, follow SD-1804 north for 8 miles.

The Corps-managed Beaver Creek campground is located in North Dakota.

Beaver Creek: May-Sep, 45 sites with electric hookups, 21 non-reservable basic sites, $8–$12, drinking water, dump, restrooms, showers, playground, swimming, hiking trails. From Linton, North Dakota, go west on Hwy-13 for 13 miles. After the highway changes to Hwy-1804, continue west for 1 mile, then follow the road south for 2 more miles. The campground is on the right. 701-255-0015.

Ohio

1)   Berlin Lake

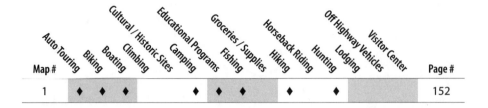

Map #													Page #
1	♦	♦	♦		♦	♦	♦		♦		♦		152

1) BERLIN LAKE

U.S. Army Corps of Engineers
7400 Bedell Road
Berlin Center, OH 44401
Phone: 330-547-3781
District: Pittsburgh

Located in northeastern Ohio, the project includes 4,400 land acres, 3,580 water acres and 70 shoreline miles. Berlin Lake is on the Mahoning River about 35 miles upstream from Warren, Ohio; it is known for its walleye fishing. From Deerfield, Ohio, travel 2 miles east on OH-224.

The campground features ranger programs in season, Memorial Day through Labor Day. The campground has a boat ramp, fishing pier, playground, swimming area and a self-guided interpretive trail. The lake is a short distance from Akron and Youngstown, where restaurants and shopping can be found.

Mill Creek: May-Sep, 92 sites with electric (some 50amp) hookups, 256 basic sites, $14–$24, drinking water, dump, restrooms, showers. From I-76 exit 54, go south on SR-534 about 5.5 miles to US-224 in Berlin Center. Go west on US-224 for 2 miles to Bedell Road, then south about .75 mile. 330-547-8180.

Oklahoma

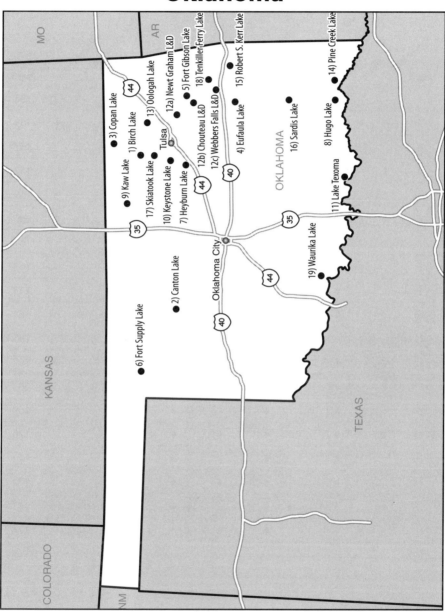

1)	Birch Lake	9)	Kaw Lake	13)	Oologah Lake
2)	Canton Lake	10)	Keystone Lake	14)	Pine Creek Lake
3)	Copan Lake	11)	Lake Texoma	15)	Robert S. Kerr Lake
4)	Eufaula Lake	12)	Locks & Dams on the	16)	Sardis Lake
5)	Fort Gibson Lake		Arkansas River	17)	Skiatook Lake
6)	Fort Supply Lake		a. Newt Graham	18)	Tenkiller Ferry Lake
7)	Heyburn Lake		b. Chouteau	19)	Waurika Lake
8)	Hugo Lake		c. Webbers Falls		

Map #	Auto Touring	Biking	Boating	Climbing	Cultural / Historic Sites	Camping	Educational Programs	Fishing	Groceries / Supplies	Hiking	Horseback Riding	Hunting	Lodging	Off Highway Vehicles	Visitor Center	Page #
1			♦			♦		♦		♦	♦	♦				155
2		♦	♦			♦		♦		♦		♦			♦	155
3			♦			♦		♦		♦	♦	♦				157
4	♦		♦			♦		♦		♦		♦		♦		157
5	♦		♦			♦		♦	♦	♦		♦			♦	159
6	♦		♦			♦	♦	♦		♦		♦			♦	160
7			♦			♦		♦		♦		♦				161
8		♦	♦			♦		♦		♦	♦	♦				162
9			♦			♦		♦		♦	♦	♦		♦		163
10			♦			♦		♦		♦		♦	♦	♦		164
11		♦	♦			♦		♦		♦	♦	♦				166
12	♦		♦			♦		♦		♦		♦			♦	167
13	♦		♦		♦	♦		♦		♦	♦	♦				168
14			♦			♦		♦		♦		♦				169
15	♦		♦			♦		♦		♦		♦				170
16			♦			♦		♦		♦		♦				171
17			♦			♦		♦		♦		♦				172
18	♦		♦		♦	♦		♦		♦		♦	♦			173
19		♦	♦			♦		♦		♦	♦	♦				174

1) BIRCH LAKE

U.S. Army Corps of Engineers
HCR 67 Box 135
Skiatook, OK 74070
Phone: 918-396-3107
District: Tulsa

Located just north of Skiatook Lake, Birch Lake has 2,584 land acres, 1,137 water acres and 27 shoreline miles. The lake is on Birch Creek in Osage County and its dam site is about 1.5 miles south of the town of Barnsdall. From Tulsa, go north on US-75, then west on SR-20 to the first light (Hwy-11), then go north to Barnsdall and turn left across from Big Heart grocery to the "T" then left to Birch Lake.

Boating, fishing and hunting (in season) are popular activities. Anglers will find walleye, crappie, catfish and several species of bass in the lake. There is a horse trail at Birch Cove.

Birch Cove, A & B Sections: Apr-Oct, 98 sites with electric hookups, $18, drinking water, dump, restrooms, showers, playground, swimming, interpretive trail. From Barnsdall, Oklahoma, travel 3.1 miles to Hwy-11 across the spillway, then .7 mile west, follow signs. 918-847-2220 or 918-396-3170.

Twin Cove: Apr-Sep, 11 sites, no hookups, non-reservable, $8. From Barnsdall, go 1.5 miles south to the camping area near the spillway. 918-396-3170.

2) CANTON LAKE

U.S. Army Corps of Engineers
HCR 65 Box 120
Canton, OK 73724
Phone: 580-886-2989
District: Tulsa

Located in western Oklahoma on the North Canadian River, the project is 2 miles north of the town of Canton. The lake has 7,910 water acres and 40 shoreline miles surrounded by 12,684 land acres. The project is accessible from I-40 exit 108. Go north on US-270 to Watonga, continue on US-270/281, then north on SR-58 to Canton. From Canton, Oklahoma, go .5 mile west on OK-51, then north on OK-58A, follow signs. The project office is southwest of the dam. The Visitor Center has an overlook with excellent views of the lake. There are displays of animals native to the area, arrowheads and historic artifacts at the Center.

Canton is noted for its fishing, especially walleye. The annual "Walleye Rodeo" event is held in May. The lake has a sandy beach. Calm waters paralleling the dam are popular for water skiing. There is an active prairie dog town at the project. Corps camping areas are located on both sides of the lake. Boat ramps and playgrounds are located at all campgrounds. Restaurants are nearby.

Big Bend: Apr-Oct, 85 sites with electric hookups, 19 basic sites, $13–$20, drinking water, dump, restrooms, showers, playground. On the west side of the lake, north of the dam. From Canton, Oklahoma, go 1.8 miles west on SR-51, then travel 4 miles north on the paved road, follow signs. 580-886-3576.

Canadian: Apr-Sep, 98 sites with electric (some 50amp) hookups and 81 electric only, $17–$20, drinking water, dump, restrooms, showers, playground, amphitheater. Near the west side of the dam. From Canton, Oklahoma, go .5 mile west on SR-51, then north on SR-58A. Travel for 2 miles, taking the left fork and go west where the highway joins a paved county road. Keep traveling west for .25 mile, then north to the campground. 580-886-3454.

Longdale: Apr-Oct, 35 sites, no hookups, 3 tent sites, $9, drinking water, restrooms. On the east side of the lake. From Canton, Oklahoma, go west on SR-51 for .2 mile, then north on Hwy-58 for 6 miles to the south city limits of Longdale. Turn left on a paved county road for 2 miles to the campground. 580-274-3454.

Sandy Cove: Apr-Oct, 35 sites with electric hookups, $16, drinking water, restrooms, showers, playground, swimming beach. On the east side of the dam. Located on the North Canadian River, 2.5 miles from the town of Canton. From Canton, Oklahoma, go west on SR-51 for .5 mile, then north on Hwy-58A for 2 miles. Take the right fork at the "Y" and continue on Hwy-58A to the north end of the dam. 580-274-3576.

3) COPAN LAKE

U.S. Army Corps of Engineers
Route 1 Box 260
Copan, OK 74022
Phone: 918-532-4334
District: Tulsa

The Copan project, located north of Tulsa near the Kansas state line, includes 12,997 land acres, 4,850 water acres and 30 shoreline miles. From US-75 (7 miles north of Dewey), go west on OK-10 for about 2 miles to the project office, on the north side of the road before crossing the lake. Maps and information are available. Wah Sha She State Park is nearby.

Swimming, boating and fishing are popular activities. The swimming beach is at Copan Point Recreation area. Horse trails are at Washington Cove and Copan Point.

Post Oak: Apr-Oct, 17 sites with electric hookups, $16–$18, drinking water, dump, restrooms, showers, hiking trail. From US-75 travel 3 miles west on SR-10. 918-532-4334.

Washington Cove: Apr-Oct, 100 sites with electric & water hookups, $14–$16, drinking water, dump, restrooms, showers. From US-75 travel west 1 mile on SR-10 then 2 miles north. 918-532-4129.

4) EUFAULA LAKE

U.S. Army Corps of Engineers
102 E. BK 200 Road
Stigler, OK 74462
Phone: 918-484-5135
District: Tulsa

Eufaula Lake is located in east-central Oklahoma and is the largest lake located entirely in the state of Oklahoma. The large 102,000-acre lake has over 600 miles of shoreline. The project is 31 miles south of Muskogee and spans across the junction of I-40 and US-69. From I-40 exit 278 (Warner), go south on US-2 for 10 miles to Porum. Turn right at the sign to Eufaula Dam and go about 5 miles, turn left and cross over the dam. The project office is about .5 mile on the east side of the road.

The lake is situated on the Canadian River, 27 miles upstream from its confluence with the Arkansas River. Camping is available at Corps-managed areas and at Robber's Cave State Park. Golf, restaurants, shopping and sightseeing are nearby.

Belle Starr: Apr-Sep, 115 sites with electric (some 50amp) and water hookups, some pull thrus, $16–$18. From I-40 exit 264, go south on US-69 to Texanna Road. Exit onto SR-150 and go east for 2 miles, then south for 2 miles, follow signs. 918-799-5843.

Broken Cove: Apr-Oct, 68 sites with electric (some 50amp) hookups, 13 basic sites, some pull thrus, $16–$18, drinking water, dump, restrooms, showers, playground, swimming. Located on Eufaula Lake near the dam. From Enterprise, Oklahoma, travel 5 miles north on SR-71, follow signs. 918-799-5843.

Dam Site East: All year, 10 sites with electric, non-reservable, $11, drinking water, restrooms. Located on the northeast side below the dam. 918-484-5135.

Dam Site South: Apr-Sep, 42 sites with electric hookups and 15 basic sites, $11–$16, drinking water, dump, restrooms, showers. Located near the dam. From Enterprise, Oklahoma, travel 6 miles north on SR-71, follow signs. 918-799-5843.

Elm Point: All year, 14 sites with electric, 3 basic sites, non-reservable, $7–$11, drinking water, dump, restrooms. From McAlester junction US-69, take SR-31 northeast for 12 miles, then northwest, follow signs. 918-484-5135.

Gentry Creek: Apr-Sep, 15 sites with electric hookups, 16 basic sites, $10–$14, drinking water, restrooms, showers. On the northwestern arm of the lake. From Checotah, Oklahoma, travel 9 miles west on US-266, follow signs. 918-799-5843.

Highway Landing East: Apr-Sep, 5 sites with electric, 4 basic sites, non-reservable, $7–$11, drinking water, restrooms. From Eufaula junction US-69, take SR-9 for 9 miles southeast, then go north, follow signs. 918-484-5135.

Highway 9 Landing: Apr-Sep, 75 sites with electric hookups, 6 basic sites, some pull thrus, $10–$16, drinking water, dump, restrooms, showers. From Eufaula, Oklahoma, travel 9 miles east on SR-9, follow signs. 918-799-5843.

Mill Creek Bay: Apr-Oct, 12 sites, no hookups, non-reservable, $7, drinking water, restrooms. From Eufaula, go 6 miles west on SR-9, then 2 miles south. 918-484-5135.

Oak Ridge: Mar-Oct, 8 sites with electric, 5 basic sites, non-reservable, $7-$11, drinking water, restrooms. From Eufaula, Oklahoma, junction US-69, go south for 6 miles, then northeast on SR-9A. 918-484-5135.

Porum Landing: Apr-Sep, 50 sites with electric hookups, some pull thrus, $16, drinking water, dump, restrooms, showers. From Porum, Oklahoma, travel 7 miles west on Texanna Road, follow signs. 918-799-5843.

5) FORT GIBSON LAKE

U.S. Army Corps of Engineers
8568 SR-251A
Fort Gibson, OK 74434
Phone: 918-682-4314
District: Tulsa

Fort Gibson Lake is located on the Grand Neosho River about 5 miles northwest of historic Fort Gibson and north of Muskogee. From I-40 exit 286, take Muskogee Turnpike north to Tahlequah/Fort Gibson exit. Travel east on Hwy-62 to the town of Fort Gibson, then take Hwy-80 north about 7 miles to the dam. The project office is on the hill on the west side of the dam. Information and maps are available. Dam tours are given.

The lake draws its name from historic Fort Gibson which played a prominent part in the military history of early day Oklahoma. A reconstructed log stockade stands on the site of the first log fort, and volunteers reenact the lifestyle of the late 1800's for various events during the year.

The lake is 7 miles above the confluence of the Neosho and Arkansas Rivers and is noted for its fishing where sportsmen will find bass, crappie and several varieties of catfish and panfish. Boat ramps are located at all campgrounds. A swimming area is at Rocky Point. A marina is located at Flat Rock Creek. Bird watchers enjoy the variety of migratory birds that pass through the area.

Blue Bill Point: Apr-Sep, 40 sites with electric (some 50amp) hookups, 3 basic sites, $16–$17, drinking water, dump, restrooms, showers. The campground sits along the banks of Flat Rock Bay. From Wagoner, Oklahoma, travel north on US-69 for 5 miles, follow signs. 918-476-6638.

Dam Site: Apr-Sep, 47 sites with electric hookups, $15, drinking water, dump, restrooms, showers. From Okay, Oklahoma, travel 6 miles east on SR-251A. 918-683-6618.

Flat Rock Creek: Apr-Sep, 25 sites with electric hookups, $14–$15, drinking water, dump, restrooms, showers. The campground sits along the banks of Flat Rock Bay. From Wagoner, Oklahoma, travel north on US-69 for 5 miles, then 3 miles east and 1 mile south follow signs. 918-476-6766.

Rocky Point: Apr-Sep, 48 sites with electric (some 50amp) hookups, $11–$17, drinking water, dump, restrooms, showers. Located on the main body of the lake surrounded by woods. From junction US-69 and SR-51 in Wagoner, Oklahoma, go 8 miles east on SR-51, then south before the bridge, follow signs. 918-462-3492.

Taylor Ferry: Apr-Sep, 92 sites with electric (some 50amp) & water hookups, 6 basic sites, $11–$17, drinking water, dump, restrooms, showers. From Wagoner, Oklahoma, travel 5 miles east on SR-51, follow signs. 918-485-4792 (34179 Marina Dr, Wagoner, OK 74467).

Wildwood: Apr-Sep, 30 sites with electric (some 50amp) & water hookups, $16, drinking water, dump, restrooms, showers, the serene campground is located along Fourteen Mile Creek and provides excellent lake access. From Fort Gibson Dam travel 5 miles north on SR-80. 918-682-4314.

6) FORT SUPPLY LAKE

U.S. Army Corps of Engineers
RR 1 Box 175
Fort Supply, OK 73841

Phone: 580-766-2701
District: Tulsa

The Fort Supply project is located in northwestern Oklahoma in Woodward County near the panhandle. It consists of 6,369 land acres, 1,786 water acres and 26 shoreline miles. From Woodward, Oklahoma, travel 13 miles northwest on US-270, then SR-3, follow signs. The Visitor Center at the project office has displays of animals native to the area, arrowheads and historic artifacts. Fishing is popular for crappie, walleye, white bass, hybrid bass and catfish. There is plenty of open shore line for bank fishing as well as piers. Boat ramps are available throughout.

A swim beach and sand dunes are on the east side of the lake. Places of interest in the area include the Fort Supply site and museum, Pioneer Museum & Art Center in Woodward and Boiling Springs State Park, just north of Woodward.

Beaver Point: Apr-Oct, 16 sites, no hookups, non-reservable, $8, restrooms. Located near the dam. 580-766-2701.

Supply Park: Mar-Nov, 96 sites with electric (some 50amp) and water hookups, 14 basic sites, some pull thrus, $13-$19, drinking water, dump, restrooms, showers, playground, swimming. From Woodward, Oklahoma, travel 9 miles northwest on US-270 to the Fort Supply lake sign. Turn west and follow for 3 miles, crossing the Fort Supply Dam, continue .75 mile to the 4-way stop. Then left and follow access road. 580-766-2001.

7) HEYBURN LAKE

U.S. Army Corps of Engineers
27349 West Heyburn Lake Road
Kellyville, OK 74039
Phone: 918-247-6391
District: Tulsa

Located south of Tulsa in the Sandstone Hills of the Osage Section central lowlands, the Heyburn project encompasses 6,344 land acres,

920 water acres and 50 shoreline miles. From I-44, exit 196 (Bristow), travel east on SR-66 for 9 miles to 257th West Ave, then north on paved road 2 miles to Heyburn Lake Road.

Three Corps-managed campgrounds all have swimming areas and boat ramps. Services and supplies are available on access roads into the lake area.

Heyburn Park: Apr-Sep, 46 sites with electric (some 50amp) hookups, some pull thrus, $14–$16, drinking water, dump, restrooms, showers, playground. Across the dam on the west side. From Bristow, Oklahoma, go 9 miles east, then left onto 257th West Ave. Follow the paved road about 3 miles. 918-247-6601.

Sheppard Point: Apr-Oct, 21 sites with electric and water hookups and 17 tent sites, $10–$16, drinking water, dump, restrooms, showers, playground. On the north side of the lake. From Sapulpa, Oklahoma, take SR-33 west for about 12 miles, then south to E0730 Road, follow signs. 918-247-4551.

Sunset Bay: All year, 14 sites, no hookups, non-reservable, $7, drinking water, dump, restrooms. On the northeast side of the dam. 918-247-6391.

8) HUGO LAKE

U.S. Army Corps of Engineers
P.O. Box 99
Sawyer, OK 74756
Phone: 580-326-3345
District: Tulsa

Located in southeastern Oklahoma near the Texas state line, the project has 28,608 land acres, 13,250 water acres and 110 shoreline miles. Hugo Lake is on the Kiamichi River about 7 miles east of Hugo and 30 miles north of Paris, TX. From the south end of Indian Nation Turnpike, the highway turns into US-70 east on the bypass. The project office is on the east side of US-70 in Hugo.

All campgrounds have boat ramps. Sportsmen find a wide variety of fish, including bass, crappie, catfish, bluegill, sunfish, carp and drum.

Speedboats and water skiers enjoy some 8,000 acres of open water.

Kiamichi Park: Apr-Sep, 87 sites with electric hookup, $9–$15, drinking water, dump, restrooms, showers, horse trail, hiking, playground, swimming. From Hugo, Oklahoma, take US-70 east for 5 miles, follow signs. 580-326-3345.

Rattan Landing: All year, 13 sites with electric, some pull thrus, non-reservable, $10, drinking water, restrooms. From Rattan, travel 4 miles west on SR-3/SR-7, then south, follow signs. 580-326-3345.

Virgil Point: Apr-Sep, 51 sites with electric hookups, $15, drinking water, dump, restrooms, showers. From Hugo, go 10 miles east on US-70, turn left at Neil's. 580-326-3345.

9) KAW LAKE

U.S. Army Corps of Engineers
9400 Lake Road
Ponca City, OK 74604
Phone: 580-762-5611
District: Tulsa

Located in northcentral Oklahoma about 25 miles east of I-35, the Kaw Lake project encompasses 33,075 land acres, 17,040 water acres and 168 shoreline miles. It is on the Arkansas River just east of Ponca City. From Ponca City, travel 9.5 miles east on US-60, turn at the sign and go north on the county road, after crossing the spillway, the project office is on the left. Maps and information are available.

Kaw Lake and the Arkansas River are noted for producing some of the state's largest catfish. In winter, the area has one of the largest populations of Bald Eagles. Numerous Corps-managed camping areas are located around the lake with numerous boat ramps and fishing piers throughout. Hikers and horseback riders are attracted to the beautiful trails along Kaw Lake's eastern shore. The Eagle View Hiking Trail, about 12 miles long, runs between Osage Cove and Burbank Landing. The Five Fingers Equestrian Trail extends from Burbank Landing to the Sarge Creek Cove area. Off-road vehicle trails are at Sarge Creek.

Designated swimming areas are at Pioneer Park and Sandy Park.

Bear Creek Cove: May-Sep, 22 sites with electric & water hookups, $13, drinking water, dump, restrooms, showers. From Newkirk, Oklahoma, on US-77, go east on the county road for 8.3 miles, then 3 miles south, follow signs. 580-762-5611.

Coon Creek: Apr-Sep, 54 sites with electric hookups, $8–$16, drinking water, dump, restrooms, showers. From junction of US-77 & SR-11, go east on SR-11 for 6 miles, then 1 mile north on a county road and 2 miles east on county road, follow signs. 580-762-5611.

McFadden Cove: Mar-Nov, 15 sites with electric hookups, non-reservable, $12, drinking water, restrooms, marina. From Ponca City, travel 7 miles east, on the north side. 580-762-5611.

Osage Cove: Mar-Nov, 97 sites with electric hookups, $16, drinking water, dump, restrooms, showers, playground. From Ponca City, travel 9 miles east across Kaw Dam, turn east on county road and travel 2 miles, follow signs. 580-762-5611.

Sandy: Apr-Oct, 12 sites with electric hookups, non-reservable, $12, drinking water, restrooms. From Ponca City, 9 miles east, .5 mile below the dam, east side. 580-762-5611.

Sarge Creek: Mar-Nov, 51 sites with electric hookups, $16, drinking water, dump, restrooms, showers, group camping area. From Kaw City, travel 2.8 miles on SR-11, follow signs. 580-762-5611.

Washunga Bay: Mar-Nov, 24 sites with electric & water hookups, $16, drinking water, dump, restrooms, showers. From Kaw City, go about 2.5 miles east on SR-11, then north on the county road for about 1 mile, then west on county road for 4.5 miles, follow signs. 580-762-5611.

10) KEYSTONE LAKE

U.S. Army Corps of Engineers
23115 West Wekiwa Road
Sand Springs, OK 74063
Phone: 918-865-2621
District: Tulsa

Noted for its blue-green water, Keystone Lake has 23,610 water acres and 330 shoreline miles. It is surrounded by 59,580 acres of public land. The project is on the Arkansas River. From Tulsa, travel 19 miles west on US-64/412 (Keystone Expressway). Look for signs to Keystone and go east on Hwy-151 toward the lake. Before crossing over the dam, turn left on West Wekiwa Road to the project office. Information and maps are available.

There are several Corps-managed camping areas at Keystone. The project features 11 boat ramps throughout, three marinas, miles of sandy beaches, two ORV areas and five short distance trails. The wildlife refuge provides extensive wildlife viewing opportunities. Keystone Lake is noted for several varieties of bass, crappie and catfish. Nearby Keystone State Park and Walnut Creek State Park have camping and cabins. Boat rentals are available at the marina. Off road vehicle trails are at the Appalachia Bay camping area.

Appalachia Bay: Apr-Oct, 18 sites, no hookups, non-reservable, drinking water, rest rooms, swimming, $8. From Sand Springs, go 10.1 miles west on US-64. Campground is on the west side of US-64. 918-243-7822.

Brush Creek: All year, 20 sites with electric hookups, non-reservable, $14, drinking water, restrooms. From Sand Springs, Oklahoma, travel 8 miles west on US-64. Campground is below the dam on the north side of the spillway. 918-865-2621.

Salt Creek North: Apr-Oct, 112 sites with electric hookups and 12 basic sites, $10–$17, drinking water, dump, restrooms, showers, playground, swimming. From Tulsa, take SR-51 west for 18 miles to Hwy-412. Go west for 12 miles to Hwy-151. Exit and go south for 2 miles to Hwy-51. Travel Hwy-51 west for 4 miles to the campground. 918-865-2845.

Washington Irving: Apr-Oct, 40 sites with electric & water hookups, $10–$17, drinking water, dump, restrooms, showers, playground, swimming, hiking trail. Located on the Arkansas arm of Keystone Lake. Heavy tree cover and low hanging limbs in some areas. From Tulsa, take US-412 west for 15 miles to Bears Glen exit. Turn left at the stop sign onto Frontage Road and drive 1 block. Turn right at the first paved road and follow 2 miles. Gates close at 10pm. 918-865-2621.

11) LAKE TEXOMA

U.S. Army Corps of Engineers
351 Corps Road
Denison, TX 75020
Phone: 903-465-4990
District: Tulsa

This project is in south-central Oklahoma on the Texas state line. It has 102,968 land acres, 88,000 water acres and 680 shoreline miles. From Denison, Texas, go 5 miles northwest on TX-91. Before the dam, turn right onto Corps Road to the project office.

Cross Timbers is a popular hiking trail that wends for 14 miles above the lake on rocky ledges and through the woodland. Also available are 40 miles of equestrian trails. Texoma is known as the "Striper Capitol of the World," one of the few reservoirs in the nation where striped bass reproduce naturally.

Swimming beaches are at Burns Run East and West and Caney Creek. Boat ramps and fishing piers are conveniently located throughout. Marinas can be found at Johnson Creek, Lakeside and Platter Flats campgrounds. Overnight accommodations, boat rentals, slip rentals and supplies are available at many of the 23 concessions located adjacent to the lake. There are two state parks and two wildlife refuges at Texoma.

Buncomb Creek: Apr-Oct, 54 sites with electric & water hookups, $16, drinking water, dump, restrooms, showers. Gates close at 10pm. From Madill, Oklahoma, travel south on SR-99 for 17 miles to Willis, then east for 1 mile on paved access road. 580-564-2901.

Burns Run East: Apr-Oct, 25 sites with electric & water hookups, 9 sites with water only, $12–$20, drinking water, dump, restrooms, showers, playground. Gates close at 10pm. From US-75 in Denison, Texas, take exit 72 to SR-91, travel north on 91 across Denison Dam 5 miles, take the first exit left. 903-465-4990.

Burns Run West: Apr-Oct, 104 sites with electric (some 50amp) & water hookups, some pull thrus, $12–$22, drinking water, dump, restrooms, showers, playground. Overlooks the main portion of the lake. Gates close at 10pm. From Denison, Texas, take US-75 exit 72 to SR-91, travel north on 91 across Denison Dam 5 miles, take the second left, follow signs for about 1.5 miles. 903-465-4990.

Caney Creek: Apr-Oct, 42 sites with electric & water hookups and 10 basic sites, $12–$18, drinking water, dump, restrooms, showers, playground. From SR-32 in Kingston, Oklahoma, take Donahoo Road south, 6 miles on access road, follow signs. 580-564-2632.

Johnson Creek: Apr-Oct, 55 sites with electric (some 50amp) & water hookups, $20, drinking water, dump, restrooms, showers. Gates close at 10pm. From Durant, Oklahoma, travel 11 miles west on SR-70. Exit off SR-70 to the north, the park entrance is 300 yards ahead. 903-465-4990.

Lakeside: Apr-Oct, 127 sites with electric & water hookups, $12–$20, drinking water, dump, restrooms, showers, horse trail, hiking trail. Gates close at 10pm. Most sites are near the water. From Durant, Oklahoma, travel 10 miles west on SR-70 to Streetman Road. Turn south on Streetman and go 4 miles to the park. 580-920-0176.

Platter Flats: All year, 16 electric-only sites, 28 equestrian sites with electric & 29 equestrian basic sites, $12–$16, drinking water, dump, restrooms, showers, horse trail, hiking trail. Gates close at 10pm. From Colbert, Oklahoma, travel 5 miles north on US-75, turn west 5 miles, follow signs.

12) LOCKS & DAMS - ARKANSAS RIVER

The Locks & Dams are part of the Arkansas River Navigation System. All are administered by the Tulsa District, Army Corps of Engineers. The waterway and pools (lakes) formed by the dams provide good areas for recreation, particularly fishing, swimming, camping and picnics in the park. Some Locks & Dams located along about 150 miles of shoreline southeast of Tulsa near the Muskogee Turnpike have camping areas. A Visitor Center at Webbers Falls in Gore, Oklahoma, features a platform where visitors can watch the lockage of barges and view a large area of the lake.

12a) Newt Graham Lock & Dam
Fort Gibson, Oklahoma, 918-682-4314

Bluff Landing: All year, 21 sites with electric & water, non-reservable, $15, drinking water, dump, restrooms, showers, boat ramp, From Broken Arrow, Oklahoma, go 12 miles east on 71st Street, follow signs. 918-775-4475.

12b) Chouteau Lock & Dam
Muskogee, Oklahoma, 918-682-4314

Afton Landing: All year, 20 sites with electric & water hookups, 2 basic sites, $10–$15, drinking water, dump, restrooms, showers, boat ramp. From Wagoner, Oklahoma, at junction of US-69 & SR-51, go 5 miles west on SR-51. 918-489-5541.

12c) Webbers Falls Lock & Dam
Gore, Oklahoma, 918-487-5252

Brewers Bend: All year, 34 sites with electric & water hookups, 8 basic sites, some pull thrus, non-reservable, $15–$18, dump, restrooms, showers, boat ramp. From Webbers Falls, travel 2 miles west on US-64, then about 5 miles north on Road N4410, follow signs. 918-489-5541.

Spaniard Creek: All year, 35 sites with electric & water hookups, non-reservable, $14–$18, dump, restrooms, showers. From Muskogee, travel 10 miles south on US 64 and then east 5 miles on Elm Grove Rd, follow signs. 918-489-5541.

13) OOLOGAH LAKE

U.S. Army Corps of Engineers
P.O. Box 700
Oologah, OK 74053
Phone: 918-443-2250
District: Tulsa

From Tulsa, go 30 miles north on US-169, then east on OK-88. Before going over the dam, turn at the project office sign. A popular sailing destination, Oologah Lake has 29,460 water acres and 209 shoreline miles. There are 36,735 acres of public land. Several Corps-managed camping areas are located around the lake. Restaurants, shopping and sightseeing are available in the area. A nearby attraction is Dog Iron Ranch, the birthplace of Will Rogers.

Big Creek Ramp: All year, 16 sites, no hookups, non-reservable, free, drinking water, restrooms. From Nowata, 5.1 miles east on US-60, then 2 miles north. 918-443-2250.

Blue Creek: Apr-Sep, 24 sites with electric hookups, 37 basic sites, $12–$16, drinking water, dump, restrooms, showers, playground. Campground is 12 miles north and east of the city of Oologah via county roads, follow signs. 918-341-4244, (13400 E 390 Rd, Claremore, OK 74017).

Hawthorn Bluff: Apr-Sep, 68 sites with electric hookups, 25 basic sites, $14–$18, drinking water, dump, restrooms, showers, playground, swimming. From Oologah, Oklahoma, travel 2 miles east on SR-88, follow signs. 918-443-2319, (12557 S Hwy 88, Oologah, OK 74053).

Redbud Bay: Apr-Oct, 12 sites with electric, non-reservable, $14, drinking water, restrooms. From Oologah go 3.2 miles east on SR-88 to the east side of the dam. 918-443-2250.

Spencer Creek: Apr-Sep, 30 sites with electric hookups, 55 basic sites, $12–$16, drinking water, dump, restrooms, showers, playground, swimming. Located 15 miles from Oologah via county roads, follow signs. 918-341-3690, (6998 S 4180 Rd, Claremore, OK 74017).

Verdigris River: Apr-Oct, 8 sites, no hookups, non-reservable, $10, drinking water, restrooms. From US-169 in Oologah, take SR-88 for 3.1 miles east to the camping area below the dam. 918-443-2250.

14) PINE CREEK LAKE

U.S. Army Corps of Engineers
Route 1, Box 400
Valliant, OK 74764
Phone: 580-933-4239
District: Tulsa

Located on Little River in McCurtain County, the project encompasses 21,559 land acres, 4,880 water acres and 74 shoreline miles. From Idabel, Oklahoma, go 18 miles west on US-70 to Valliant, then 1.5 miles north on county road (Dalton Street), follow brown signs to the project office.

The four Corps-managed campgrounds all have boat ramps. Fishing piers can be found at Little River, Lost Rapids and Pine Creek. Swimming is at Little River and Pine Creek.

Little River Park: Mar-Nov, 62 sites with electric (50amp) and water hookups, 17 basic sites, $10–$18, drinking water, dump, restrooms, showers, playground, hiking trail. Park gates close at 10pm. From Broken Bow, Oklahoma, take SR-3 for 23 miles, follow signs. 580-876-3720.

Lost Rapids: All Year, 16 sites with electric & water hookups and 14 basic sites, $8–$12, restrooms, dump, group camping area. From Broken Bow, travel west on SR-3 for 22 miles, follow signs. 580-876-3720.

Pine Creek Cove: Mar-Nov, 40 sites with electric (50amp) & water hookups, $10–$15, drinking water, dump, restrooms, showers, playground, group camping area. From Valliant, Oklahoma, travel north on Pine Creek Road for 7 miles to the access road, follow signs. 580-933-4215.

Turkey Creek: All Year, 10 sites with electric & water hookups and 24 basic sites, $8–$12, drinking water, dump, restrooms, showers, playground, group camping area. From Broken Bow, travel west on SR-3 for 28 miles, follow signs. 580-876-3720.

15) ROBERT S. KERR LAKE

U.S. Army Corps of Engineers
R.S. Kerr Navigation Office
Sallisaw, OK 74955
Phone: 918-775-4475
District: Tulsa

From I-40 exit 307, travel 8 miles south on US-59. The navigation office is near the powerhouse. Drive past the convenience store and look for the brown sign for the office, turn right. The project consists of 21,913 land acres, 42,000 water acres and 260 shoreline miles.

Boat ramps are located at the campgrounds and there is a marina at Applegate Cove. Swimming areas are located at all campgrounds and there is a playground at Cowlington Point.

Applegate Cove: May-Sep, 27 sites with electric & water hookups, $15, drinking water, dump, restrooms, showers. From Sallisaw, Oklahoma, travel 8 miles south on US-59, then 3 miles west on the paved county road, follow signs. 918-775-4475.

Cowlington Point: May-Sep, 32 sites with electric & water hookups, $15, drinking water, dump, restrooms, showers. From Sallisaw, Oklahoma, travel 12 miles south on US-59, then 4 miles west on the paved county road, follow signs. 918-775-4475.

Short Mountain Cove: May-Sep, 32 sites with electric & water hookups, $10–$15, drinking water, dump, restrooms, showers. From Sallisaw, Oklahoma, travel 12 miles south on US-59, then 2 miles west on the paved county road, follow signs. 918-775-4475.

16) SARDIS LAKE

U.S. Army Corps of Engineers
HC 60 Box 175
Clayton, OK 74536
Phone: 918-569-4131
District: Tulsa

Located in southeastern Oklahoma, 5 miles north of Clayton, the lake covers 14,360 water acres and has 117 miles of shoreline. From McAlester, go 36 miles southeast on OK-1, then 15 miles south on OK-2. The project office is on OK-2, about a mile past the parks. Maps are available. The project is situated at the western tip of the Ouachita Mountain Range. Fishing is a popular activity providing excellent opportunities to catch crappie, catfish and walleye.

Potato Hills Central: Apr-Sep, 94 sites with electric & water, $15, drinking water, dump, restrooms, showers, playground, hiking. Campground gates close at 10pm. From McAlester, Oklahoma, go south on US-69 for 4 miles, then south on Indian Nations Turnpike for 26 miles to Daisy, OK. Go east on SR-43 for 33 miles to Sardis Lake office. Then go north on SR-2 for 2 miles. 918-569-4131.

Potato Hills South: Apr-Oct, 20 sites, no hookups, no dump, $8, restrooms, swimming, playground. From Clayton, Oklahoma, take SR-2 for 2.5 miles north, follow signs. 918-569-4131.

Sardis Cove: Apr-Oct, 22 sites with electric hookups and 23 basic sites, non-reservable, $8-$12, drinking water, dump, restrooms, no showers, boat ramp. From SR-2, go 8.3 miles west on SR-43, follow signs. 918-569-4637.

17) SKIATOOK LAKE

U.S. Army Corps of Engineers
HCR 67 Box 135
Skiatook, OK 74070
Phone: 918-396-3107
District: Tulsa

Located in Osage County, about 25 miles northwest of Tulsa, Skiatook has 10,190 water acres, 100 miles of shoreline and 10,130 land acres. The lake is on Hominy Creek about 5 miles west of the town of Skiatook. From Tulsa, take SR-11 northwest for about 20 miles into Skiatook, then west on OK-20, travel through the town of Skiatook and continue another 4 miles to Lake Road. Travel south on Lake Road for 2 miles to the project office, where maps and information are available.

Sport fishing is a primary activity at the lake. A sand beach and swimming area is located at Tall Chief Cove. Boat rentals and supplies are available at the marina. Golf is nearby.

Bull Creek Peninsula: All year, 41 sites, no hookups, non-reservable, $8, restrooms. From the dam, 7.8 miles west on SR-20, then 3.7 miles northeast, access is after the second bridge crossing on the lake. 918-396-2444.

Tall Chief Cove: Apr-Oct, 50 sites with electric & water hookups, 10 tent sites, from $20, drinking water, dump, restrooms, showers. From Tulsa, Oklahoma, take US-75 north to SR-20 (Skiatook exit). Turn west on SR-20 about 15 miles, then left on Lake Road, follow signs about 5 miles. 918-288-6820.

Twin Points: Apr-Oct, 54 sites with electric (50amp) and water hookups, $20, drinking water, dump, restrooms, showers, playground, swimming. From Tulsa, Oklahoma, take US-75 north to Skiatook exit, then SR-20 west for about 20 miles. Turn right at the entrance sign on SR-20 and follow for 2 miles. 918-396-1376.

18) TENKILLER FERRY LAKE

U.S. Army Corps of Engineers
Route 1, Box 259
Gore, OK 74435
Phone: 918-487-5252
District: Tulsa

Nestled in the Cookson Hills of eastern Oklahoma, the Tenkiller project has 17,734 land acres, 12,800 water acres and 130 shoreline miles. From Muskogee, Oklahoma, travel 21 miles southeast on OK-10, then 7 miles east on OK-10A to Hwy-100. Turn left on Hwy-100 and go 1 mile to the project office on the right.

The lake is known as Oklahoma's Clear Water Wonderland. Camping may be found at the many Corps-managed facilities around the lake as well as Tenkiller State Park and Cherokee Landing State Park. Attractions at the lake include marinas, golf, three floating restaurants and many islands to explore.

Fishing, boating and scuba diving are popular. Boat ramps can be found at all campgrounds. Three nature trails vary in length from 1.25 to over 2 miles. Spectacular vistas, rock formations and many species of wildlife can be observed.

Carters Landing: All year, 10 sites with electric & water hookups, 15 basic sites, non-reservable, $8–$11. From Tahlequah, Oklahoma, go 4 miles southeast on US-62, then 6.6 miles south on SR-82, then 2 miles northeast on the access road. 918-487-5252.

Chicken Creek: Jan-Sep, 104 sites with electric (some 50amp) hookups (some with water), $14–$18, drinking water, dump, restrooms, showers, playground. From Gore, Oklahoma, go 17.5 miles northeast on Hwy-100, then turn left and go 1.75 miles northwest on the paved access road, follow signs. 918-487-5252.

Cookson Bend: Jan-Sep, 64 sites with electric (some 50amp) hookups, and 62 basic sites, $10–$18, drinking water, dump, restrooms, showers, playground, swimming beach, marina concession at the entrance to the park. From Tahlequah, Oklahoma, go 17.5 miles southeast on Hwy-82, then right for 2 miles on the paved access road, follow signs. 918-487-5252.

Elk Creek Landing: Jan-Sep, 6 sites with electric hookups, 23 basic sites, $10–$15, drinking water, dump, restrooms, showers. Swimming, public marina. From Tahlequah, Oklahoma, go 14.5 miles southeast on Hwy-82, then right on the paved access road, follow signs. 918-487-5252.

Pettit Bay: Jan-Sep, 7 full hookup sites, 17 sites with electric & water, 63 electric-only and 13 basic sites, $10–$18, drinking water, dump, restrooms, showers, playground, swimming, public marina. From Tahlequah, Oklahoma, go 8.5 miles south on Hwy-82, then right on Indian Road 2 miles south, then left for 1 mile on paved access road, follow signs. 918-487-5252.

Snake Creek: Jan-Sep, 104 electric (some 50amp) only sites and 3 basic sites, $10–$18, drinking water, dump, restrooms, showers, playground, swimming, public marina, group camping area. From Gore, Oklahoma, go 15 miles northeast on Hwy-100, then turn left and go .5 mile west on the paved access road, follow signs. 918-487-5252.

Strayhorn Landing: Jan-Sep, 47 sites with electric hookups, $15–$18, drinking water, dump, restrooms, showers, playground, marina, swimming, hiking trail. From Gore, Oklahoma, go 6 miles northeast on Hwy-100, then north on Hwy-10A for 1.5 miles, then east on the paved access road, follow signs. 918-487-5252.

19) WAURIKA LAKE

U.S. Army Corps of Engineers
Route 1, Box 68
Waurika, OK 73573
Phone: 580-963-2111
District: Tulsa

Located on Beaver Creek, a tributary of the Red River, the project has 12,505 land acres, 10,100 water acres and 80 shoreline miles. The town of Waurika is near the junction of US-70 & US-81. Go left on US-70 for 1.5 miles to Main Street in Waurika. Turn right onto Main Street (at the Waurika Quick Mart), stay on Main Street (turns into Hwy-5) for 6 miles. At the brown Waurika Lake sign, turn right to the project office. Maps are available. Fishing, boating and water skiing are popular activities.

Chisholm Trail Ridge: May-Sep, 95 sites with electric & water hookups, $14–$16, drinking water, dump, restrooms, showers, playground, swimming. From the city of Waurika, go 5 miles northwest on SR-5, then 3 miles north on Advent Road and 1 mile west on county road. 580-439-8040.

Kiowa Park: Apr-Oct, 180 sites with electric & water hookups, some pull thrus, $14–$16, drinking water, dump, restrooms, showers, playground, swimming beach, group camping area. From Waurika, travel 8 miles northwest on SR-5, then 3 miles north on the county road to the park entrance. 580-963-9031.

Moneka North: Mar-Oct, 38 sites, no hookups, non-reservable, $8, drinking water, restrooms. From Hastings, go 3.7 miles east on SR-5, then north for .8 mile. 580-963-2111.

Wichita Ridge: All year, 10 sites with electric hookups, 16 basic sites, non-reservable, $8–$12, restrooms. From Hastings, go 1.2 miles east on SR-5, then 3 miles north, 1 mile west and 2.1 miles north. 580-963-2111.

Oregon

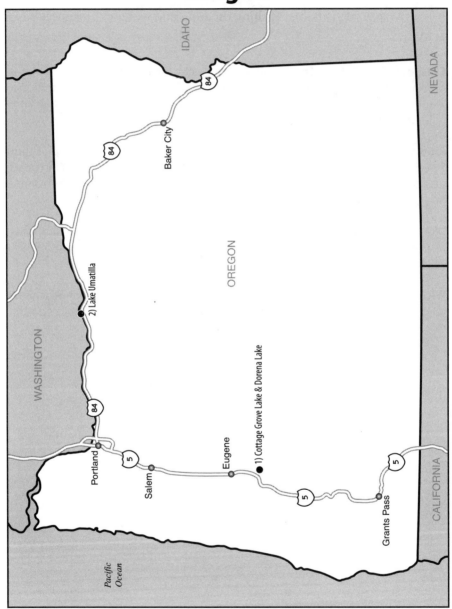

1) Cottage Grove Lake & Dorena Lake
2) Lake Umatilla

Map #	Auto Touring	Biking	Boating	Climbing	Cultural / Historic Sites	Camping	Educational Programs	Fishing	Groceries / Supplies	Hiking	Horseback Riding	Hunting	Off Highway Vehicles	Lodging	Visitor Center	Page #
1		♦	♦			♦		♦		♦						177
2		♦				♦		♦		♦					♦	178

1) COTTAGE GROVE LAKE & DORENA LAKE

U.S. Army Corps of Engineers
75819 Shortridge Hill Road
Cottage Grove, OR 97424
Phone: 541-942-5631
District: Portland

Cottage Grove and Dorena Lakes are both set in the Willamette Valley, about 20 miles south of Eugene and on the east side of I-5. The lakes are nestled in the valley's rolling, wooded hill country. The area is managed to provide a habitat for a wide variety of wildlife species of birds and animals. Cottage Grove is accessed from I-5 exit 172 and Dorena from I-5 exit 174. There are Corps-managed camping areas at both lakes. Both campgrounds have playgrounds and there is a swimming area at Pine Meadows.

Pine Meadows: May-Sep, 93 sites, no hookups, $10-$15, drinking water, dump, restrooms, showers, amphitheater. At Cottage Grove Lake. From I-5 exit 172, turn left on London Road for about 3 miles, then turn left on Cottage Grove Reservoir Road, 3 miles to the campground. 541-942-8657 (75166 Cottage Grove Reservoir Rd, Cottage Grove, OR 97424).

Schwarz Park: Apr-Sep, 63 sites, no hookups, $13, drinking water, dump, restrooms, showers, interpretive trail, 12-mile bike path nearby. At Dorena Lake. From I-5 exit 174, turn left on Row River Road and travel 5 miles to the campground on the left. 541-942-5631 (34909 Shoreview Dr, Cottage Grove, OR 97424).

2) LAKE UMATILLA

U.S. Army Corps of Engineers
P.O. Box 564
The Dalles, OR 97058
Phone: 541-296-1181
District: Portland

John Jay Dam is 216 miles upstream from the mouth of the Columbia River and is located at exit 109 off I-84 in northern Oregon. The project consists of a navigation lock, spillway, powerhouse and fish passage facilities on both shores of the 76-mile long lake. The Visitor Center has a fish viewing window and self-guided tours. Water recreation is plentiful on the John Day River and along the lake.

Note: The Cliffs and Plymouth camping areas are on the Washington side of Lake Umatilla and are listed in the Washington section of this guide.

LePage Park: Apr-Oct, 22 sites with electric & water hookups, 20 tent sites, $12-$20, some pull thrus, drinking water, dump, restrooms, showers, fish cleaning station, swimming, water skiing. From I-84 exit 114, the campground is located on the eastbound side of the interstate. Westbound travelers must go under the roadway, follow signs. 541-506-7816.

Pennsylvania

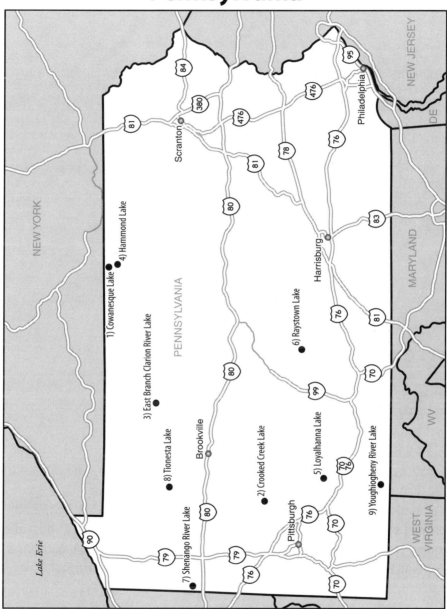

1) Cowanesque Lake
2) Crooked Creek Lake
3) East Branch Clarion River Lake
4) Hammond Lake
5) Loyalhanna Lake

6) Raystown Lake
7) Shenango River Lake
8) Tionesta Lake
9) Youghiogheny River Lake

Map #	Auto Touring	Biking	Boating	Climbing	Cultural / Historic Sites	Educational Programs	Camping	Groceries / Supplies	Fishing	Hiking	Horseback Riding	Hunting	Lodging	Off Highway Vehicles	Visitor Center	Page #
1			♦				♦	♦	♦	♦		♦				180
2	♦	♦	♦				♦	♦	♦	♦	♦	♦	♦			181
3	♦		♦				♦		♦	♦		♦				181
4		♦	♦				♦		♦	♦	♦	♦			♦	182
5		♦	♦				♦	♦	♦	♦		♦				183
6		♦	♦				♦		♦	♦	♦	♦				183
7	♦	♦	♦		♦	♦			♦			♦		♦		184
8	♦		♦		♦	♦	♦	♦	♦	♦		♦				185
9		♦	♦		♦	♦	♦	♦	♦	♦	♦	♦				186

1) COWANESQUE LAKE

U.S. Army Corps of Engineers
RR1 Box 65
Tioga, PA 16946
Phone: 570-835-5281
District: Baltimore

Located north of the town of Tioga and near the New York state line, the project consists of 2,212 land acres, 1,085 water acres and 17 shoreline miles. It is off US-15, between PA-49 and CR-58052. Cowanesque is popular for fishing, boating, hiking and hunting (in season).

The campground is on the north side of the lake. Ranger programs are presented at the campground in season. Other activities include water skiing, baseball, swimming and a playground.

Tompkins: May-Sep, 17 full hookup sites, 67 sites with electric (some 50amp) and water hookups and 16 tent sites, $18-$30, drinking water, dump, restrooms, showers, laundry, interpretive trail, fish cleaning station. Travel on US-15 north to the Cowanesque River Bridge in Lawrenceville, PA. Turn west on Bliss Road, travel 1.5 miles. 570-835-5281.

2) CROOKED CREEK LAKE

U.S. Army Corps of Engineers
RD3 Box 323A
114 Park Main Road
Ford City, PA 16226
Phone: 724-763-3161
District: Pittsburgh

The project has 2,511 land acres, 400 water acres and 15 shoreline miles. The lake is located about 48 miles southeast of Pittsburgh and just south of Kittanning. From Kittanning, Pennsylvania, travel 7 miles south on SR-66, then east on SR-2019 to the park management office.

Crooked Creek Rangers developed the Corps' first Auto Tour Trail that takes in the local history of Armstrong County and local townships. Visitors learn about the one-room schools of 1867, the first water-powered sawmill and depreciation lands awarded soldiers of the American Revolutionary War. Ranger interpretive programs are presented in season at the campground.

Crooked Creek: May-Sep, 50 sites, no hookups, non-reservable, $10, drinking water, dump, restrooms, showers, playground, group camping area. From Ford City, Pennsylvania, go south for 5 miles on SR-66, then .1 mile east on SR-2019/W.T. Heilman Road, follow signs. 724-763-3161.

3) EAST BRANCH CLARION RIVER LAKE

U.S. Army Corps of Engineers
631 East Branch Dam Road
Wilcox, PA 15870
Phone: 814-965-2065
District: Pittsburgh

This 1,160-acre lake is situated in scenic northeast Pennsylvania, 14 miles northeast of Johnsburg. From I-80 exit 97, travel north 36 miles on US-219 into Wilcox, turn right at the sign and go 2 miles, continue to follow signs. The lake has 20 shoreline miles and is surrounded by 424 land acres. Popular activities include fishing, boating and water skiing. Elk State Park is also located at the lake.

East Branch: Mar-Oct, 16 sites with electric hookups, 16 basic sites, 9 tent sites, non-reservable, $12–$15, dump, restrooms, showers. From Wilcox, follow signs. 814-965-2065.

4) HAMMOND LAKE

U.S. Army Corps of Engineers
RR1 Box 65
Tioga, PA 16946
Phone: 570-835-5281
District: Baltimore

Hammond Lake is located south of the town of Tioga and west of US-15. It is north of Wellsboro on PA-287 which is accessible from US-15. The lake has 685 surface acres of water. Boating, sailing and fishing are popular activities.

In the Endless Mountains of north-central Pennsylvania, the area offers excellent wildlife viewing. The campground is located on the east shore of the lake. Ranger programs are presented in season at the amphitheater. Display gardens are located near the Visitor Information Center. There is a mile-long Archery Trail with targets and two tree stands. Other activities include water skiing, swimming, ball fields and playgrounds.

Ives Run: Apr-Oct, 80 full hookup sites (50amp), 25 sites with electric (some 50amp) & water and 57 basic sites, $18-$28, drinking water, dump, restrooms, showers, laundry, interpretive trail. From Tioga, travel south 5 miles on SR-287 and exit east at the sign. 570-835-5281, (710 Ives Run Lane, Tioga, PA 16946).

5) LOYALHANNA LAKE

U.S. Army Corps of Engineers
440 Loyalhanna Dam Road
Saltsburg, PA 15681
Phone: 724-639-9013
District: Pittsburgh

The 400-acre lake, located 32 miles east of Pittsburgh, is 4 miles long. The project is .75 mile south of Saltsburg on PA-981. From Pittsburgh go east on US-22 to PA-981, then north, follow signs.

There are numerous biking and hiking trails at the lake as well as the Black Willow Water Trail, a unique self-guided boating trail. Brochures and trail maps are available at the ranger booth at the Bush Recreation Area. A boat ramp is located at the campground. Fishing is popular from inlet coves and backwater areas. The lake contains plentiful crappie, bullhead, catfish, bluegill, bass and carp.

Bush: May-Oct, 49 wooded sites, some with electric & water hookups, non-reservable, $16-$22, dump, restrooms, showers (fee), group camping area. From Saltsburg, go south on SR-981 past the dam, then 1 mile on Bush Road. 724-639-9013.

6) RAYSTOWN LAKE

U.S. Army Corps of Engineers
RD1 Box 222
Hesston, PA 16647
Phone: 814-658-3405
District: Baltimore

The lake is located in south-central Pennsylvania, east of Altoona and north of the Pennsylvania Turnpike. From US-22 in Huntington, Pennsylvania, travel south on PA-26 to Hesston. The park headquarters is 2 miles east of PA-26 at Hesston. Raystown Lake, the largest entirely within the state of Pennsylvania, extends 27 miles and covers 8,300 acres.

There is a full service marina at the lake. Ranger programs are presented in season at Seven Points. Other amenities include ball fields, playgrounds and swimming beaches. Golf is nearby. Nearby attractions include the Lincoln and Indian Caverns, Altoona Railroad Museum and the Swigart Antique Car Museum.

Seven Points: Mar-Oct, 150 sites with electric (some 50amp) hookups (some with water) and 6 tent sites, $20-$25, drinking water, dump, restrooms, showers, interpretive trail. From the PA Turnpike travel US-30 to PA-26. Take PA-26 to Saxton and continue north for 17.5 miles to the turnoff for Hesston and Seven Points, then 4 miles to the campground. 814-658-3405.

Susquehannock: May-Sep, 45 basic sites and 17 tent sites, no hookups, $12, drinking water, NO dump, restrooms, hiking trail. From Huntington, Pennsylvania, take PA-26 south for 6 miles, then east on unmarked Rt-3011 (Hesston Road). Travel 3 miles and turn left onto Bakers Hollow Road, 3 miles to the campground. 814-658-6806.

7) SHENANGO RIVER LAKE

U.S. Army Corps of Engineers
2442 Kelly Road
Hermitage, PA 16148
Phone: 724-962-7746
District: Pittsburgh

Located in the Shenango River Valley, the lake is 21 miles northeast of Youngstown, Ohio, and near the PA/OH state line. From I-80 exit 4B, go north on SR-18 for about 7 miles. Take the Birchwood Drive exit and go south on SR-18 for about .25 mile and turn right onto West Lake Drive, follow signs. The project covers 15,071 acres and the lake is 11 miles long.

History buffs will enjoy exploring the remnants of the Erie Extension Canal, sections of which are on project property. Other local attractions include the Kidd Mill Covered Bridge and the Great Blue Heron Sanctuary.

Corps-managed camping is on the north shore of the lake. Activities available at the campground include volleyball, water skiing, swimming, interpretive trail and playground. Also located at the campground are a boat ramp, fishing pier and marina. Fishing enthusiasts will find bass, walleye and a variety of panfish in the lake.

Shenango: May-Sep, 228 sites with electric (some 50amp) hookups, 97 basic sites and 5 tent sites with electric, $17-$22, drinking water, dump, restrooms, showers, laundry. From I-80 exit 4b, take SR-18 north about 6 miles until crossing the causeway. (The park is on the left side of the divided highway.) Continue north on SR-18 about 1/4 mile. Exit right at Birchwood Drive to the turnaround to SR-18 south. Before crossing the causeway again, turn right onto West Lake Road. 724-646-1124.

8) TIONESTA LAKE

U.S. Army Corps of Engineers
P.O. Box 539
Tionesta, PA 16353
Phone: 814-755-3512
District: Pittsburgh

Tionesta Lake winds through the rugged hills of northwestern Pennsylvania. It is situated in Forest County where nearly half the county is public land. From Tionesta, travel 1.5 miles south on PA-36 to the 3,184-acre project. The lake is 6.3 miles in length.

The Tionesta Indian Festival is held annually in August. The Forest County History Center in nearby Tionesta is open daily, May to October. Areas nearby include AlleghenyNational Forest and Cooks Forest State Park.

Ranger programs are presented in season at the campgrounds. There are marinas and boat ramps at the campgrounds.

Kellettville: Apr-Oct, 20 sites, no hookups, non-reservable, $10, drinking water, dump, restrooms. From Kellettville, Pennsylvania, take Forest Road 127 southwest across the bridge. 814-755-3512.

Outflow: All year, 39 sites, no hookups, non-reservable, $7-$10, drinking water, dump, restrooms. From Tionesta, Pennsylvania, go .5 mile south on SR-36, follow signs. 814-755-3512.

Tionesta Recreation Area: May-Sep, 78 full hookup sites (some 50amp), $25, dump, restrooms, showers, laundry, playground, hiking trail, public marina. From Tionesta, Pennsylvania, go .5 mile south on SR-36, follow signs. 814-755-3512 or 814-755-3592.

9) YOUGHIOGHENY RIVER LAKE

U.S. Army Corps of Engineers
497 Flanigan Road
Confluence, PA 15424
Phone: 814-395-3242
District: Pittsburgh

In the heart of the Laurel Highlands and spanning the Mason-Dixon line between Pennsylvania and Maryland, the lake is 16 miles long. It is located southeast of Uniontown, Pennsylvania, and just south of the town of Confluence. The project office is .5 mile south of Confluence on PA-281.

Nearby Ohiopyle State Park is noted for some of the best whitewater in the east. Ranger programs are presented in season in the campground amphitheater. Of the three Corps-managed campgrounds, one is in Maryland, two are in Pennsylvania.

Mill Run: All year, 30 sites, no hookups, non-reservable, $12, drinking water, dump, restrooms. Located in Maryland at the far southern end of the project and subject to low water conditions; it is advisable to call ahead. (Near I-68 Maryland exit #4), from the town of Friendsville, go north for about 5 miles, following the brown Corps signs. 814-395-3242

Outflow: All year, 36 sites with electric hookups (some 50amp), 15 basic sites and 10 tent-only, $10-$22, drinking water, dump, restrooms, showers. From Confluence, Pennsylvania, travel south on SR-281 and go over the Casselman and Youghiogheny Rivers. Make an immediate left into the campground. From US-40 in Maryland, take

US-281 north for 7 miles to just past the Youghioghney River entrance. Turn right into the campground. 814-395-3242.

Tub Run: May-Sep, 32 sites with electric hookups, 57 basic sites and 12 tent sites, $18-$22, drinking water, dump, restrooms, showers, laundry. From Confluence, Pennsylvania, travel south over the Casselman and Youghioghney Rivers. Go 4 miles and turn left on Tub Run Road. 814-395-3242.

South Carolina

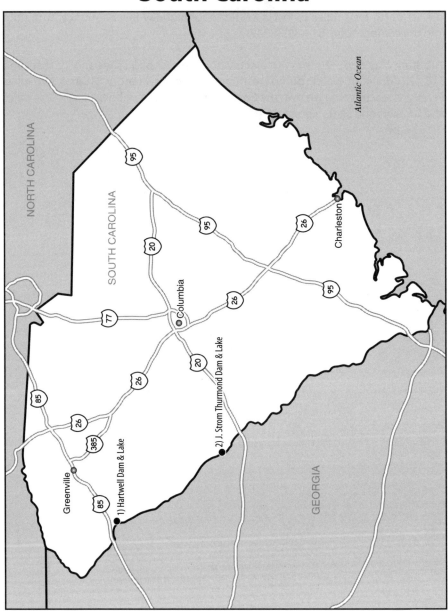

1) Hartwell Dam & Lake
2) J. Strom Thurmond Dam & Lake

Map #	Auto Touring	Biking	Boating	Climbing	Cultural / Historic Sites	Educational Programs	Camping	Fishing	Groceries / Supplies	Hiking	Horseback Riding	Hunting	Lodging	Off Highway Vehicles	Visitor Center	Page #
1	◆	◆			◆	◆	◆		◆		◆				◆	189
2	◆	◆		◆	◆	◆	◆	◆	◆	◆		◆	◆		◆	190

1) HARTWELL DAM & LAKE

U.S. Army Corps of Engineers
5625 Anderson Highway (US-29)
Hartwell, GA 30643
Phone: 706-856-0300
District: Savannah

Hartwell is one of the most popular Corps lakes in the nation. The dam is located just off US-29 on the SC/GA border. The Hartwell Visitor Center is located 1 mile past the dam on the Georgia side (5 miles north of Hartwell, Georgia). Guided tours of the dam and power plant are offered. Many lake access areas can be reached from I-85. Hartwell Lake comprises 56,000 acres of water with a shoreline of 962 miles. Over 20,000 acres of public land surround the lake.

Boat ramps are located around the lake. A private marina provides boating services and supplies. Swimming areas are provided at all campgrounds. Sailing is a popular activity at the lake. Boating safety courses are offered annually.

Four Corps-managed camping areas are located on the South Carolina side of the lake. The Anderson Jockey Lot, the largest flea market in the south, is nearby.

Note: See the Georgia section for additional project campgrounds.

Coneross Park: May-Oct, 94 sites with 50amp electric & water hookups and 12 basic sites, $14-$26, drinking water, dump, restrooms, showers, playground. Gates close at 10pm. From I-85 in SC, take exit 11 to Hwy-24 toward Townville. Go 1.5 miles past Townville and turn right onto Coneross Creek Road, follow signs. 888-893-0678.

Oconee Point: May-Sep, 70 waterfront sites with 50amp electric & water hookups, $22-$46, drinking water, dump, restrooms, showers, playground. All sites are waterfront. From I-85 exit 11 in SC, take SR-24 toward Townville, South Carolina, and continue 1.5 miles past Townville. Turn right on Coneross Creek Road and go 2.5 miles, turn south on South Friendship Road, 3 miles. 888-893-0678.

Springfield: Apr-Sep, 79 sites with 50amp electric & water hookups, most sites are waterfront, $22, drinking water, dump, restrooms, showers, playground. From I-85 exit 14, take SR-187 to Providence Church Road, follow signs. 888-893-0678.

Twin Lakes: Mar-Nov, 102 sites with 50amp electric & water hookups, $18-$20, drinking water, dump, restrooms, showers, playground, most sites are waterfront. Located 5 miles from Clemson. From I-85 exit 14, take SR-187 north toward Pendleton. Immediately after passing Clemson Research Center, turn left on Fants Grove Road, follow signs. 888-893-0678.

2) STROM THURMOND DAM & LAKE

U.S. Army Corps of Engineers
510 Clarks Hill Highway
Clarks Hill, SC 29821
Phone: 864-333-1100 or 800-533-3478
District: Savannah

Thurmond Lake is a long, relatively narrow body of water that extends from the dam (just north of Augusta, GA) to 29 miles up the Savannah River, 46 miles up the Little River and 6 miles up the Broad River. It is one of the most visited Corps lakes in the nation. With a shoreline of 1,200 miles and 71,000 acres of water, it straddles the SC/GA border. The Visitor Center (open 7 days a week, excluding Thanksgiving, Christmas & New Years Day) is located on the South Carolina side of the dam. Corps rangers are on duty throughout the year at the lake. From I-20 exit 183 (in GA), the dam is north on US-221.

The Corps manages 13 campgrounds at the Thurmond Project; of these, four are located in South Carolina: On the north segment of the waterway, Hawe Creek is five miles from historic McCormick where visitors will find sightseeing, shopping and restaurants. It is near two state parks and golf is also nearby. Mount Carmel, north of McCormick, is in the Old Ninety-Six tourism area. Modoc is in the south end near the dam; it has a swimming area.

All the campgrounds have easy access to boat ramps and fishing. Fish species include bass, bream, crappie and catfish. Fishing piers and bank fishing areas are numerous. Navigational maps are available at area stores and marinas.

Note: See the Georgia section for additional project campgrounds.

Hawe Creek: Apr-Sep, 34 sites, electric (50amp), & water hookups, some pull thrus, $20–$22, dump, restrooms, showers, marina. Located one mile from the Dorn Sportfishing facility. From junction US-221/US-378 in McCormick, southwest on US-378, then south 4 miles on Park Road. 864-443-5441.

Leroys Ferry: All year, 10 sites, no hookups, non-reservable, $6, drinking water. From Wellington, South Carolina, go 4 miles southwest. 864-333-1100.

Mt. Carmel: Apr-Sep, 21 sites with electric (50amp) & water hookups and 22 tent sites, some pull thrus, $18–$22, dump, restrooms, showers, laundry, 30-foot RV length limit. A quiet, remote campground with many sites near the shoreline. From McCormick, go northwest on Hwy-28 to Hwy-81 into Mt. Carmel, follow signs. 864-391-2711.

Modoc: Apr-Nov, 49 sites with electric (50amp) and water hookups, some pull thrus, $16–$42, dump, restrooms, showers, laundry, playground, hiking, many waterfront sites, beautiful views. From I-20 exit 200 (in GA), River Watch Pkwy, turn right and go 2 miles to Hwy-28 west (Furys Ferry Road), turn right and go 13 miles to Clarks Hill, SC. Continue northwest on Hwy-221 for 4 miles. 864-333-2272.

South Dakota

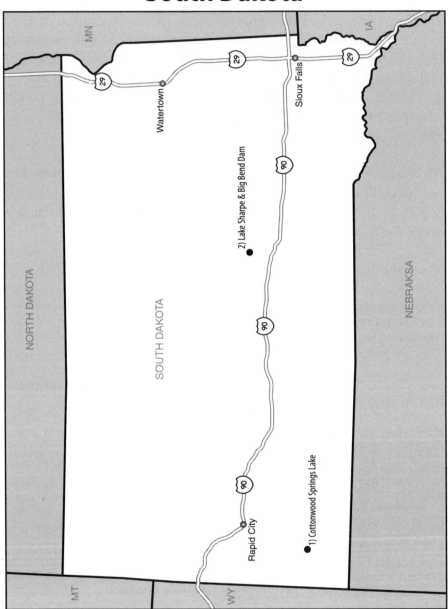

1)   Cottonwood Springs Lake
2)   Lake Sharpe & Big Bend Dam

Map #	Auto Touring	Biking	Boating	Climbing	Cultural/Historic Sites	Educational Programs	Camping	Fishing	Groceries/Supplies	Hiking	Horseback Riding	Hunting	Off Highway Vehicles	Lodging	Visitor Center	Page #
1			♦				♦	♦		♦		♦				193
2			♦			♦	♦	♦		♦		♦				194

1) COTTONWOOD SPRINGS LAKE

U.S. Army Corps of Engineers
HC 69 Box 74
Chamberlain, SD 57325
Phone: 605-745-5476
District: Omaha

The project is located in the southwestern corner of South Dakota on Cottonwood Creek, 3.5 miles west of Hot Springs. The lake is nestled in the rugged hills and evergreen trees of the southern Black Hills. It is a popular off-the-beaten-path destination for nature lovers. The most frequent recreational activities include hiking, fishing and boating (electric motors only). There is excellent wildlife viewing from the campground, so bring your binoculars.

Cottonwood Springs: May-Sep, 18 rustic sites in a hillside setting, no hookups, non-reservable, $5, drinking water, restrooms, NO dump, 35-foot RV length limit. On the south end of Hot Springs along US-385/18, turn west on US-18 truck bypass, go 1.5 miles on the bypass to the stop sign, turn west on US-18 for 3.5 miles, follow signs. Turn right onto CR-17 (gravel) for 1.2 miles to the Cottonwood access road. 605-745-5476.

2) LAKE SHARPE & BIG BEND DAM

U.S. Army Corps of Engineers
Big Bend Project
HC 69, Box 74 -- 33573 N. Shore Road
Chamberlain, SD 57325
Phone: 605-245-2255
District: Omaha

Lake Sharpe has 56,000 water acres and 200 miles of shoreline. It is located in the heart of South Dakota's "Indian Country." The project office is at the dam near the North Shore camping area. From Sioux Falls, travel west on I-90 to Reliance (exit 248), then northwest on SD-47 to the dam.

Big Bend takes its name from the unique bend in the Missouri River, 7 miles upstream from the dam, where the river makes almost a complete loop before returning south. There are 19 recreation areas at Lake Sharpe. The Corps manages 3 campgrounds at the lake.

Left Tailrace: Apr-Sep, 81 sites with electric hookups, non-reservable, $14, drinking water, dump, restrooms, showers. From Reliance, South Dakota, (west of Chamberlain, which is on the Missouri River), travel on SD-47 north for 14 miles. Take the highway across the powerhouse structure and take the first turn right (about 1/4 mile). 605-245-2255.

North Shore: May-Sep, 24 sites, no hookups, non-reservable, free. Two miles from Fort Thompson. Go across the crest of the dam, take the second left. (Sign says Administration – North Shore Area.) 605-245-2255.

Old Fort Thompson: May-Sep, 13 sites, no hookups, non-reservable, free, drinking water, dump, restrooms, showers. Located below the dam on the east side of the spillway, one-half mile to Fort Thompson. 605-245-2555.

Tennessee

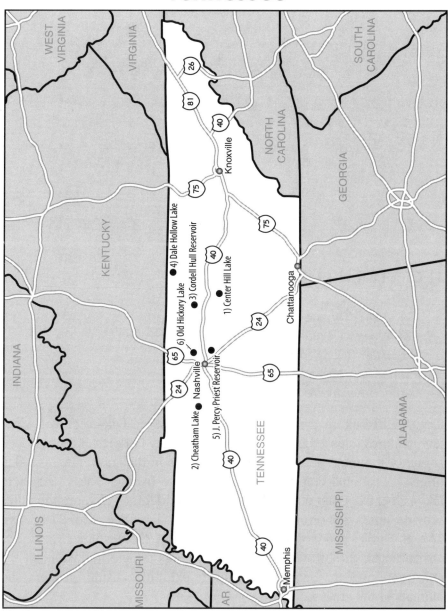

1) Center Hill Lake
2) Cheatham Lake
3) Cordell Hull Reservoir
4) Dale Hollow Lake
5) J. Percy Priest Reservoir
6) Old Hickory Lake

Map #	Auto Touring	Biking	Boating	Climbing	Cultural/Historic Sites	Camping	Educational Programs	Fishing	Groceries/Supplies	Hiking	Horseback Riding	Hunting	Lodging	Off Highway Vehicles	Visitor Center	Page #
1			◆			◆	◆	◆	◆	◆		◆			◆	196
2	◆		◆			◆	◆		◆	◆		◆			◆	197
3		◆	◆			◆	◆		◆	◆	◆	◆	◆	◆	◆	198
4		◆	◆				◆	◆	◆	◆	◆	◆			◆	199
5	◆		◆			◆	◆		◆	◆	◆	◆			◆	200
6	◆		◆			◆	◆	◆	◆	◆		◆			◆	201

1) CENTER HILL LAKE

U.S. Army Corps of Engineers
158 Resource Lane
Lancaster, TN 38569
Phone: 931-858-3125
District: Nashville

Center Hill Lake is a popular fishing destination. Due to cooler water temperatures released from the dam, the Carney Fork River downstream is one of the most productive trout fisheries in the state. The lake also offers exceptional crappie, bass and walleye fishing. The 18,220-acre lake is located about 60 miles east of Nashville. Its 415 shoreline miles provide much opportunity for recreational activities. From I-40 exit 268, go 5 miles south on TN-96, follow signs to the Resource Manager's Office where the Information Center features a pictorial history of the construction of the dam and a wildlife exhibit focusing on birds and animals of the area.

There are several commercial marinas at the lake. Camping is found at three Corps-managed areas. Rangers conduct boating and water safety programs. Facilities of interest at the lake include: Edgar Evins State Park, the Evins Appalachian Center for Crafts, Burgess Falls State Natural Area and Rock Island State Park.

Floating Mill: Apr-Oct, 54 sites with electric (some 50amp) and water hookups, 16 basic sites, 32 basic tent sites and 16 family tent sites with electric & water, $14-$24, drinking water, dump, restrooms, showers, laundry, interpretive trail, playground, fish cleaning station, swimming. From I-40 exit 273, take US-56 for 5 miles to Hurricane Dock Road. At the store turn right, follow signs. 931-858-4845.

Long Branch: Apr-Oct, 5 full hookup sites (50amp), 55 sites with electric (some 50amp) & water hookups, $20-$24, drinking water, dump, restrooms, showers, laundry, playground, fish cleaning station, good trout fishing below the dam. From I-40 exit 268, follow US-96 west for 5 miles to the end of Center Hill Dam on SR-141, follow signs to the Long Branch Recreation Area. 615-548-8002.

Ragland Bottom: Apr-Oct, 41 sites with electric (some 50amp) and water hookups, 16 basic tent sites and 10 tent sites with electric & water, $14-$24, drinking water, dump, restrooms, showers, laundry, interpretive trail, swimming. From Smithville, Tennessee, take US-70 northeast for 8 miles, turn on Ragland Bottom Road, follow signs. The campground is located 1 mile from Slego Bridge. 931-761-3616.

2) CHEATHAM LAKE

U.S. Army Corps of Engineers
1798 Cheatham Dam Road
Ashland City, TN 37015
Phone: 615-792-5697
District: Nashville

Cheatham Lake is part of the Cumberland River located about 35 miles west of Nashville on SR-12/Ashland City Highway. The lake has 320 shoreline miles. From Nashville, take SR-12 west through Ashland City, then another 12 miles to Cheap Hill. Turn left onto Cheatham Dam Road, follow brown signs. The project office is located on the right just before the dam. Maps and information are available.

Two Corps-managed camping areas include Lock A, close to the lock & dam on the lake and on the Cumberland River, and Harpeth River Bridge, situated where SR-49 crosses the scenic Harpeth River. Camping elsewhere on public lands along the shoreline is prohibited. Canoe rentals are available at nearby Narrows of the Harpeth State Park. Riverfront Park in Nashville is popular for summertime concerts and festivals.

Harpeth River Bridge: Apr-Oct, 15 sites with electric & water hookups, non-reservable, $7–$9, restrooms, boat ramp, playground. From Ashland City, Tennessee, go west on SR-49 for 6 miles to the bridge. 615-792-4195.

Lock A: Apr-Oct, 45 sites with electric(50amp) & water hookups including 7 tent sites, $19-$23, drinking water, dump, restrooms, showers, laundry. From Ashland City, Tennessee, take SR-12 west for 12 miles to Cheap Hill. Turn left on Cheatham Dam Road, travel west for 4 miles. 615-792-3715.

3) CORDELL HULL RESERVOIR

U.S. Army Corps of Engineers
71 Corps Lane
Carthage, TN 37030
Phone: 615-735-1034
District: Nashville

The lake, located 50 miles east of Nashville, has 11,960 water acres and 381 shoreline miles. From I-40 exit 258, travel north on TN-53 to Carthage, then SR-25 and SR-263; follow signs to the Resource Manager's Office & Visitor Center where information and maps are available.

Camping is in designated areas only: Defeated Creek and Salt Lick campgrounds and the primitive camping area at the horse trail. Two commercial marinas have boating supplies and services and restaurants. The Bluegrass Festival held annually in June is nearby.

Defeated Creek: Apr-Sep, 63 full hookup sites (some 50amp), 92 sites with electric (some 50amp) & water hookups, $15-$26, drinking water, dump, restrooms, showers, laundry, playground, swimming, tennis courts, trailhead nearby. From Carthage, Tennessee, go 4 miles west on SR-25, then north on US-80 and east on SR-85, follow signs. 615-774-3141.

Salt Lick Creek: May-Sep, 31 full hookup sites, 119 sites with electric & water hookups, some pull thrus, $15-$26, drinking water, dump, restrooms, showers, laundry, playground, swimming. From Carthage, Tennessee, go 4 miles west on SR-25, then north on US-80, then east on SR-85 to Gladice, turn right on Smith Bend Road, follow signs. 931-678-4718.

4) DALE HOLLOW LAKE

U.S. Army Corps of Engineers
5050 Dale Hollow Dam Road
Celina, TN 38551
Phone: 931-243-3136
District: Nashville

The Dale Hollow project is located northeast of Nashville near the Kentucky state line. The 27,700-acre lake, with its 620 miles of shoreline is 4 miles east of the town of Celina. The Dale Hollow National Fishery, located just below the dam is open to visitors daily, 7-3:30. It features a Visitor Center, aquarium and various displays and exhibits. From I-40 exit 280, travel 17 miles north on TN-56, then 23 miles north on TN-53 to Celina, follow signs.

Camping is available at four Corps-managed areas as well as Dale Hollow State Park. All Corps campgrounds have a playground and amphitheater. Dale Hollow Lake is a popular destination for scuba divers.

Dale Hollow Dam: Apr-Oct, 79 sites with electric (some 50amp) & water, $17-$24, drinking water, dump, restrooms, showers, laundry, fish cleaning station, bike trail, hiking trail, volleyball, basketball. From Celina, take TN-53 for 2 miles northwest. Turn right on Dale Hollow Dam Road, then second right onto the campground road, follow signs. 931-243-3554.

Lillydale: Apr-Sep, 93 sites with electric (some 50amp) & water hookups, 5 basic sites, 11 tent and 15 primitive island sites, $10-$24, drinking water, dump, restrooms, showers, laundry, hiking trail, swimming, volleyball. From I-40 exit 288, take SR-111 north. At about 3.5 miles north of Livingston, go north on CR-294 (Willow Grove Road) for 13.3 miles. Turn right onto Lillydale Road, follow signs. 931-823-4155.

Obey River: Apr-Oct, 96 sites with electric (some 50amp) and water hookups, 11 basic sites and 25 tent sites, $12-$24, drinking water, dump, restrooms, showers, laundry, largest swimming beach on the lake, ball courts, public marina. From I-40 exit 288, travel north on SR-111. About 15 miles past Livingston, follow signs. 931-864-6388.

Willow Grove: May-Sep, 63 sites with electric (some 50amp) and water hookups and 21 tent sites, $12-$24, drinking water, dump, restrooms, showers, laundry, swimming, volleyball, water skiing. From I-40 exit 288, north on SR-111. At about 3.5 miles north of Livingston, take CR-294 (Willow Grove Road) north for 16 miles, follow signs. 931-823-4285.

5) J. PERCY PRIEST RESERVOIR

U.S. Army Corps of Engineers
3737 Bell Road
Nashville, TN 37214
Phone: 615-889-1975
District: Nashville

The project is located 10 miles east of Nashville. The Visitor Center, on the west side of the dam, is open on weekdays. From I-40 exit 219 (Stewarts Ferry Pike) go right to the first stop light, then left on Bell Road and take the second right at the Visitor Center sign.

Corps-managed camping is found in three areas at the lake. Boat ramps are conveniently located throughout. There are four commercial marinas and the Nashville Shores Water Park is at the lake. Nearby points of interest include The Hermitage, Opreyland and the Grand Ole Opry, Opry Mills shopping area and the Nashville Speedway.

Anderson Road: Apr-Sep, 37 sites, no hookups, $12-$14, drinking water, dump, restrooms, showers, laundry. From I-40 exit 219 (Stewarts Ferry Pike), turn right on Stewarts Ferry Pike and go straight on Bell Road 5 miles, then left on Smith Springs Road. Go 1 mile and turn left on Anderson Road for 1 mile. 615-361-1980.

Poole Knobs: May-Oct, 57 sites with electric (some 50amp) and water hookups, 24 basic sites and 6 tent sites, $10-$24, some pull thrus, drinking water, dump, restrooms, showers, laundry. From I-24 exit 66B, go right on Sam Ridley Parkway for 3 miles, exit right onto Hwy-41 north (Murfreesboro Pike) 1.5 miles, then right on Fergus Road for 2 miles, then right on Jones Mill Road for 4 miles, follow signs. 615-459-6948.

Seven Points: Apr-Oct, 60 sites with electric (some 50amp) & water hookups, $20-$24, drinking water, dump, restrooms, showers, laundry. From I-40 exit 221B, go right on Old Hickory Blvd, then left on Bell Road, right on New Hope Road for 1 mile, then left on Stewarts Ferry Pike for 1 mile, follow signs. 615-889-5198.

6) OLD HICKORY LAKE

U.S. Army Corps of Engineers
No. 5 Power Plant Road
Hendersonville, TN 37075
Phone: 615-822-4846
District: Nashville

Located 10 miles northeast of metropolitan Nashville, the lake has 22,500 acres of water. The Visitor Center is in the Rockland Recreation Area in Hendersonville. From I-65 (north of Nashville) exit onto Vietnam Veterans Blvd, travel to exit #3, proceed to the town of Hendersonville and get into the right lane. Turn right at the traffic light onto Rockland Road, follow signs. The Center features displays, exhibits and video programs. Maps and information are available. A display narrated by a country and western star depicts the history and development of the Cumberland River.

Old Hickory Lake is conveniently close to Opreyland USA. Many parks and recreation areas are located along the large waterway. The Old Hickory Nature Trail on the south side of the dam is part of the National Trail System. Wildlife viewing is excellent.

Cages Bend: Apr-Oct, 42 sites with electric (some 50amp) & water hookups, $19-$23, drinking water, dump, restrooms, showers, laundry, playground. From I-65, north of Nashville, exit onto Vietnam Veterans Blvd East and follow until it joins Gallatin Road/Hwy-31E, then right on Cages Bend Road South, then left onto Benders Ferry Road, follow signs. 615-824-4989.

Cedar Creek: Apr-Oct, 59 sites with electric (some 50amp) & water hookups, $19-$23, drinking water, dump, restrooms, showers, laundry, playground, swimming. From I-40, east of Nashville, exit onto Old Hickory Blvd North. Turn right on Lebanon Road, then left onto Andrew Jackson Parkway to the first red light, continue straight on Saundersville Road for 10 miles, follow signs. 615-754-4947.

Texas

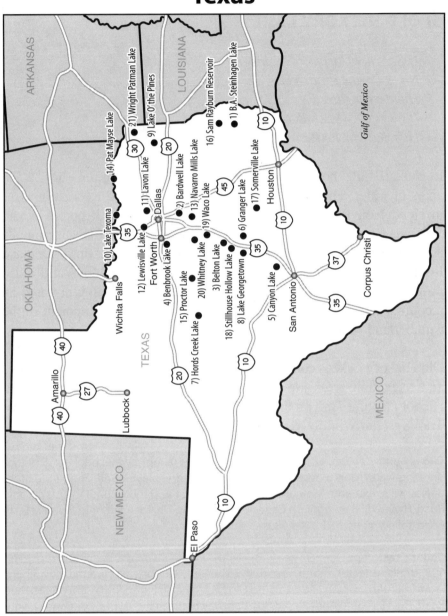

1) B.A. Steinhagen Lake	8) Lake Georgetown	15) Proctor Lake
2) Bardwell Lake	9) Lake O' The Pines	16) Sam Rayburn Reservoir
3) Belton Lake	10) Lake Texoma	17) Somerville Lake
4) Benbrook Lake	11) Lavon Lake	18) Stillhouse Hollow Lake
5) Canyon Lake	12) Lewisville Lake	19) Waco Lake
6) Granger Lake	13) Navarro Mills Lake	20) Whitney Lake
7) Hords Creek Lake	14) Pat Mayse Lake	21) Wright Patman Lake

Map #	Auto Touring	Biking	Boating	Climbing	Cultural / Historic Sites	Camping	Educational Programs	Fishing	Groceries / Supplies	Hiking	Horseback Riding	Hunting	Lodging	Off Highway Vehicles	Visitor Center	Page #
1		♦	♦			♦		♦	♦	♦		♦	♦			204
2	♦		♦		♦	♦		♦		♦	♦	♦				204
3	♦	♦	♦		♦	♦		♦		♦		♦	♦		♦	205
4	♦		♦		♦	♦		♦		♦	♦	♦				207
5	♦	♦	♦			♦	♦	♦		♦	♦	♦	♦			208
6	♦	♦	♦			♦		♦		♦	♦	♦	♦			209
7			♦			♦		♦		♦		♦	♦			209
8	♦	♦	♦			♦		♦		♦		♦				210
9	♦		♦			♦		♦		♦		♦				211
10		♦	♦			♦		♦		♦	♦	♦	♦			212
11	♦		♦		♦	♦		♦		♦	♦	♦				213
12	♦		♦		♦	♦		♦		♦	♦	♦				214
13	♦		♦			♦		♦	♦	♦		♦				214
14	♦		♦			♦		♦		♦		♦				215
15			♦			♦		♦		♦		♦	♦			216
16	♦		♦			♦		♦	♦	♦	♦	♦	♦			217
17	♦		♦			♦		♦		♦		♦	♦	♦		218
18	♦	♦	♦		♦	♦		♦		♦	♦	♦			♦	219
19	♦	♦	♦		♦	♦	♦	♦		♦	♦	♦				220
20	♦		♦			♦		♦	♦	♦	♦	♦				221
21	♦	♦	♦		♦	♦		♦		♦		♦			♦	222

1) B.A. STEINHAGEN LAKE

U.S. Army Corps of Engineers
890 FM-92
Woodville, TX 75979
Phone: 409-429-3491
District: Fort Worth

Located in east-central Texas about 75 miles north of Beaumont, Steinhagen Lake has 13,800 water acres. From Jasper, Texas, go 15 miles west on US-190, then 5 miles south on FM-92 to the project office.

RV camping may be found at two Corps-managed areas (Campers Cove is closed for renovation) as well as Hen House Ridge and Walnut Ridge areas of Dies State Park.

Magnolia Ridge: All year, 34 sites with electric & water hookups, 7 sites with water only, some pull thrus, $10-$16, drinking water, dump, restrooms, showers. On the northwest side of the lake. From Woodland, Texas, go east on US-190 for 11 miles to FM-92 (caution light), turn north on FM-92 and travel 1.5 miles. 409-283-5493.

Sandy Creek: All year, 65 sites with electric & water hookups, 6 basic sites, some pull thrus, $10-$18, drinking water, dump, restrooms, showers, swimming. From Jasper, Texas, go west on US-190 for 10 miles, then south on FM-777 for 2 miles, then west on CR-155 for 2.5 miles, follow signs. 409-429-3491 or 409-384-6166.

2) BARDWELL LAKE

U.S. Army Corps of Engineers
4000 Observation Drive
Ennis, TX 75119
Phone: 972-875-5711
District: Fort Worth

Located 35 miles southeast of Dallas in north-central Texas, the lake is 5.4 miles long and 1.2 miles wide. It covers 3,500 water acres. From Dallas take I-45 south to exit 247, then US-287 north/Barton Pkwy toward Waxahachie. Travel north 3.4 miles to Ensign Road. Turn left and go 1.5 miles to Observation Dr. Turn right and go 1.5 miles to the lake headquarters.

The Corps manages three camping areas and three swimming beaches. A private marina is located at the lake. Local attractions include the Texas Motorplex Drag Racing facility, Railroad and Cultural Heritage Museum, the Old Train Depot and the oldest mapped Blue Bonnet Trails known in Texas. The National Polka Festival, featuring dancing and Czech cuisine, is held annually during Memorial Day weekend in Ennis.

High View Park: All year, 39 sites with electric (some 50amp) & water hookups, $14-$16, drinking water, dump, restrooms, showers, swimming, public marina. Gates close at 10pm. From Ennis, Texas, I-45 exit 247, exit onto the US-287 bypass. Travel 4.5 miles and exit at Bardwell Lake sign. Turn left onto Hwy-34 and go 2.5 miles southwest. Turn left immediately past the Fina Station onto High View Park Road. Travel .2 mile to the entrance. 972-875-5711, (260 High View Rd, Ennis, TX 75119).

Mott Park: Apr-Sep, 33 sites with electric & water hookups and 7 basic sites, $16, drinking water, dump, restrooms, showers, swimming. Campground is on the western shore. Gates close at 10pm. From Ennis, Texas, I-45 exit 247, exit onto the US-287 bypass. Travel 4.5 miles and exit at Bardwell Lake sign. Turn left onto Hwy-34 and go 3.5 miles southwest, then left onto FM-985 and go 1.6 miles southeast. 972-875-5711, (957 FM-985, Ennis, TX 75119).

Waxahachie: All year, 65 sites with electric & water hookups and 7 basic sites, $14-$18, drinking water, dump, restrooms, showers, nature trail, equestrian trail. On the western shore. From I-45 exit 247, exit onto the US-287 bypass. Travel 4.5 miles and exit at Bardwell Lake sign. Turn left onto Hwy-34 and go 3 miles southwest to Bozek Road, turn right 1.5 miles to the campground. 972-875-5711, (930 Bozek Rd, Ennis, TX 75119).

3) BELTON LAKE

U.S. Army Corps of Engineers
3110 FM-2271
Belton, TX 76513
Phone: 254-939-2461
District: Fort Worth

The project office is located south of the lake (1 mile south of US-190 on FM-1670 in Belton). The 12,300-acre lake is adjacent to Fort Hood army base. From Belton go 3 miles north on TX-317, then 2 miles west on FM-439 and 1 mile north on FM-2271.

The Miller Springs Nature Area, located below the dam, includes a hiking trail along the Leon River, a restored historic bridge and several wildlife viewing areas. A mural painted on the spillway wall of Belton Dam depicts the history of the Bell County area. Six Corps-managed camping areas are suitable for RVs. Camping is also available at the Fort Hood Recreation area.

Cedar Ridge: All year, 68 sites with electric (some 50amp) & water hookups, some pull thrus, $16-$32, drinking water, dump, restrooms, showers, laundry, playground, swimming, basketball. From I-35 exit 299 in Temple, Texas, take SR-36 west toward Gatesville. Turn left on Cedar Ridge Park Road. 254-986-1404, (3740 FM-1670, Belton, TX 76513).

Iron Bridge: All year, 5 sites, no hookups, non-reservable, free, restrooms, From I-35 go west on SR-36 for about 11 miles, then north on Iron Bridge Road. 254-939-2461.

Live Oak Ridge: All year, 48 shaded sites with electric (some 50amp) & water hookups, $16-$18, drinking water, dump, restrooms, showers, laundry. From I-35 exit 299 in Temple, Texas, exit to FM-2305, travel west to FM-2271 and turn left 1.5 miles. 254-780-1738.

Westcliff: All year, 27 sites with electric & water hookups, some pull thrus, 4 tent-only sites, $10-$16, drinking water, dump, restrooms, showers, playground, swimming. From I-35 exit 294 in Belton, Texas, exit onto 6th Ave/FM-93 west. Turn north onto 317 (Main Street) for 2 miles. Turn west on FM-439 (Lake Road) for 4 miles. Turn right on Sparta Road and then right on Westcliff Park Road. 254-939-9828.

White Flint: All year, 13 sites with 50 amp electric & water hookups, some pull thrus, $18, drinking water, dump, restrooms. From I-35 exit 299 in Temple, Texas, take SR-36 west about 11 miles and cross the bridge to the north side. 254-939-2461.

Winkler: Mar-Oct, 15 paved sites with water hookups, no electric, non-reservable, $10, drinking water, restrooms, showers, 35-foot RV length limit. A popular fishing camp. From I-35 exit 299 go west on SR-36 for about 12 miles. Exit to the right 2 miles past White Flint. 254-986-1579 or 3419, (11740 Winkler Park Rd, Moody, TX 76557).

4) BENBROOK LAKE

U.S. Army Corps of Engineers
7001 Lakeside Drive
Fort Worth, TX 76132
Phone: 817-292-2400
District: Fort Worth

The 3,770-acre lake is 12 miles southwest of Fort Worth on the south side of Benbrook and just south of I-20. It is on the Clear Fork of the Trinity River and is situated partially within the city limits of Fort Worth. From I-20 exit 429A, take US-377 for 2.5 miles southwest to the lake. The Corps office is then 2 miles east on Winscott Road and Lakeside Drive.

A 7-mile horseback and hiking trail, located on the west side of the lake, is part of the National Trail System. There is a model airplane field at Holiday Park. Sightseeing and special events all year long are found at nearby Fort Worth, known as the city "Where the West Begins."

Holiday Park: All year, 79 sites with electric (some 50amp) & water hookups, 24 basic sites, $10-$20, drinking water, dump, restrooms, showers. From I-20 exit 429A, take US-377 to Granbury. Go southwest for 5.7 miles, then east onto Pearl Ranch Dr, go 2 miles. 817-292-2400.

Mustang: All year, 14 basic sites, $10, drinking water, dump, restrooms. From I-20 exit 429A, take US-377 south for 6 miles, then 1 miles east on FM-1187, then north on CR-1025 (Ben Day-Murrin Road) for 1.5 miles, follow signs. 817-292-2400.

Rocky Creek: Apr-Sep, 21 sites, no hookups, non-reservable, $10, drinking water, dump, restrooms. From I-20 exit 429A, take US-377 south, then southeast on FM-1187 for 7 miles, then north on CR-1089 for 3.6 miles. At junction CR-1150 exit south to the park. 817-292-2400.

5) CANYON LAKE

U.S. Army Corps of Engineers
601 C.O.E. Road
Canyon Lake, TX 78133
Phone: 830-964-3341
District: Fort Worth

The 8,240-acre lake is located northeast of San Antonio on the Guadalupe River in Comal County. From I-35 exit 191 take FM-306 northwest 14 miles and turn left onto Lake Access Road. The road to the dam, scenic overlook and lake office is less than one mile on the right.

Four camping areas are available from the Corps. Interpretive programs are presented by rangers at Potters Creek, the largest campground located on the north shore of the lake. Scuba diving is a popular activity at the lake. There are several private resorts and state recreation areas at the lake. Hill Country sightseeing, restaurants and shopping are nearby.

Canyon Park: Mar-Sep, 150 sites, no hookups, non-reservable, $8-$12, restrooms. Located on the north shore of the lake near Hancock. From I-35 exit 191 (north of New Braunfels), go west on Canyon Park Road for 17.5 miles. 830-964-3341.

Cranes Mills: Mar-Sep, 46 sites, no hookups, non-reservable, $8-$12, drinking water, dump, restrooms, showers. Gates close at 10pm. From I-35 exit 191 (Canyon Lake), go west on FM-306 for about 14 miles. Turn left on FM-2673 just after the Guadalupe River crossing. The park is located at the westernmost end of FM-2673 and South Cranes Mill Road. 830-964-3341.

North Park: Mar-Nov, 19 campsites, no hookups, non-reservable, $8-$12, drinking water, dump, restrooms. No showers and no boat ramp. Gates close at 10pm. From I-35 exit 191, take FM-306 west for 18.5 miles. 830-964-3341.

Potters Creek: All year, 92 sites with electric (some 50amp) and water hookups and 17 tent sites with electric & water, many lakefront sites, $14-$34, drinking water, dump, restrooms, showers, swimming. From I-35 exit 191, take Canyon Park Rd (FM-306) west for 21 miles, turn left on Potters Creek Road for 2.7 miles. The campground is on the north side of the lake. Campground gates close at 10pm and there is no re-entry after that time. 830-964-3341.

6) GRANGER LAKE

U.S. Army Corps of Engineers
3100 Granger Dam Road
Granger, TX 76530
Phone: 512-859-2668
District: Fort Worth

The 4,400-acre lake is located 35 miles northeast of Austin. From I-35 (at Round Rock) take US-79 east to SR-95 in Taylor. Take SR-95 north through Taylor to Circleville, then north to Granger. The dam is located 7 miles east of Granger via FM-971 on the San Gabriel River.

There are three Corps-managed camping areas and boat ramps are conveniently located. Gates close at 10pm at all campgrounds. The bike and hike trail is popular and there is an equestrian trail. Wildlife viewing is excellent at the project.

Taylor: Mar-Sep, 48 sites with electric & water hookups, $12-$18, drinking water, dump, restrooms, showers. From I-35 go east on US-79, then north on SR-95 north, then east on FM-1331 for 5 miles. 512-859-2668.

Willis Creek: All year, 27 sites with electric & water hookups, $14-$18, drinking water, dump, restrooms, showers. An equestrian camping area (non-reservable) is located directly across from Willis Creek Park. From I-35 go east on US-79, then north on SR-95, turn right on CR-346 and go 4 miles. 512-859-2668.

Wilson H. Fox: All year, 58 sites with electric (some 50amp) and water hookups, $14-$26, drinking water, dump, restrooms, showers, swimming, playground. From I-35, take US-79 east, then SR-95 north to FM-1331, east on FM-1331 for about 7 miles. 512-859-2668.

7) HORDS CREEK LAKE

U.S. Army Corps of Engineers
230 Friendship Park Road
Coleman, TX 76834

Phone: 325-625-2322
District: Fort Worth

The 510-acre lake is located in Coleman County, in the northern portion of the Texas Hill Country, 55 miles south of Abilene. From Coleman, go west for 8 miles on FM-153. Hords Creek is a popular fishing destination.

Lakeside: All year, 16 full hookup sites (some 50amp), 36 sites with electric (some 50amp) & water hookups, some pull thrus, $16-$26, drinking water, dump, restrooms, showers, swimming. From Coleman, Texas, take Hwy-153 west for 8 miles to the lake, follow signs. 325-625-2322 ext 15.

Flat Rock: May-Oct, 10 full hookup sites, 50 sites with electric (some 50amp) & water hookups, some pull thrus, $16-$44, drinking water, dump, restrooms, showers, swimming. From Coleman, Texas, go 8.7 miles west on Hwy-153, go south across the dam, then west to the park, follow signs. 325-625-2322 ext 15.

8) LAKE GEORGETOWN

U.S. Army Corps of Engineers
500 Lake Overlook Drive
Georgetown, TX 78628
Phone: 512-930-5253
District: Fort Worth

The 1,310-acre lake is located 25 miles north of Austin, west of I-35 in the Texas Hill Country. From I-35 (Georgetown) travel west on Williams Drive about 3.5 miles to D.B. Wood, turn left to the project entrance.

A 16-mile hiking trail features varied scenery and there is a challenging mountain biking trail. A washed pebble beach is located at Russell Park. Two Corps-managed camping areas are suitable for RVs. Gates close at 10pm.

Cedar Breaks: All year, 64 sites with electric & water hookups, $18, drinking water, dump, restrooms, showers. Campground is on the south side of the lake. From I-35, take FM-2338 west for 3.5 miles to Cedar Breaks Road, then south 2 miles, follow signs. 512-930-5253 or 512-819-9046, (500 Cedar Breaks Rd, Georgetown, TX 78633).

Jim Hogg Park: All year, 148 sites with electric hookups, $18-$26, drinking water, dump, restrooms, showers. From I-35, take FM-2338 west for 6 miles to Jim Hogg Road, then south 2 miles. 512-930-5253 or 512-819-9046.

9) LAKE O' THE PINES

U.S. Army Corps of Engineers
2669 FM-726
Jefferson, TX 75657
Phone: 903-665-2336
District: Fort Worth

Located in the Piney Woods of northeast Texas, 9 miles south of Jefferson, the project includes 18,700 water acres and 9,000 land acres. It is situated between I-30 to the north and I-20 to the south. From Texarkana, Texas, take US-59 south to Jefferson, then west on SR-49 for 4 miles to FM-726, then west 2 miles to the project office near the dam.

There are 11 boat ramps located throughout plus four Corps-managed camping areas. Private campgrounds around the lake also have full service camping. Restaurants, shopping and sightseeing are nearby. Many festivals are held in local towns. Antique shopping is popular.

Alley Creek: Mar-Sep, 49 sites with electric & water hookups and 15 tent-only sites, $12-$38, drinking water, dump, restrooms, showers, swimming, group camping area for RVs. From Jefferson TX, travel 4 miles northwest on SR-49, then turn left on FM-729 and travel 12 miles west to the park entrance. 903-755-2637 or 903-755-2336, (Rt 1 Box 2282, Jefferson, TX 75657).

Brushy Creek: All year, 63 sites with electric (some 50amp) and water hookups, some pull thrus and 40 tent-only sites, $10-$36, drinking water, dump, restrooms, showers, swimming. From Jefferson, Texas, go 4 miles northwest on SR-49, then 3.5 miles west on FM-729, then south for 4.8 miles on FM-726 past the dam, follow signs. 903-777-3491.

Buckhorn Creek: Mar-Sep, 57 sites with electric & water hookups and 38 tent-only sites, $12-$38, drinking water, dump, restrooms, showers. From Jefferson, Texas, travel 4 miles northwest on SR-49, then turn left on FM-729 and 3.5 miles west, then turn left on FM-726 and travel 2.4 miles south to the park. 903-665-8261.

Johnson Creek: All year, 63 sites with electric & water hookups, some pull thrus, and 22 tent-only sites, $12-$26, drinking water, dump, restrooms, showers, swimming, group camping area for RVs. From Jefferson, Texas, travel 4 miles northwest on SR-49, then left on FM-729 for 8.5 miles west to the park entrance. 903-755-2435 or 903-665-2336.

10) LAKE TEXOMA

U.S. Army Corps of Engineers
351 Corps Road
Denison, TX 75020
Phone: 903-465-4990
District: Tulsa

This project is on the Texas/Oklahoma state line. It has 102,968 land acres, 88,000 water acres and 680 shoreline miles. From Denison, Texas, go 5 miles northwest on TX-91. Before the dam, turn right onto Corps Road to the project office.

Cross Timbers is a popular hiking trail that wends for 14 miles above the lake on rocky ledges and through the woodland. Of the 15 Corps-managed campgrounds, the 3 that are located in Texas are listed below. See the Oklahoma section of this guide for additional campgrounds at Lake Texoma. Accomodations, boat rentals and supplies are available at the many marinas located at the lake. Wildlife viewing within the project is excellent.

Dam Site: All year, 20 sites with electric & water hookups, $10-$16, dump, restrooms, showers. From Denison, Texas, travel 5 miles north on SR-91. The camping area is on the south side of the dam. 903-463-6455.

Juniper Point: Apr-Oct, 44 sites with electric & water hookups, 26 basic sites, $12-$18, drinking water, dump, restrooms, showers. From Whitesboro, Texas, travel 13 miles north on Hwy-377. The campground is on both sides of the highway as the highway enters the Willis Bridge crossing into Oklahoma. 903-523-4022.

Preston Bend: Apr-Oct, 26 sites with electric & water hookups and 12 sites with water, $12-$16, dump, restrooms, showers. From Pottsboro, Texas, travel 9 miles north on Hwy-120, follow signs. 903-786-8408.

11) LAVON LAKE

U.S. Army Corps of Engineers
3375 Skyview Drive
Wylie, TX 75098
Phone: 972-442-3141
District: Fort Worth

The 21,400-acre lake is located 30 miles northeast of Dallas. From Wylie, go 3 miles east on TX-78, then 1 mile north on CR-434 to the park headquarters.

There are three Corps-managed camping areas and a private marina available to RVs. The project features hiking, equestrian and bike trails operated by the county. Off road vehicles are prohibited at the lake. The Heard Natural Science Museum & Wildlife Sanctuary in nearby McKinney, Texas, features natural history exhibits and nature trails.

Clear Lake: Mar-Sep, 23 sites with electric & water hookups, $18, dump, restrooms, showers. From Princeton, go 9 miles south on FM-982 (changes to CR-735). Watch for Clear Lake signs. Take FM-436 and follow to dead end. 972-442-3014.

East Fork: All year, 50 sites with electric (50amp) & water hookups and 12 tent only sites, some pull thrus, &10-$18, drinking water, dump, restrooms, showers, horse trail, public marina. From Wylie, Texas, take Hwy-78 east to FM-389 (Eubanks). Go north on FM-389, stay to the right at the fork and continue on FM-389 to the park. 972-442-3014.

Lavonia: Feb-Sep, 38 sites with electric & water hookups and 15 tent only sites, $10-$18, drinking water, dump, restrooms, showers, swimming. Gates locked at 10pm. From Wylie, Texas, take Hwy-78 east to CR-486 (Lake Road), follow signs. 972-442-3141, (1301 CR-486, Lavon, TX 75166).

12) LEWISVILLE LAKE

U.S. Army Corps of Engineers
1801 North Mill Street
Lewisville, TX 75057
Phone: 469-645-9100
District: Fort Worth

The 28,980-acre lake is adjacent to Interstate 35E at exit 457A northwest of Dallas. The project office located on Mill Street is open on weekdays.

Three hiking and equestrian trails are on project land. There is one Corps-managed campgrounds as well as a private campground. Golf is nearby. Boat rentals are available at the marina. In the heart of the Dallas-Fort Worth Metroplex, there are many sightseeing, shopping and restaurant opportunities in the area.

Hickory Creek: All year, 116 sites with electric (some 50amp) and water hookups and 10 tent sites, $10-$20, drinking water, dump, restrooms, showers, laundry, swimming, playground, convenience store. From I-35 exit 457B, follow the service road to the overpass leading to the southbound access service road and follow to Turbeville Road, then right to Point Vista Road. Turn left for 1 mile to the park. 469-645-9100.

13) NAVARRO MILLS LAKE

U.S. Army Corps of Engineers
1175 FM-667
Purdon, TX 76679
Phone: 254-578-1431
District: Fort Worth

The 5,070-acre lake is 71 miles south of Dallas and 18 miles west of Corsicana, Texas. From Corsicana, go 20 miles southwest on TX-31 then 1 mile north on FM-667.

There are 4 Corps-managed campgrounds at the lake. Points of interest in

Corsicana, the Fruit Cake Capital, include Collin Street Bakery, Pioneer Village and an Indian art and crafts exhibit at the Gooch Library.

Liberty Hill: All year, 98 sites with electric (some 50amp) & water (14 with sewer hookup), $14-$32, some pull thrus, drinking water, dump, restrooms, showers, swimming, playground, convenience store, public marina. From Dawson, junction of SR-31 & FM-709, travel north on FM-709 for 4 miles. 254-578-1431.

Oak: All year, 5 full hookup sites (some 50amp) and 43 sites with electric (some 50amp) & water hookups, $16-$20, drinking water, dump, restrooms, showers, interpretive trail, swimming. From junction of SR-31 & FM-667 (38 miles northeast of Waco) travel 1.5 miles north on FM-667 to the park. 254-578-1431.

Pecan Point Park: Apr-Sep, 5 sites with electric (some 50amp) & water hookups and 30 basic sites, $8-$10, drinking water, dump, restrooms, hiking, biking, some lakefront sites. From junction of SR-31 & FM-667 (38 miles east of Waco) travel about 5 miles north on FM-667 to the intersection of FM-744. Go 3 miles on FM-744, then 2 miles south on FM-1578 to CR-3360 west for .2 mile. 254-578-1431.

Wolf Creek: Apr-Sep, 50 sites with electric & water hookups and 22 basic sites, $12-$24, drinking water, dump, restrooms, showers. From junction of SR-31 & FM-667 (38 miles northeast of Waco) travel about 3 miles north on FM-667 to FM-639 for 2 miles west. 254-578-1431.

14) PAT MAYSE LAKE

U.S. Army Corps of Engineers
P.O. Box 129
Powderly, TX 75473
Phone: 903-732-3020
District: Tulsa District

The 5,990-acre lake is located in the Red River Basin in Lamar County. The damsite is on Sanders Creek, a tributary of the Red River, about 12 miles north of Paris, TX. From Paris, take US-271 north for 15 miles, then FM-906 west for 3 miles to the lake.

Two Corps-managed camping areas are available and boat ramps are conveniently located. A few miles north of the project area are the famed Red River Bottoms where waterfowl congregate in great numbers.

Pat Mayse East & West: All year, 103 sites with electric & water hookups, $10-$15, dump, restrooms, showers, swimming. Gates close at 10pm. Sites at Pat Mayse East are non-reservable. From Paris, Texas, junction US-271, travel north for 12 miles to FM-906 west, then 4 miles to FM-197. Turn west for 3 miles to CR-35810, turn left 1 mile to CR-35800, turn left into the park. 903-732-4955 or 903-732-3020.

Sanders Cove: All year, 86 sites with electric & water hookups and 3 tent sites, $15, drinking water, dump, restrooms, showers, swimming. Gates close at 10pm. From Paris, Texas, take US-271 north for 12 miles to FM-906 west, then 1 mile to CR-35920, follow signs. 903-732-4956 or 903-732-3020.

15) PROCTOR LAKE

U.S. Army Corps of Engineers
2180 FM-2861
Comanche, TX 76442
Phone: 254-879-2424
District: Fort Worth

The 4,610-acre lake is located 97 miles southwest of Fort Worth in the historic territory of the Comanche Indians. From Comanche, Texas, go 5 miles east on US-377, then 2 miles north on FM-2861. Proctor Lake is a popular destination for sportsmen, birders and naturalists.

There are three full service Corps campgrounds at the lake, which is a popular fishing destination for Hybrid Striper and Crappie. Boat ramps, fish cleaning stations and swimming areas are at all campgrounds.

Copperas Creek: All year, 7 full hookup sites, 60 sites with electric hookups, $16-$32, drinking water, dump, restrooms, showers. From Comanche, Texas, take US-67/377 northeast for 5 miles, then left on FM-2861 for 2.5 miles. 254-879-2498 or 254-879-2424.

Promontory: Apr-Sep, 69 sites with electric (some 50amp) and water hookups and 30 basic sites, $8-$32, drinking water, dump, restrooms, showers, swimming. From Comanche, Texas, take SR-16 north for 12 miles to the town of Downing, then turn right on FM-2318 for 5 miles. 254-893-7545.

Sowell Creek: All year, 11 full hookup sites (50amp) and 50 sites with electric (some 50amp) & water hookups, $16-$32, drinking water, dump, restrooms, showers, swimming. From Comanche, Texas, take US-67/377 east for 12 miles to the town of Proctor, then left on FM-1476 west for 2 miles to RR-6, turn left .5 mile. 254-879-2322.

16) SAM RAYBURN RESERVOIR

U.S. Army Corps of Engineers
Rt-3 Box 486
Jasper, TX 75951
Phone: 409-384-5716
District: Fort Worth

Sam Rayburn Lake is the largest body of water within the State of Texas. It is in the Piney Woods, 18 miles north of Jasper. With 114,500 surface acres and 750 miles of shoreline, the project spans five counties. From Jasper, Texas, go 15 miles northwest on TX-63, then east on TX-255 and follow signs to the project office located next to Overlook Park.

A 28-mile hiking trail is in nearby Sabine National Forest. Restaurants, shopping and sightseeing can be found in local towns. 16 boat ramps are located conveniently throughout. There are six Corps-managed areas for RV camping.

Ebenezer: All year, 10 sites with electric & water hookups, 9 basic sites and 11 tent sites, equestrian camping at selected sites, $9-$18, drinking water, dump, restrooms, laundry. No boat ramp at this campground. From Jasper, Texas, take US-96 north about 12 miles to the intersection of FM-255, then west on 255 about 8 miles. 409-384-5716.

Hanks Creek: All year, 47 sites with electric (some 50amp) & water hookups, $16-$18, drinking water, dump, restrooms, showers. From Zavalla TX, take SR-147 northeast for .25 mile, then north on FM-2109 for 8 miles to FM-2801. Turn right (east) on FM-2801 for 2 miles. 409-384-5716.

Mill Creek: All year, 110 sites with electric (some 50amp) & water hookups, $16-$18, drinking water, dump, restrooms, showers, swimming, playground. From Jasper TX, take US-96 north for 18 miles to Brookland TX, then Loop-149 for 2 miles to the intersection with Spur-165. Go west 1 mile. 409-384-5716.

Rayburn: All year, 24 sites with electric (some 50amp) and water hookups, 22 basic sites, $11-$18, drinking water, dump, restrooms, showers, laundry, playground, swimming. On the north shore. From Pineland, Texas, take FM-83 west for 10 miles, then south on FM-705 for 11 miles, then west on FM-3127 for 1.5 miles. 409-384-5716.

San Augustine: All year, 100 sites with electric & water hookups (including 5 tent-only), $16-$18, drinking water, dump, restrooms, showers, interpretive trail, swimming beach, playground, volleyball, basketball, horseshoes. From Pineland, Texas, take FM-83 west 6 miles, then south on FM-1751 for 4 miles. 409-384-5716.

Twin Dikes: All year, 9 full hookup sites (some 50amp), 10 sites with electric (some 50amp) and water hookups, 27 basic sites, $12-$18, drinking water, dump, restrooms, showers, laundry. From Jasper, Texas, take US-96 north for 13 miles, then west on Recreation Road (FM-255) for 5 miles. 409-384-5716.

17) SOMERVILLE LAKE

U.S. Army Corps of Engineers
6500 Thornberry Drive
Somerville, TX 77879
Phone: 979-596-1622
District: Fort Worth

Located 84 miles east of Austin and northwest of Houston, the project consists of 11,000 water acres and 19,000 land acres. From Austin, Texas, take US-290 east to Brenham, then SR-36 north for about 11.5 miles to FM-1948. Turn left, cross the railroad tracks and turn right, follow the road for about 4 miles across the dam and turn left into the office complex to the project office where information is available.

Two Corps-managed camping areas are located at Somerville Lake. Swimming areas can be found at Birch Creek and Nails Creek State Parks. Off road vehicles are prohibited.

Rocky Creek: All year, 82 sites with electric & water hookups and 121 basic sites, $12-$22, drinking water, dump, restrooms, showers, laundry. From Austin, Texas, take US-290 east, then SR-36 north for 11.5 miles, then left on FM-1948 for 5 miles, follow signs. 979-596-1622.

Yequa Creek: All year, 47 sites with electric & water hookups, 26 sites with water and 9 basic sites, $14-$20, drinking water, dump, restrooms, showers. From Austin, Texas, take US-290 east to Brenham, then SR-36 north for 11.5 miles, then left on FM-1948 for 2.5 miles, follow signs. 979-596-1622.

18) STILLHOUSE HOLLOW LAKE

U.S. Army Corps of Engineers
3740 FM-1670
Belton, TX 76513
Phone: 254-939-2461
District: Fort Worth

The 6,430-acre lake is located near Fort Hood, and 80 miles north of Austin. From Belton, go 5 miles southwest on US-190, then 4 miles left on FM-1670. The Clark Falls Environmental Center is located below the dam and includes a hiking trail along the Lampasas River, a spring-fed creek with a waterfall and several wildlife viewing points. There are hiking, biking and equestrian trails at the lake.

There are two Corps-managed campgrounds. Swimming is available at both campgrounds and at Stillhouse Park. Boat ramps, fishing docks and fish cleaning stations are conveniently located. Nearby historic sites include the Stage Coach Inn in Salado.

Dana Peak: All year, 25 sites with electric & water hookups and 10 tent sites, $16-$26, most sites are close to the shoreline, drinking water, dump, restrooms, showers, swimming. From I-35 in Belton, Texas, take US-190 west to Simmons Road exit. Cross under the highway and turn west on FM-2410, then south on Commanche Gap Road, 5 miles, follow signs. 254-698-4282.

Union Grove: All year, 37 sites with electric (some 50amp) & water hookups (including 7 tent sites), some pull thrus, $16-$32, most sites are along the shoreline, drinking water, dump, restrooms, showers, swimming. From I-35 in Salado, take FM-2484 exit and travel west about 5 miles. 254-947-0072.

19) WACO LAKE

U.S. Army Corps of Engineers
3801 Zoo Park Drive
Waco, TX 76708
Phone: 254-756-5359
District: Fort Worth

The 7,270-acre lake is on the northwest side of Waco. In McLennan County, the project is entirely within the city limits of Waco. From I-35 exit 330, go west on TX-6, exit at Twin Bridges, follow signs.

Special use areas at the project include a model airplane area and a soccer complex. There are three Corps-managed camping areas; free educational programs and live exhibits are presented every Saturday night during the summer at the amphitheater in Reynolds Creek Park. Camping is also available at the Waco Marina. The marina features a floating restaurant. Dogs on leashes are permitted on the six-mile hiking and biking trail. Nearby Cameron Park is the largest municipal park in the country. The nation's oldest suspension bridge (1870) still in operation is located in Waco. Golf is nearby.

Airport: All year, 50 sites with electric (50amp) & water hookups (some have sewer) and 13 tent sites, some pull thrus, $12-$24, dump, restrooms, showers. Located on the north shore of the lake .25 mile west of the dam. From I-35 take exit 339 (Lake Shore Dr.) and exit west, travel to Airport Road, then right for 2 miles, follow signs. 254-756-5359.

Midway: All year, 27 sites with electric (some 50amp) and water hookups (some with sewer), $12-$36, dump, restrooms, showers. Located on the east shore of the South Bosque River. From I-35 exit 330, take SR-6 for about 5 miles and take the Midway Park exit. Circle under the bridge .5 mile on the service road. 254-756-5359.

Reynolds Creek: All year, 94 sites with electric (some 50amp) & water hookups and 6 tent sites, $12-$20, dump, restrooms, showers. From I-35 exit 330, take SR-6 north for 7 miles to Speegleville Road, exit right and go 1 mile to the stop sign, go straight and curve left, 1 mile to the entrance, follow signs. 254-756-5359.

20) WHITNEY LAKE

U.S. Army Corps of Engineers
285 Corps Road 3602
Clifton, TX 76634
Phone: 254-694-3189
District: Fort Worth

The 23,560-acre lake, located in the Prairies and Lakes region of Texas, is 65 miles south of Fort Worth and 35 miles north of Waco on the Brazos River. From I-35 exit 368 take SR-22 west 12 miles to Whitney, continue on SR-22 and follow signs to the dam.

Seven Corps-managed parks are suitable for RVs. Additional camping can be found at private parks and a state park on the lake. There are 11 boat ramps conveniently located around the lake. There is excellent wildlife viewing throughout the project.

Cedar Creek: All year, 20 sites, non-reservable, free, drinking water, restrooms. From Whitney Lake Dam, take SR-22 east to the city of Whitney, then FM-993 north about 5 miles, then turn left on CR-2604, follow signs. 254-694-3189.

Cedron Creek: Apr-Sep, 57 sites with electric (some 50amp) & water hookups, $16-$20, drinking water, dump, restrooms, showers, playground, swimming, convenience store. From I-35 exit 368 (Hillsboro), take SR-22 west for 12 miles into Whitney, then Hwy-933 north for 3 miles, then left on FM-1713 and cross the bridge over the lake. Turn at the first road on the left and follow signs. 254-694-3189.

Kimball Bend: All year, 36 sites with electric (50amp) and water hookups, $20, drinking water, restrooms, dump, showers. From Koppert, TX go north on Hwy-56 for about 2.5 miles, then right onto Hwy-174 about 2.3 miles, then left into park (just before the bridge). 254-694-3189.

Lofers Bend East & West Areas: All year, 136 sites with electric (some 50amp) & water hookups, some pull thrus, $12-$20, drinking water, dump, restrooms, showers. Gates close at 10pm. From I-35 exit 368 (Hillsboro), take SR-22 west for 12 miles into Whitney, continue 7 miles and turn right before the dam. Follow the park road to the 4-way stop. Turn left to West Lofers or turn right to East Lofers. 254-694-3189.

McCown Valley: All year, 52 sites with electric (some 50amp) & water hookups, some pull thrus, $12-$20, drinking water, dump, restrooms, showers, horseshoes, swimming, equestrian camping area. From I-35 exit 368, take SR-22 west and go 12 miles into Whitney, exit at FM-933 north for 2.5 miles, then FM-1713 for 6 miles west, follow signs. 254-694-3189.

Plowman Creek: All year, 24 sites with electric & water hookups and 10 sites with water only, $12-$16, dump, restrooms, showers, playground, basketball, convenience store. From Kopper, Texas, travel 1 mile south on FM-56, follow signs. 254-694-3189.

Steele Creek: All year, 21 sites, no hookups, non-reservable, free, drinking water, restrooms. From FM-927, go 1 mile east on FM-56, then northeast on the gravel road. 254-694-3189.

21) WRIGHT PATMAN LAKE

U.S. Army Corps of Engineers
P.O. Box 1817 – 64 Clear Springs Park
Texarkana, TX 75501
Phone: 903-838-8781
District: Fort Worth

Located on the Sulphur River, 9 miles southwest of Texarkana, the lake covers about 33,000 water acres. From Texarkana, go south on US-59 for 9 miles, then west on FM-2148 to the lake entrance. The project is nestled in the southern pine woods near the Arkansas border.

Four camping areas are available for RVs. A trail system connects Rocky Point and Piney Point campgrounds. Swimming beaches are located at North Shore area and at Atlanta State Park. Restaurants, shopping, sightseeing and riverboat gaming are nearby. Wildlife viewing is excellent, especially in winter when many migratory birds, including Bald Eagles, are in the area.

Clear Spring: All year, 85 sites with electric (some 50amp) and water hookups and 15 tent-only sites, $10-$22, drinking water, dump, restrooms, showers, swimming beach, playground, basketball, horseshoes. From Texarkana, take US-59 south, then west on FM-2148 to the lake entrance, follow the park road west. 903-838-8781 or 903-838-8636.

Malden Lake: All year, 39 sites with electric (some 50amp) & water hookups, $18-$36, drinking water, dump, restrooms, showers. From I-30 exit 201, travel on SR-8 south, through Maud, Texas, and continue south about 6 miles. Malden Park is on the north side of the lake. 903-585-2497.

Piney Point: Mar-Sep, 49 sites with electric (some 50 amp) & water hookups and 20 tent-only sites, non-reservable, $16-$20, drinking water, dump, restrooms, showers, hiking trail, volleyball. From Texarkana, take US-59 south for 12 miles. Take the first right past the Sulphur River Bridge, follow signs. 903-838-8781.

Rocky Point: All year, 14 full hookup sites (some 50amp) and 110 sites with electric (some 50amp) and water hookups, many waterfront sites, $16-$22, drinking water, dump, restrooms, showers, laundry, swimming, playground, interpretive trail. Located on the eastern shore of the lake. From Texarkana, take US-59 south to the lake. The park is just south of the dam on the right. 903-838-8781.

Vermont

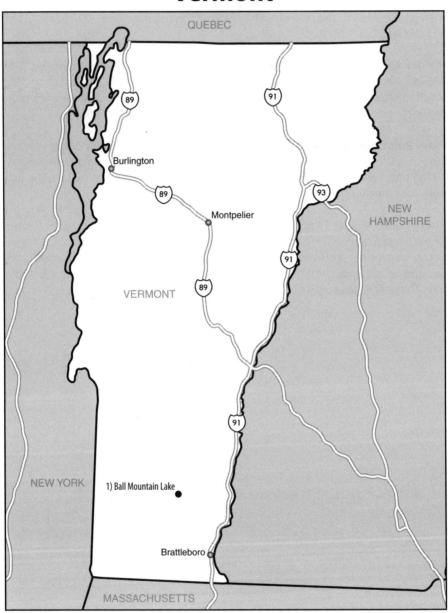

1) Ball Mountain Lake

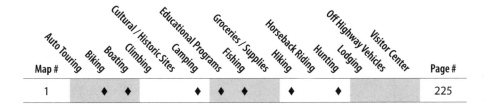

Map #	Auto Touring	Biking	Boating	Climbing	Cultural / Historic Sites	Camping	Educational Programs	Fishing	Groceries / Supplies	Hiking	Horseback Riding	Hunting	Lodging	Off Highway Vehicles	Visitor Center	Page #
1		♦	♦				♦	♦	♦		♦		♦			225

1) BALL MOUNTAIN LAKE

U.S. Army Corps of Engineers
88 Ball Mountain Lane
Jamaica, VT 05343
Phone: 802-874-4881
District: New England

The 75-acre lake surrounded by 965 land acres is located some 30 miles northwest of Brattleboro in southern Vermont. The project is a popular destination for outdoor recreation in summer and winter. From Brattleboro, travel north on SR-30 to the town of Jamaica and follow signs to the dam and project office.

The camping area, located about 5 miles north of the Ball Mountain Lock & Dam, is nestled in the Green Mountains along the Winhall Brook. Most sites are streamside. Interpretive programs are presented by park rangers in the campground amphitheater. Other amenities at the campground include a ballfield, playground, volleyball and basketball courts. On two weekends each year (in April and September) Ball Mountain Dam releases water for whitewater rafting, canoeing and kayaking.

Winhall Brook: Apr-Oct, 23 sites with electric & water hookups and 88 basic sites, $18-$22, drinking water, dump, restrooms, showers, swimming, hiking trails. From Brattleboro, Vermont, take SR-30 north to Rt-100. Go 2.5 miles north on Rt-100 to Winhall Station Road, then 1 mile to the campground. 802-874-4881, (919 Winhall Station Rd, South Londonderry, VT 05155).

Virginia

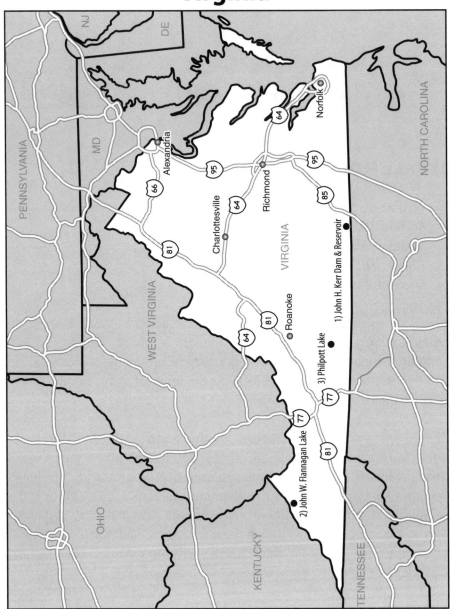

1)   John H. Kerr Dam & Reservoir
2)   John W. Flannagan Lake
3)   Philpott Lake

Map #	Auto Touring	Biking	Boating	Climbing	Cultural/Historic Sites	Camping	Educational Programs	Fishing	Groceries/Supplies	Hiking	Horseback Riding	Hunting	Lodging	Off Highway Vehicles	Visitor Center	Page #
1		♦	♦			♦		♦	♦	♦		♦			♦	227
2			♦			♦		♦		♦		♦				228
3		♦	♦			♦		♦		♦		♦			♦	229

1) JOHN H. KERR DAM & RESERVOIR

U.S. Army Corps of Engineers
1930 Mays Chapel Road
Boydton, VA 23917
Phone: 434-738-6143
District: Wilmington

The project, with 50,000 water acres, 70,000 land acres and 900 miles of wooded, cove-studded shoreline, stretches across the VA/NC state line. The Visitor Center, adjacent to the dam next to North Bend Park, is open on weekdays. The Tanner Environmental Education Center is just down the road at the intersection of Mays Chapel Road & Rt-4 (which leads across the dam). The Tanner Center is open Thursday to Sunday, Memorial Day through Labor Day. From Richmond, take I-85 south to exit 12, then US-58 west to VA-4 south to the dam and Visitor Center.

There are 30 recreation areas at the project. The reservoir is widely known for bass fishing. Four Corps campgrounds as well as Virginia State Parks and North Carolina State Parks are available for RV camping. Boat ramps and fishing piers are conveniently located throughout. Ranger programs are presented in season at North Bend.

Buffalo Park: May-Sep, 19 sites, no hookups, $15, drinking water, dump, restrooms, showers, swimming. From Clarksville, Virginia, travel 8 miles west on US-58 to Buffalo Springs Road (SR-1501) to Carters Point Road. 434-738-6143.

Longwood Park: Apr-Oct, 34 sites with electric (some 50amp) & water hookups and 24 basic sites, $15-$30, drinking water, dump, restrooms, showers, swimming, playground. Gates close at 11pm. From Clarksville, Virginia, take US-15 south about 5 miles, follow signs. 434-738-6143 or 434-374-2711.

North Bend: Apr-Oct, 94 sites with electric & water hookups and 155 basic sites, $15-$20, drinking water, dump, restrooms, showers, interpretive trail, swimming, playground. Gates close at 11pm. From South Hill, Virginia, take US-58 west to SR-4 (Buggs Island Road) and follow for 6 miles and bear right at the dam to the park entrance. 434-738-0059.

Rudds Creek: Apr-Oct, 75 sites with electric (50amp) & water hookups and 24 basic sites, $15-$30, drinking water, dump, restrooms, showers, swimming. Gates close at 11pm. From Boydton, Virginia, travel 2 miles west on US-58 and follow signs into the recreation area. 434-738-6827 or 434-738-6143.

2) JOHN W. FLANNAGAN LAKE

U.S. Army Corps of Engineers
Rt 1 Box 268
Haysi, VA 24256
Phone: 276-835-9544
District: Huntington

Located in the Cumberland Mountains on the Kentucky state line, the 1,145 acre lake is northwest of the town of Haysi. The project lands adjoin the Jefferson National Forest. From US-460 take SR-80 into Haysi. Take VA-63, VA-614 and VA-739 (7 miles), to the dam, follow signs. The project office and Visitor Center are located at the dam.

There are three Corps-managed camping areas at the project. Boat ramps are conveniently located and a marina has docking facilities and supplies.

Cranesnest: May-Sep, 25 sites, no hookups, non-reservable, $10-$12, drinking water, dump, restrooms, showers. From Clintwood go 2 miles southeast on SR-83, then north. 276-835-9544.

Lower Twin: May-Sep, 15 sites with electric hookups, 17 basic sites, non-reservable, $10-$12, drinking water, dump, restrooms, showers, amphitheater. From SR-739, go 3 miles west on SR-611 and exit southeast on SR-683. 276-835-9544.

Pound River: May-Sep, 23 sites, no hookups, non-reservable, $10-$12, drinking water, dump, restrooms, showers. From Clintwood go .2 mile west on SR-83, then 2 miles north on SR-631. 276-835-9544.

3) PHILPOTT LAKE

U.S. Army Corps of Engineers
1058 Philpott Dam Road
Bassett, VA 24055
Phone: 276-629-2703
District: Wilmington

Philpott Lake is located south of Roanoke, northwest of Martinsville, and west of US-220. Over 6,000 acres of surrounding land, 3,000 acres of water and a power plant make up the Philpott project. From Roanoke, go south on US-220 to the Bassett, Virginia, exit. Travel west on VA-57 for about 6 miles to Philpott Dam Road. Look for the brown directional sign and turn right, 1 mile to the Visitor Assistance Center which is open daily 9-5, April to October. An overlook at Philpott Park gives visitors a spectacular view of the lake and the Blue Ridge Mountains.

Goose Point: Apr-Oct, 53 sites with electric (50amp) & water and 10 basic sites, some pull thrus, $18-$22, drinking water, dump, restrooms, showers, swimming, playground, amphitheater. From US-220 take the Bassett, Virginia, exit onto VA-57 and go about 10 miles to Goose Point Road (follow brown directional sign). Turn right and go 5 miles on the paved park road. 276-629-1847.

Horseshoe Point: May-Sep, 15 sites with electric & water and 34 basic sites, some pull thrus, $18-$22, drinking water, dump, restrooms, showers, swimming, playground. The park is located in a rural and sparsely populated part of Franklin County near the small community of Henry. From US-220, turn onto Henry Road (SR-605) and go 8 miles. Turn left onto Horseshoe Point Road, follow signs. 540-365-7385, (3950 Horseshoe Point Rd, Henry, VA 24102).

Jamison Mill: Apr-Oct, 5 sites with electric hookups and 4 basic sites, some pull thrus, non-reservable, $18-$21, drinking water, dump, restrooms, showers. From Henry, Virginia, travel 5 miles northwest on CR-605, then 2 miles south on CR-778. 276-629-2703.

Salthouse Branch: Apr-Oct, 26 sites with electric (50amp) & water and 67 basic sites, $18-$22, drinking water, dump, restrooms, showers, interpretive trail, swimming, playground, amphitheater. From US-220, turn onto Henry Road (SR-605), go 6 miles, turn left onto Knob Church Road, go 2 miles and turn left onto the Salthouse Branch access road. 540-365-7005, (620 Salthouse Branch Rd, Henry, VA 24102).

Washington

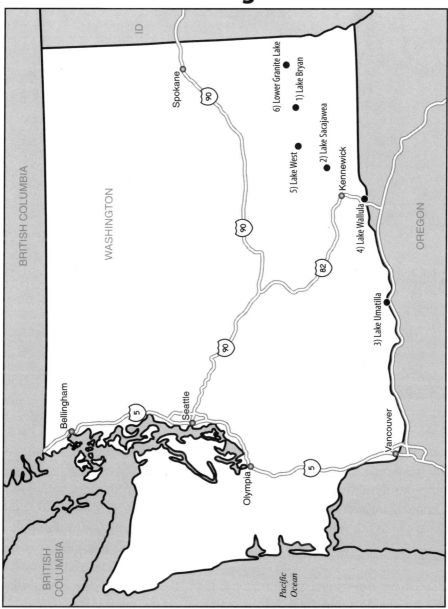

1) Lake Bryan
2) Lake Sacajawea
3) Lake Umatilla

4) Lake Wallula
5) Lake West
6) Lower Granite Lake

Map #	Auto Touring	Biking	Boating	Climbing	Cultural / Historic Sites	Camping	Educational Programs	Groceries / Supplies	Fishing	Horseback Riding	Hiking	Hunting	Off Highway Vehicles	Lodging	Visitor Center	Page #
1			♦			♦			♦		♦		♦	♦		♦	232
2			♦		♦	♦	♦	♦	♦	♦	♦		♦			♦	233
3			♦			♦			♦		♦					♦	234
4	♦		♦		♦	♦	♦	♦	♦		♦			♦		♦	235
5			♦			♦	♦	♦	♦		♦		♦			♦	236
6	♦	♦	♦			♦	♦	♦	♦	♦	♦			♦		♦	236

1) LAKE BRYAN

U.S. Army Corps of Engineers
1001 Little Goose Dam Road
Dayton, WA 99328
Phone: 509-751-0240
District: Walla Walla

Lake Bryan and Little Goose Dam are located just west of the Lower Granite area. The lake is in a remote part of the Lower Snake River and the landscape features steep canyon walls and few trees. The lake is 45 miles north of Walla Walla and 8 miles northeast of Starbuck. A Visitor Center is on the south end of the dam – follow the Little Goose Dam access road north out of the town of Starbuck. Lake Bryan is a popular destination for fishing and hunting and semi-primitive camping.

Three Corps-managed camping areas listed below are all primitive. Full-service campgrounds with RV hookups are at the nearby Boyer Park & Marina and Central Ferry Park.

Illia Landing: All year, free primitive camping, non-reservable, drinking water, restrooms, fishing pier, boat ramp. From the Lower Granite Dam, go 3 miles west on Almota Ferry Road. 509-751-0240.

Little Goose Landing: All year, free primitive camping, non-reservable, restrooms, fishing pier, boat ramp. From the town of Starbuck, go 9 miles northeast on Little Goose Dam Road. 509-751-0240.

Willow Landing: All year, free primitive camping, non-reservable, restrooms, fishing pier, boat ramp. From Central Ferry State Park go 1 mile south on Hwy-127, then 4 miles east on Deadman Road and 5 miles north on Hasting Hill Road. 509-751-0240.

2) LAKE SACAJAWEA

U. S Army Corps of Engineers
1215 East Ainsworth
Pasco, WA 99301
Phone: 509-547-2048
District: Walla Walla

Lake Sacajawea is formed by the Ice Harbor Dam and is the first of the reservoir/lakes in the Lower Snake River Project in southeastern Washington. The lake stretches for 31 miles between the Ice Harbor Lock & Dam northward to the Lower Monumental Lock & Dam. To reach the Visitor Center from junction US-12 in Burbank travel on SR-124 east for 5.5 miles, then 2.5 miles north on Monument Dr. The Visitor Center is on the south end of the dam and features a fish viewing room and exhibits on the early inhabitants of the region. It is open daily April through October.

Three of the six Corps-managed areas offer full-service camping for RVs. Ranger programs are presented in season at the Charbonneau amphitheater. The lake has great appeal to boaters and anglers and the white sandy beaches are an attractive feature.

Charbonneau: Apr-Oct, 15 full hookup sites, 39 sites with electric hookups, $18-$22, some pull thrus, drinking water, dump, restrooms, showers, playground, swimming, public marina. All sites are paved and shaded. From Pasco WA, take US-12 east. After crossing the Snake River Bridge, take the next left onto SR-124. Travel east on 124 through Burbank WA and pass the turnoff to the Visitor Center, continue eastbound on SR-124 and turn left, heading north on Sun Harbor Dr. Follow Sun Harbor Dr for

1.5 miles, then turn left on Charbonneau Road. 509-547-2048, (642 Campground Rd, Burbank, WA 99323).

Fishhook Park: May-Sep, 41 sites with electric & some with water hookups, 20 basic sites and 20 tent sites, $14-$22, drinking water, dump, restrooms, showers, swimming, playground. From Pasco, Washington, take US-12 east and, after crossing the Snake River Bridge, go east on SR-124 for 19 miles, then left (north) on Fishhook Park Road for 4 miles. 509-547-2048, (4562 Fishhook Park Rd, Prescott, WA 99348).

Lake Emma: All year, free primitive camping, non-reservable, no services. From Pasco-Kahlotus Hwy, go west 3 miles on Murphy Road. 509-547-2048.

Matthews: All year, free primitive camping, non-reservable, restrooms, boat ramp, fishing pier. From Burbank, travel 26 miles east on Hwy-124, then 8.6 miles north on Lyons Ferry Road to Clyde, 15.2 miles north (left) on Lower Monumental Road, go left 1 mile before the dam, then east 1 mile. 509-547-2048.

Walker: All year, free primitive camping, non-reservable, no services. From Burbank, travel 26 miles east on Hwy-124, then 8.6 miles north on Lyons Ferry Road to Clyde, then 4 miles northwest (left) on Lower Monumental Road, then 9.2 miles west on Wooden Road. 509-547-2048.

Windust Park: Apr-Sep, 24 sites, no hookups, free, drinking water, dump, restrooms, showers, swimming, playground. From Pasco, Washington, take the Pasco-Kahlotus Highway for 30 miles to Burr Canyon Road, then 6 miles to the campground. 509-547-2048, (5262 Burr Canyon Rd, Pasco, WA 00301).

3) LAKE UMATILLA

U.S. Army Corps of Engineers
P.O. Box 564
The Dalles, OR 97058
Phone: 541-296-1181
District: Portland

John Day Dam and Lake Umatilla is 216 miles upstream from the mouth of the Columbia River and is located at exit 109 off I-84 in northern Oregon. The project consists of a navigation lock, spillway, powerhouse and fish passage facilities on both shores of the 76-mile long lake. Water recreation is plentiful on the John Day River and along the lake.

Corps-managed campgrounds are on both the Oregon and Washington sides of Lake Umatilla and are listed in their respective state sections of this guide.

Cliffs: All year, free primitive camping, non-reservable, restrooms, boat ramp. Near the dam, north of US-97. 541-296-1181.

Plymouth: Apr-Oct, 17 full hookup sites, 15 sites with electric (some 50amp) & water hookups, $18-$24, drinking water, dump, restrooms, shower, laundry, swimming, playground, boat launch. The campground is nestled in the high desert along the Columbia River. From Kennewick, Washington, go south 23 miles on I-82 to exit 131, then west on SR-14 for 1.5 miles to the campground. 541-506-7816.

4) LAKE WALLULA

U.S. Army Corps of Engineers
82925 Devore Road
Umatilla, OR 97882
Phone: 541-922-2268
District: Walla Walla

Lake Wallula was formed by McNary Lock & Dam on the WA/OR border. It is located along the Columbia River in eastern Washington. North of the junction of I-82 (exit 1) & US-730, the Visitor Center is 1 mile north of Umatilla, and features interpretive displays and fish viewing rooms.

On the northern sector of the lake, near the junction of US-12 & US-730 is an area known as Wallup Gap, where the canyon narrows. The Gap is the site of colorful Indian lore and is a place where interesting natural phenomenon occurred during an ancient catastrophic event known as the Great Missoula Floods. Ranger programs in season are presented in the campground amphitheater. The campground is convenient to the Tri Cities where there are shopping malls and other activities. The McNary National Wildlife Refuge is next to Hood Park.

Hood Park: May-Sep, 69 paved and shady sites with electric (some 50amp) hookups, $11-$22, drinking water, dump, restrooms, showers, swimming, playground, horseshoes, basketball. From Pasco, Washington, take US-12 east. After crossing the Snake River Bridge, take the next left at the junction of SR-124 to the park entrance. 509-547-2048.

5) LAKE WEST

U.S. Army Corps of Engineers
5520 Devil's Canyon Road
Kahlotus, WA 99335
Phone: 509-282-3219
District: Walla Walla

The second reservoir of the four major locks & dams of the Lower Snake River Project, Lake West consists of 6,590 water acres. It is nestled in a remote section of the river where visitors can enjoy the scenic surrounding countryside. A Visitor Center is on the northwest end of the dam. Travel 41.5 miles northeast of Pasco, WA on the Pasco-Kahlotus Hwy, go 6 miles south on Devil's Canyon Road. At the Lower Monumental Lock & Dam, visitors can watch barge traffic pass through the 100-foot tall navigation locks.

Primitive camping is offered at three Corps-managed areas. Full service camping is available at Lyons Ferry Marina.

Ayer Boat Basin: All year, free primitive camping, non-reservable, restrooms, boat ramp, fishing pier. From Burbank, travel 26 miles east on SR-124, then 24 miles north through Clyde and Pleasant View to Ayers, follow signs. 509-282-3219.

Devils Bench: All year, free primitive camping, non-reservable, restrooms, boat ramp, fishing pier. From Kahlotus, go south on SR-263 for 6 miles. 509-282-3219.

Riparia: All year, free primitive camping, non-reservable, restrooms. From Little Goose Dam, go 3 miles west on North Shore Road. 509-282-3219.

6) LOWER GRANITE LAKE

U. S. Army Corps of Engineers
885 Almota Ferry Road

Pomeroy, WA 99403
Phone: 509-843-1493
District: Walla Walla

Lower Granite Lake is located in deep southeastern Washington along the Lower Snake and Clearwater Rivers near the WA/ID border at Clarkson, WA and Lewiston, ID. A Visitor Center at the dam features a fish viewing room that allows visitors an up-close look at the many species of fish in the Lower Snake River, as well as movies and interactive displays. To reach the dam from Pomeroy, travel west on US-12 to SR-127 to Lower Deadman Road, then east to the dam. Maps and information about camping and area attractions are available. The dam and lake are in the heart of the Lewis & Clark expedition area. Nez Perce Historical Park is about 10 miles east of Lewiston on US-12.

The lake adjoins the towns of Clarkson, Washington and Lewiston, Idaho where a series of 22 levees have been designated as the Clearwater & Snake River National Recreation Trail for walking, bicycling and running. The three Corps-managed camping areas listed here are all primitive camping areas. Sites with hookups for RVs can be found at Hells Gate State Park (on the Idaho side of the historic Lewis & Clark area) and at private RV parks on the Washington side. Sightseeing, shopping and restaurants are in the area. Golf is nearby.

Camping areas listed below are managed by the Corps of Engineers Clarkston Resources Office, 100 Fair St, Clarkston, WA.

Blyton Landing: All year, free primitive camping, non-reservable, restrooms, fishing pier, boat ramp. From Lewiston, Idaho, go 20 miles west on CR-9000 (North Shore Snake River Road). 509-751-0240.

Nisqually John Landing: All year, free primitive camping, non-reservable, restrooms, fishing pier, boat ramp. From Lewiston, Idaho, go 15 miles west on CR-9000 (North Snake River Road). 509-751-0240.

Wawawai Landing: All year, free primitive camping, non-reservable, restrooms, fishing pier, boat ramp. From Lewiston, Idaho, go 28 miles west on CR-9000 (North Snake River Road) –or– 19 miles southwest of Pullman on Wawawai Road. 509-751-0240.

West Virginia

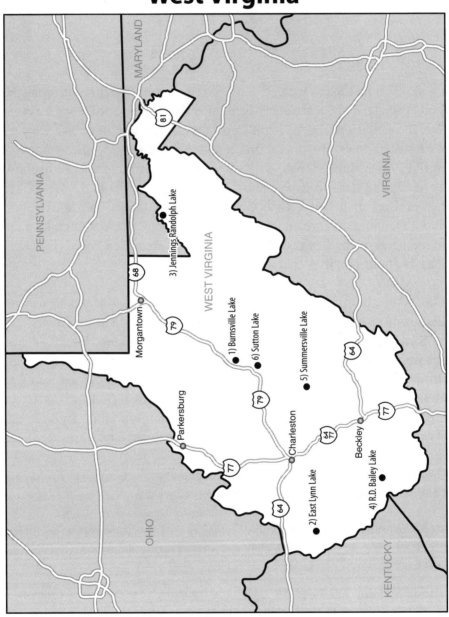

1) Burnsville Lake
2) East Lynn Lake
3) Jennings Randolph Lake
4) R.D. Bailey Lake
5) Summersville Lake
6) Sutton Lake

Map #	Auto Touring	Biking	Boating	Climbing	Cultural / Historic Sites	Camping	Educational Programs	Fishing	Groceries / Supplies	Hiking	Horseback Riding	Hunting	Lodging	Off Highway Vehicles	Visitor Center	Page #
1	♦		♦			♦	♦		♦	♦	♦	♦	♦	♦		♦	239
2	♦	♦	♦			♦			♦		♦		♦		♦	♦	240
3	♦		♦			♦	♦		♦	♦	♦		♦	♦			240
4		♦	♦			♦			♦		♦	♦	♦			♦	241
5	♦	♦	♦	♦	♦	♦			♦		♦	♦	♦	♦			242
6	♦	♦	♦			♦			♦		♦	♦	♦			♦	242

1) BURNSVILLE LAKE

U.S. Army Corps of Engineers
HC 10 Box 24
Burnsville, WV 26335
Phone: 304-853-2371
District: Huntington

The 968-acre lake is located northeast of Charleston, just east of I-79 at exit 79. It is on the Little Kanawha River three miles north of Burnsville. From I-79 exit 79, follow SR-5 to the Visitor Center at the dam. Wildlife viewing is excellent at the project.

There are two camping areas at the project. Boat rentals and supplies are available at the marina. The Bulltown Historical Village gives visitors a chance to see pioneer life during the Civil War era. Civil War re-enactments are held locally.

Bulltown: May-Sep, 204 sites with electric (some 50amp) hookups, $20-$26, drinking water, dump, restrooms, showers, laundry, interpretive trail, swimming, playground, horseshoes, basketball. From I-79 exit 67 (Flatwoods), travel north on US-19 for 10 miles and follow signs to the campground. 304-452-8006.

Rifle Run: Apr-Nov, 6 full hookup sites, 48 sites with electric & water hookups and 6 tent sites, $6-$18. From I-79 exit 79, go east on SR-5 for 3 miles. 304-853-2583.

2) EAST LYNN LAKE

U.S. Army Corps of Engineers
HC 85 Box 35-C
East Lynn, WV 25512
Phone: 304-849-2355
District: Huntington

The project, located south of Huntington near the Kentucky state line, covers 25,000 acres of land and water. The lake is on the Twelvepole Creek, 12 miles south of the town of Wayne. From Huntington, travel south on SR-152 to Wayne, then take SR-37 to the lake office and Visitor Center. Trail maps and information are available.

The Environmental Interpretive Center is located at the Overlook area. It features wildlife exhibits.

East Fork: May-Oct, 169 sites with electric hookups, $18-$30, drinking water, dump, restrooms, showers, swimming, nature trail, horseshoes, playground. From Huntington, I-64 exit 8, go south on SR-152 to Wayne, then east on SR-37 for 19 miles, follow signs. 304-849-5000 or 304-849-2355..

3) JENNINGS RANDOLPH LAKE

U.S. Army Corps of Engineers
P.O. Box 247
Elk Garden, WV 26717
Phone: 304-355-2346
District: Baltimore

The project, with a total of 4,500 acres of land and water, is located on the North Branch Potomac River in Garrett County, Maryland, on the West Virginia state line. From Cumberland, Maryland, travel south on US-220 then west on US-50, then north on WV-42 to WV-46 east, follow project signs.

There is an excellent trout stream at the project. Several whitewater releases are done each year when rafters put in to enjoy an 8-mile ride downstream. Along the way they pass through a wilderness area filled with history and natural beauty. A resident pair of Bald Eagles has been breeding at the lake since the late 1990's and they usually fledge two young a year.

Robert W. Craig Campground: Apr-Sep, 70 sites with electric hookups and 12 basic sites, $18-$22, drinking water, dump, restrooms, showers, interpretive trail, swimming beach, basketball, horseshoes. From Cumberland, Maryland, take US-220 south to US-50 west to WV-42 north, then north to WV-46 east, follow signs. 304-355-2346.

4) R.D. BAILEY LAKE

U.S. Army Corps of Engineers
Drawer 70
US Route 52 North
Justice, WV 24851
Phone: 304-664-3220
District: Huntington

This beautiful 1,005-acre lake is in the rugged terrain of deep southwestern West Virginia. The dam is on the Guyandotte River near the town of Justice. From Justice take SR-52 east and turn left at the R.D. Bailey sign.

The Visitor Center overlooks the lake and provides a breathtaking view of the dam, lake and surrounding forest. Viewing telescopes are mounted on the observation deck. The Center is open on weekdays. A marina is at the lake. Golf is nearby.

Guyandotte: Memorial Day-Labor Day, 94 sites with electric hookups, some pull thrus, non-reservable, $12-$14, drinking water, restrooms, showers, laundry. Camp sites are spread along a scenic 6-mile stretch of the Guyandotte River and the camppground is divided into four sections. From the dam, go 1.1 miles to US-52, then 2.2 miles south on SR-52, then 5.8 miles south on SR-97. 304-664-3220 or 304-664-9587 (24-hour information line).

5) SUMMERSVILLE LAKE

U.S. Army Corps of Engineers
2981 Summersville Lake Road
Summersville, WV 26651
Phone: 304-872-3412
District: Huntington

Summersville is the largest lake in central West Virginia. It is located 69 miles east of Charleston. From I-79 exit 57, travel south on US-19. At Mount Nebo take SR-129 west for 3 miles to the project office at the dam.

The project is noted for its spectacular cliffs and whitewater on the river. Technical rock climbing and whitewater rafting are available year-round nearby, with whitewater releases below the dam on the Gauley River in September and October. A marine & dive shop is located on the lake. Shopping and restaurants are in Summersville. Civil War historic sites are nearby.

Battle Run: May-Oct, 110 sites with electric hookups, $16-$24, drinking water, dump, restrooms, showers, laundry, swimming, playground, hiking trail, bike trail, public marina. Located 5 miles south of Summersville. From US-19 go 4 miles west on SR-129, follow signs. 304-872-3459.

6) SUTTON LAKE

U.S. Army Corps of Engineers
P.O. Box 426
South Stonewall Street
Sutton, WV 26601
Phone: 304-765-2816
District: Huntington

The project is located 70 miles north of Charleston in the wooded hills of central West Virginia. There are 1,440 water acres and 20,000 land acres. The lake winds 14 miles along the Elk River with many coves along the 45 miles of shoreline. From I-79 exit 64, take the Sutton/Gassaway exit, go north on Rt-4 and follow signs to Sutton Dam. The project office is at the dam, 1 mile east of Sutton.

Three Corps-managed camping areas are located at the lake. Local attractions include a riding stable, canoe livery, outlet mall and bowling alley. There is a marina at the lake.

Bakers Run – Mill Creek: May-Oct, 79 sites with electric hookups, some pull thrus, non-reservable, $12-$14, drinking water, dump, restrooms, showers, swimming. From I-79 exit 62, go 2 miles to Sutton, then 4 miles south on old US-19 (CR-19/40), then 12 miles east on CR-17. 304-765-2816 or 304-765-5631.

Bee Run: All year, 12 sites, no hookups, all pull thrus, non-reservable, $5, 20-foot RV length limit, drinking water, restrooms. From I-79 exit 67, go 1 mile east on SR-4, then 1.2 miles east on SR-15, turn right. 304-765-2816.

Gerald Freeman Campground: May-Oct, 74 sites with electric hookups and 84 basic sites (some have water hookups), $16-$22, drinking water, dump, restrooms, showers, laundry, marina. From I-79 exit 67, turn right on SR-4 and go 1 mile, then left on SR-15 and follow for 12 miles to the camping area. 304-765-2816 or 304-765-7756.

Wisconsin

1) Eau Galle River Lake
2) Mississippi River Camping
   a) DeSoto - Blackhawk Park
   b) Potosi - Grant River

Map #	Auto Touring	Biking	Boating	Climbing	Cultural / Historic Sites	Camping	Educational Programs	Fishing	Groceries / Supplies	Hiking	Horseback Riding	Hunting	Lodging	Off Highway Vehicles	Visitor Center	Page #
1	◆		◆			◆		◆		◆	◆					245
2	◆		◆			◆		◆		◆						245

1) EAU GALLE RIVER LAKE

U.S. Army Corps of Engineers
P.O. Box 190
W500 Eau Galle Dam Road
Spring Valley, WI 54767
Phone: 715-778-5562
District: St. Paul

This 150-acre lake is surrounded by recreation areas including the campground, beach, hiking and equestrian trails and boat launches. The project is located just north of Spring Valley, Wisconsin, and 50 miles east of Minneapolis, Minnesota. Local attractions, sightseeing and shopping are nearby. The Highland Ridge campground is about 4 miles south of I-94. Golf courses, gift stores and other attractions are nearby.

Highland Ridge: Apr-Dec, 35 sites with electric hookups, 3 basic and 7 tent sites, some equestrian sites, some pull thrus, $14-$24, drinking water, dump, restrooms, showers (fee), interpretive trail, playground. From I-94 exit 24, take CR-B south about 2 miles. Go east on CR-N for 2 miles, then south on CR-NN, follow signs. 715-778-5562.

2) MISSISSIPPI RIVER CAMPING

U.S. Army Corps of Engineers
District: Rock Island (309-794-4522)
District: St. Paul (507-895-6341)

Of the 15 Corps-managed campgrounds that dot the shoreline along the upper Mississippi River, two are in Wisconsin: Grand River Campground in Potosi and Blackhawk Park in De Soto. Directions to the camping areas are included with the listings, as are campground phone numbers.

Fishing and boating are major attractions of Mississippi River camping. Watching river traffic is a popular pastime. Historic sites can be found along the river as well as scenic drives.

2a) De Soto - Blackhawk Park

Blackhawk Park: Apr-Nov, 65 sites with electric (some 50amp) and 99 basic sites, $22, drinking water, dump, restrooms, showers (coin-operated), swimming, boat ramps, playground, volleyball, horseshoe pits. From LaCrosse, Wisconsin, travel 25 miles south on Hwy-35 and turn right on CR-B1. 608-648-3314, (E590 County Rd Bl, Desoto, WI 54624).

2b) Potosi - Grant River

Grant River Campground: Apr-Oct, 63 sites with 50amp electric hookups and 10 tent sites, $10-$16, drinking water, dump, restrooms, showers, boat ramp, playground. From Potosi, Wisconsin, go south for 2 miles on SR-133, turn left on River Lane, follow signs. 563-582-0881 or 800-645-0248.

Appendix A

About the Army Corps of Engineers

The U.S. Army Corps of Engineers is familiar to many of us from the Corps' involvement in dam construction to control river overflows, building lake reservoirs or producing hydroelectric power.

The Corps of Engineers is the steward of lands and waters at Corps water resource projects. It has responsibility for managing our nation's water resources infrastructure. The Corps systems for navigation, flood control and storm damage reduction, together with its efforts to restore aquatic ecosystems make an important contribution to the national welfare.

As a leading provider of outdoor recreation on federally-managed lands, the Corps recreation base is built primarily around the water. Consequently, the Corps has a dedicated focus on water safety. Rangers present water safety programs in season at many of the projects. Corps developed water safety programs, materials and information are available from the Corps at http://watersafety.usace.army.mil/

Part of the Army Corps of Engineers' charter is to open river and lakeside areas to the public and to provide recreational opportunities for fishing, boating and camping. Corps camping facilities are clean and well-maintained. The Corps operates 2,500 recreation areas at 463 projects (mostly lakes) and leases an additional 1,800 sites to state or local recreation authorities or private interests.

The Corps hosts about 360 million visits a year at its lakes, beaches and other areas and estimates that 25 million Americans (one in ten) visit a Corps project at least once a year. Supporting visitors to Corps recreation areas generates 600,000 jobs.

About Corps Projects

• Corps RV campsites generally have other basic amenities not mentioned in the individual listings such as picnic tables, lamp posts, fire rings and grills.

• Recreational opportunities are affected by high and low water marks that may impede shoreline access. Call the project office for information about current conditions.

• Fishing and hunting licenses are required in most states. Contact the state for information about hunting and fishing regulations, requirements, licensing and seasons.

• Directional signs to Corps projects are standard throughout the country. Look for the brown signs with white lettering.

• Camping fees listed are valid as of press time and are subject to change.

• Many Corps lakes have campgrounds that are not managed by the Corps, such as state parks and private concessionaires who lease space at the lake. These campgrounds generally do not accept Senior Pass or Access Pass discount cards, but it's always a good idea to ask.

• Corps campgrounds are subject to change without notice. New parks may be opened or existing parks closed or consigned to other agencies or concessionaires at any time.

• When a campground season of operation is listed as ending in September, it generally is the day after Labor Day.

Appendix B

General Rules for Corps Campgrounds

Camping
- If you are staying at a campground, you must camp only in those places specifically provided or marked.
- All vehicles, RVs and trailers must be parked on your campsite or driveway. Driving or parking off road is not permitted.
- Quiet hours are between 10 pm and 6 am. Please be considerate.
- Camping longer than 14 consecutive days is generally not allowed. At Corps of Engineers projects, 14 days within any 30 day period is the typical limit.
- The number of camping units per campsite varies and is set locally.

Sanitation
- Help prevent pollution by keeping garbage, litter and foreign substances out of lakes, streams and other waters.

Campfires
- Obey any restrictions on fires. Fires may be limited or prohibited at certain times.
- Within campgrounds and other recreation areas, fires may only be built in fire rings, stoves, grills or fireplaces provided for that purpose.
- Be sure your fire is completely extinguished before leaving. Do not leave your fire unattended. You are responsible for keeping fires under control.

Vehicle Operation
- Drivers must obey all traffic signs and operate their vehicles in accordance with posted regulations and applicable federal, state and local laws.
- Vehicles must be parked in designated areas only.

- Use of vehicles within campgrounds and other recreation areas is limited to entering and leaving those areas.

Pets and Animals
- Pets must be restrained or on a leash at all times while in developed recreation areas.
- Pets (except guide dogs) are not allowed in swimming areas or sanitary facilities.
- Saddle or pack animals are only allowed where authorized by posted instructions.

Fireworks
- Use of fireworks or other explosives within campgrounds and other recreation areas is prohibited.

Public Property
- Preserve and protect your Corps project areas. Leave natural areas the way you found them.
- Do not carve, chip, cut or damage any live trees.

Campsite Reservations

Recreation.gov (a private one-stop reservation service), handles all federal recreation reservations including Corps of Engineers campgrounds. Reservations may be made through this service for any of the campgrounds listed in this book (except those indicated as non-reservable). Campgrounds or selected sites listed as non-reservable are not handled by recreation.gov; call the project office for information.

There are two ways to make campsite reservations:

- On the Internet at www.recreation.gov. You may check availability and make a reservation online anytime.

- Call toll-free 1-877-444-6777 to check availability and make reservations over the phone. Telephone hours of operation are:

March 31 to October 31, 10am-midnight EST and November 1 to February 28, 10am-10pm EST.

When making a reservation you will be asked to provide the following information:

- Campground name, project and state,
- Arrival and departure dates,
- Type of site required,
- Number of people in your party,
- Discount, if applicable, including the number on your Senior Pass or Access Pass,
- Method of payment (Visa, MasterCard, American Express, Discover).

Individual sites may be reserved up to 6 months in advance. Reserved sites will be held until checkout time on the day following your scheduled arrival. Cancellation fees will be assessed for changes, cancellations and no-shows.

Appendix C

Volunteers Are Vital

As the steward of almost 12 million acres of land and water, the U.S. Army Corps of Engineers offers many volunteer positions in recreation and natural resources management. These include:

- Campground hosting
- Presenting educational programs
- Writing and editing materials for publication
- Developing computer programs
- Distributing information at visitor centers
- Conducting interpretive tours of dam sites

Volunteers generally swap their talents and services for a free campsite and amenities. A large contingent of willing volunteers apply each year to work at Corps projects. They like the spacious and tidy campsites and the clean, well-kept appearance of the recreation areas. They enjoy being outdoors and socializing with other campers. A volunteer assignment usually lasts for a camping season, about 6 months or so, and volunteers commit to about 18-20 hours a week.

The Corps maintains a Nationwide Volunteer Clearinghouse, a toll-free hotline, and a website for individuals who are interested in offering their time and talent to the Corps. Callers to the Clearinghouse toll-free number should be prepared to provide information about their interests, talents and the locations where they'd like to volunteer.

The Clearinghouse is basically a matchmaker, pairing up skilled, enthusiastic workers with people at Corps projects who need their services. You can log on to www.orn.usace.army.mil/volunteer/ to view volunteer positions available or call the Clearinghouse at 1-800-865-8337 to receive a Point of Contact list for your area of interest.

Appendix D

Money Saving Programs

Frequent visitors to Corps of Engineers projects can get significant savings with the America the Beautiful Senior Pass or Access Pass, recreation passes issued by the federal government. Both of these passes are honored at Corps of Engineers-managed campgrounds. The passes provide a 50 percent discount on federal use fees charged for facilities and services such as camping, swimming, parking, boat launching, and tours. In some cases where use fees are charged, only the pass signee will be given the 50 percent price reduction. It does not cover or reduce special recreation permit fees or fees charged by concessionaires.

Senior Pass
This pass is for citizens of the United States who are 62 or older. The cost for a Senior Pass is $10; proof of age must be shown. It is a lifetime entrance pass to national parks, monuments, historic sites, recreation areas, and national wildlife refuges that charge an entrance fee. The Senior Pass admits the pass signee and any accompanying passengers in a private vehicle. Senior Passholders get 50% off camping fees at Corps-managed campgrounds.

Access Pass
This pass is for citizens of the United States who are blind or permanently disabled. The Access Pass is free; proof of medically determined permanent disability or eligibility for receiving benefits under federal law must be shown. It is a lifetime entrance pass to national parks, monuments, historic sites, recreation areas, and national wildlife refuges that charge an entrance fee. The passport admits the pass signee and any accompanying passengers in a private vehicle. Access Passholders get 50% off camping fees at Corps-managed campgrounds.

Where to Get A Senior Pass or Access Pass
Senior Pass or Access Pass must be obtained in person. They are available at offices of the National Park Service, Bureau of Land

Management, U.S. Forest Service, U.S. Fish & Wildlife Service and Bureau of Reclamation. The Corps of Engineers honors the passes but does not issue them.

America the Beautiful Senior Pass and Access Pass replace the Golden Age and Golden Access Passports issued before 2007. However, existing Golden Age and Golden Access Passports remain valid for the lifetime of passholders.

Appendix E

District Offices

Albuquerque District
U.S. Army Corps of Engineers
4101 Jefferson Plaza NE
Albuquerque, NM 87109
505-342-3171
www.spa.usace.army.mil

Baltimore District
U.S. Army Corps of Engineers
P.O. Box 1715
Baltimore, MD 21203
410-962-2809
www.nab.usace.army.mil

Fort Worth District
U.S. Army Corps of Engineers
P.O. Box 17300
Fort Worth, TX 76102
817-886-1326
www.swf.usace.army.mil

Huntington District
U.S. Army Corps of Engineers
502 8th Street
Huntington, WV 25701
304-399-5211
www.lrh.usace.army.mil

Jacksonville District
U.S. Army Corps of Engineers
701 San Marco Blvd
Jacksonville, FL 32207
904-232-2234
www.saj.usace.army.mil

Kansas City District
U.S. Army Corps of Engineers
700 Federal Building
601 East 12th Street
Kansas City, MO 64106
816-389-3486
www.nwk.usace.army.mil

Little Rock District
U.S. Army Corps of Engineers
Attn: PAO (CESWL-PA)
P.O. Box 867
Little Rock, AR 72203
501-324-5551
www.swl.usace.army.mil

Louisville District
U.S. Army Corps of Engineers
P.O. Box 59
Louisville, KY 40201
502-315-6766
www.lrl.usace.army.mil

Mobile District
U.S. Army Corps of Engineers
P.O. Box 2288
Mobile, AL 36628
251-690-2505
www.sam.usace.army.mil

Nashville District
U.S. Army Corps of Engineers
P.O. Box 1070
Nashville, TN 37202
615-736-7161
www.lrn.usace.army.mil

New England District
U.S. Army Corps of Engineers
696 Virginia Road
Concord, MA 01742
978-318-8238
www.nae.usace.army.mil

Omaha District
U.S. Army Corps of Engineers
106 S 15th St
Omaha, NE 68102
402-995-2417
www.nwo.usace.army.mil

Pittsburgh District
U.S. Army Corps of Engineers
William S. Moorehead Federal Bldg
1000 Liberty Avenue Room 2200
Pittsburgh, PA 15222
412-395-7500
www.lrp.usace.army.mil

Portland District
U.S. Army Corps of Engineers
P. O. Box 2946
Portland, OR 97208
503-808-4510
www.nwp.usace.army.mil

Rock Island District
U.S. Army Corps of Engineers
P.O. Box 2004
Rock Island, IL 61204
309-794-5729
www.mvr.usace.army.mil

Sacramento District
U.S. Army Corps of Engineers
1325 J Street
Sacramento, CA 95814
916-557-7461
www.spk.usace.army.mil

Saint Louis District
U.S. Army Corps of Engineers
1222 Spruce Street
St. Louis, MO 63103
314-331-8002
www.mvs.usace.army.mil

Saint Paul District
U.S. Army Corps of Engineers
190 5th Street East
St. Paul, MN 55101
651-290-5108
www.mvp.usace.army.mil

San Francisco District
U.S. Army Corps of Engineers
1455 Market St Room 1667
San Francisco, CA 94103
415-503-6804
www.spn.usace.army.mil

Savannah District
U.S. Army Corps of Engineers
P.O. Box 889
Savannah, GA 31402
912-652-5279
www.sas.usace.army.mil

Seattle District
U.S. Army Corps of Engineers
P.O. Box 3755
Seattle, WA 98124
206-764-3750
www.nws.usace.army.mil

Tulsa District
U.S. Army Corps of Engineers
1645 South 101 East Ave
Tulsa, OK 74128
918-669-7342
www.swt.usace.army.mil

Vicksburg District
U.S. Army Corps of Engineers
4155 Clay Street
Vicksburg, MS 39183
601-631-5412
www.mvk.usace.army.mil

Walla Walla District
U.S. Army Corps of Engineers
201 North Third Avenue
Walla Walla, WA 99362
502-527-7020
www.nww.usace.army.mil

Wilmington District
U.S. Army Corps of Engineers
69 Darlington Ave
Wilmington, NC 28403
919-251-4606
www.saw.usace.army.mil

Index